Treasure truth — restore trust!

Blessings,

Betty De Meussenn

FOREWORD by JOEL AARON
Georgia Association of Broadcasters 2009 Radio Personality of the Year

DISSED TRUST

AMERICA'S CRISIS OF TRUTH, FAITH, AND FREEDOM

WILLIAM DEMERSSEMAN

WESTBOW
PRESS
A DIVISION OF THOMAS NELSON

Check out _dissedtrust.com_ to order additional copies of Dissed Trust or to share your thoughts online.

WestBow Press books may be ordered through booksellers or by contacting:

WestBow Press
A Division of Thomas Nelson
1663 Liberty Drive
Bloomington, IN 47403
www.westbowpress.com
1-(866) 928-1240

ISBN: 978-1-4497-0367-7 (sc)
ISBN: 978-1-4497-0368-4 (dj)
ISBN: 978-1-4497-0366-0 (e)

Library of Congress Control Number: 2010937600

Printed in the United States of America

WestBow Press rev. date: 10/07/2010

In memory of my beloved brother David,
faithful and fearless disciple of Jesus Christ,
who richly blessed countless lives,
most of all mine.

October 26, 1955 – May 3, 2010
John 10:10   Philippians: 1:21

*Characterized by the current **DissedTrust**, people will continue to reject 'establishment' institutions, expecting them to lie, cheat and abuse employees, communities and the environment. However, rich rewards will go to any institution that can reach the bar of trust.*

-- Faith Popcorn, from her BrainReserve Trend Forecast for 2008[1]

---

1   "Faith Popcorn's BrainReserve Trend Forecast for 2008," Reuters.com. http://www.reuters.com/article/pressRelease/idUS121541+02-Jan-2008+MW20080102. Internet.

CONTENTS

Foreword

By Joel Aaron

The headlines today are inescapable. Unemployment at nearly 10 percent and REAL unemployment nearly double that. A contracting economy with credit drying up. Sweeping government legislation to lay the regulatory groundwork for a nationalization of health care and our financial transactions. The disturbing trends in U.S.-international relations. A $14 trillion dollar debt ceiling we are dangerously close to meeting and $65 trillion dollars in unfunded government liabilities on Social Security and Medicare.

Society breaks down along lines of trust. Engineering distrust in society has become the forte of many in today's governing class. It is a ruse, a plan designed to transfer trust from God, communities, families and self to a bureaucracy seeking more control. The goal becomes presenting government as the solution to whatever ails us. *Dissed Trust* cuts through the pedantic clutter to reveal the true crisis in our country and charts a course for recovery. When we address this crisis for what it is, many of the headlines will begin to fix themselves. For our crisis, ultimately, is not one of economic malaise, the "right" party in power, unemployment or spending. America suffers a crisis of character. Overcoming this crisis means regaining lost trust where it counts - in communities capable of self government.

William expertly goes to the root of our current American crisis and what is driving the economic, social, political and diplomatic headlines; the casualty of trust comes screaming at the reader from every page. This book is not just excellent. The Left will fear it.

"Virtue or morality is a necessary spring of popular government."
- George Washington

"Only a virtuous people are capable of freedom. As nations become corrupt and vicious, they have more need of masters."
– Benjamin Franklin

Introduction

America needs help.

She has been lied to, misled and manipulated. Politicians dupe her. The media mock her. Bureaucrats betray her. Her friends talk about her behind her back. Scientists falsify reports to her. Professional athletes cheat on her. At times, even the clergy fail her.

America has trust issues.

It is difficult to trust any institution, corporation, organization, or public figure. In a March 2010 study by the Pew Research Center, respondents expressed negative views toward banks and financial institutions (69 percent), Congress (65 percent), the federal government (65 percent), large corporations (64 percent), the national news media (57 percent), federal agencies and departments, (54 percent), and the entertainment industry (51 percent).[2]

Public images rarely bear relation to reality. Tiger Woods, the world's greatest golfer, learned how quickly a favorable image can evaporate when his extramarital affairs were exposed in November 2009. His scandal left experts wondering whether the day of multi-million dollar endorsement contracts were over. "There has to be trust and he's just taken a grenade to any kind of traditional agreement that you'd normally have," said John Sweeney, director of sports communications at the University of North Carolina at Chapel Hill's School of Journalism and Mass Communication.[3] The Woods scenario was only the latest in a string of sports scandals ranging from performance enhancing drugs to murderous mistresses.

Trust in government has fallen precipitously in the last half-century. In 1958, the National Election Survey's research indicated that 73 percent of people trusted the government to do what is right most or all of the time; that figure dropped as low as 34 percent in the wake of Watergate. After the terrorist attacks of 9/11, a CBS News/*New York Times* poll reported that 55 percent of Americans trusted government to do what is right always or most of the time. In 2008, the number fell to an all-time

---

2   "Distrust, Discontent, Anger and Partisan Rancor," People-Press.org. http://people-press. org/report/606/trust-in-government. Internet.

3   Fredrix, Emily. "Tiger Inc's image crash to make sponsors cautious," Newsmax.com. http:// www.newsmax.com/Entertainment/US-Woods-Celebrity-Endorsements/2009/12/15/ id/342672. Internet.

low of 17 percent.[4] Following an April 2009 cabinet meeting, President Barack Obama reminded government officials, "We also have a deficit, a confidence gap when it comes to the American people. And we've got to earn their trust."[5]

What Obama euphemistically refers to as a "confidence gap" is actually a Grand Canyon-sized deficit of trust. A large and growing number of hard-working, tax-paying, patriotic Americans no longer trust their government; instead, they fear it.[6]

This book is not only about the lack of integrity, and corresponding deficit of trust in society and government. It is about the government's betrayal of the public trust. It is about the loss of principles of Truth, and the corresponding threat to freedom. It is about the government's lack of accountability and responsibility. It is about government that is taxing and spending to oblivion. It is about government that disdains the Constitution, accepts no limits on its power, and denies individual liberties protected by the Constitution as unalienable rights. It is about a government that, more and more, openly defies the rule of law and is intrusive, secretive, arrogant, duplicitous, and even contemptuous of the citizenry. It is about the public's justified fears of a corrupt and coercive political establishment led by officials whose values are light years away from those of our founders and of most modern Americans. It is about a government that seeks to marginalize religion by stretching the concept of church-state separation to absurdity so that allegiance to the state will have no competition. It is about a government that esteems political correctness above even the protection of its own citizens. It is about a government that indoctrinates, intimidates, and abuses its power.

America's national debt increases by $2.2 billion every single day, yet the current administration boasts of its plan to whittle $100 million dollars from the budget in 90 days. That is like telling your spouse, "Honey, I

---

4   "Trust in Government Nears All-Time Low," CBS4.com. http://cbs4.com/national/cbs. poll.government.2.1499189.html. Internet.

5   "Remarks by the President after Meeting with the Cabinet," WhiteHouse.gov. http:// www.whitehouse.gov/the_press_office/Remarks-by-the-President-after-Cabinet-meeting-4/20/09/. Internet.

6   In a February 2010 poll by CNN/Opinion Research, 56 percent of respondents answered "yes" when asked "Do you think the federal government has become so large and powerful that it poses an immediate threat to the rights and freedoms of ordinary citizens, or not?" The margin of sampling error in the survey was plus or minus 3 percentage points. Steinhauser, Paul. "CNN Poll: Majority says government a threat to citizens' rights," CNN.com. http://politicalticker.blogs.cnn.com/2010/02/26/cnn-poll-majority-says-government-a-threat-to-citizens-rights/?fbid=H3RuHSdf_69. Internet.

bought a 747, a castle in France, and a new Porsche today, but don't worry, we just saved $100 on our life insurance." Token budget cuts only heighten the sense that the American people are being played for fools.

Obama correctly identified the trust gap, but he has yet to acknowledge that growing the government and trampling individual liberties will not close the gap. According to a February 2010 CBS News/*New York Times* survey taken shortly after Obama's first State of the Union address, the number of Americans who trusted government to do what is right always or most of the time was only 19 percent, down from a still dismal 23 percent the previous August. Congress fared even worse in the survey, registering a 15 percent approval rating, down from 26 percent a year earlier. President Obama's job approval rating stood at 46 percent approval/45 percent disapproval, a collapse of 22 points in ten months.[7]

A March 2010 Pew Research Center poll reported similar findings, showing favorable ratings for Congress declining by half from the previous year. Favorable ratings for both major political parties registered record lows in the survey. An astounding 77 percent of respondents indicated they were frustrated (56 percent) or angry (21 percent) with the federal government. In the Pew study, average trust in government over the course of the Obama administration registered 22 percent, seven points lower than that of any administration dating back to John F. Kennedy[8]

Then again, who trusts polls?

The Obama administration takes a for-us-or-against-us view of the American public, and applies a double standard of justice accordingly. Under this distorted version of justice, tax-evading bureaucratic colleagues are appointed to plum political positions while law-abiding dissenters are categorized as possible terrorists.

Early in his term, Obama highlighted this double standard by nominating a string of unqualified candidates for senior government posts.

---

7   "Trust in Government Nears All-Time Low," CBS4.com. http://cbs4.com/national/cbs. poll.government.2.1499189.html. Internet. Only 8 percent of respondents answered "yes" to the question of whether "most members of Congress deserve re-election." "The President, Congress, and Dissatisfaction with Government," CBS News/ New York Times Poll. http://www.cbsnews.com/htdocs/pdf/poll_Obama_Congress_021110.pdf?t ag=contentMain;contentBody. Internet.

8   "Distrust, Discontent, Anger and Partisan Rancor," People-Press.org. http://people-press. org/report/606/trust-in-government. Internet. Average trust in government, according to the Pew study, registered below 30 percent during only two other administrations – Jimmy Carter's and Bill Clinton's.

While vetting potential nominees for 487 Senate-approved positions is a formidable task, a disturbingly high number of Obama's early nominees to major cabinet positions came under fire for failure to pay many thousands of dollars of personal income taxes. Despite Obama's assurances to the contrary, the back-tax debacle illustrated that his politically elite friends play by a different set of rules than the average American taxpayer.

The most jarring example of this double standard was Treasury Secretary Timothy Geithner's failure to pay approximately $34,000 in owed taxes. Geithner's confirmation was an insult to tax-paying Americans and an impeachment of Obama's promise to build a new culture of personal responsibility in Washington. The treasury secretary is in charge of the Internal Revenue Service, the federal agency responsible for collecting taxes, so he should have an unassailable record regarding his own tax payments.

Geithner's bungle was categorized as an honest mistake, but he is a financially savvy operative who should be expected to understand the tax code. In the 1990s, Geithner was a senior official in the Treasury Department under President Bill Clinton. He worked for the International Monetary Fund (IMF) between 2001 and 2004. When Obama nominated him as treasury secretary, Geithner was in his fifth year as president of the Federal Reserve Bank of New York. Leaders from both sides of the aisle lauded his nomination, citing his intellect, competence, and understanding of the nation's financial needs; yet when it came to paying his taxes, Geithner consistently addressed the task in an admittedly incompetent and perfunctory manner. At his Senate confirmation hearing, he described mistakes on his past tax returns as careless and avoidable, though unintentional.[9] It strains credulity to believe Geithner's mistakes were anything less than willfully negligent. Most audits no doubt turn up a few minor infractions or unsubstantiated claims, but Geithner's tax infractions spanned a period of many years and multiple areas of the tax code.

During his time at the IMF, Geithner was required to pay his own Social Security and Medicare taxes since his official status for tax purposes was self-employed. He annually signed and submitted paperwork at the IMF that acknowledged his self-employment tax obligation. The IMF booklet, which Geithner acknowledged receipt of, instructed employees that "you pay the employee's share of U.S. Social Security taxes."[10] In 2006,

---

9   Friedman, Emily. "Geithner Calls Tax Gaffe 'Careless Mistake," ABCNews.com. http://abcnews.go.com/Business/Economy/story?id=6691508&page=1. Internet.
10   McKinnon, John D. and Davis, Bob. "IMF Informed Geithner on Taxes," John D. McKinnon and Bob Davis, Wall Street Journal. http://online.wsj.com/article/SB123194884833281695.html. Internet.

an IRS audit covering the years 2003 and 2004 found that he had failed to pay self-employment taxes in those years.[11]

Even after Geithner paid back taxes and interest of $17,230, he failed to amend his 2001-2002 tax returns to pay the overdue self-employment taxes. He paid the additional $25,970 in back taxes and interest only after his nomination, when Obama's vetting team revealed the obligation. Senate Finance aides expressed concerns that Geithner, or his accountant, seized upon the IRS's statute of limitations to avoid further back-tax payments.[12]

In his "new era of personal responsibility," Obama resolutely defended his nominee; he was not the only Democrat willing to put politics ahead of principle. Senate Finance Committee Chairman Max Baucus (D-MT), who has a long record of seeking to close the "tax gap,"[13] defended Geithner's contributions to the tax gap as "innocent mistakes."[14]

The American people have a right to expect leadership by example. At a minimum, the public has a right to expect personal diligence from prospective public servants in the areas that they will exercise professional oversight. Geithner's appointment to oversee the IRS as treasury secretary can only magnify public distrust of government.

In the wake of public outcry over Geithner's appointment, Nancy Killefer's and Tom Daschle's nominations were quickly derailed when their own income tax issues came to light.

On February 3, 2009, the White House reported that Nancy Killefer, Obama's nominee for chief performance officer for the federal government, had withdrawn her name from consideration due to controversy over a

---

11   Hagenbaugh, Barbara and Kirchoff, Sue. "Timothy Geithner says he regrets tax mistakes," USAToday.com. http://www.usatoday.com/money/economy/2009-01-21-geithner-hearing_N.htm. Internet.

12   The IRS statute of limitations for back taxes is triggered after three years. It should be noted that the statute of limitations had not been triggered for the 2004 and 2005 tax years when Geithner was notified about his mistake in 2006. Only during the vetting process in late 2008 did he pay the additional $5000 additional taxes and interest due for these and other infractions, such as improper charitable-contribution deductions and an improper small-business deduction Geithner also wrongly claimed expenses for summer camps in calculating his dependent care tax credit on 2001, 2004 and 2005 returns. When the accountant who prepared his 2006 return informed Geithner that payments to overnight camps were not allowable expenses, Geithner did not file amended returns for the affected years until 2008. Weisman, Jonathan. "Geithner's Tax History Muddles Confirmation," Wall Street Journal. http://online.wsj.com/article/SB123187503629378119.html. Internet.

13   The IRS estimated in 2007 that the annual tax gap was approximately $290 billion a year. Senator Baucus once called the tax gap "an affront to all the rest of us who pay our taxes."

14   Friedman, Emily. "Geithner Calls Tax Gaffe 'Careless Mistake," ABCNews.com. http://abcnews.go.com/Business/Economy/story?id=6691508&page=1. Internet.

$946.69 tax lien against her home for failure to pay unemployment and payroll taxes on household help. Killefer was aware of the fact that she was required to pay the taxes, but the Associated Press reported that Killefer stopped paying taxes on her household help three years after she left her treasury post in the Clinton administration.[15]

The same day that Killefer withdrew her nomination, former Senate Minority Leader Tom Daschle withdrew from consideration for secretary of Health and Human Services (HHS) after it was revealed that he failed to pay over $100,000 in taxes for a limousine service he received. On January 2, 2009, three weeks after his nomination was announced, Daschle paid $140,167 for back-taxes and interest owed for the years 2005-2007. The errors, uncovered in the vetting process, included taxes on $80,000 of consulting income and $255,000 of income from the free use of a chauffeur and driver. Even after paying these taxes, unresolved tax issues relating to free travel, entertainment services, and unsubstantiated charitable donation deductions remained.[16] After the disclosure, but before Daschle's withdrawal, Obama said he was "absolutely" standing by his nominee.[17]

Two days after Daschle and Killefer withdrew their nominations, Labor Secretary-designate Hilda L. Solis became the fourth senior administration nominee in a month to encounter problems relating to unpaid taxes. The Senate cancelled its scheduled confirmation hearing on Solis after reports surfaced that Solis' husband had fifteen outstanding local and state tax liens on his Los Angeles repair shop.[18]

One incident of tax evasion is unfortunate. Two cases could be a coincidence. But four senior-level nominees with tax evasion skeletons in their closets evince a blatant disregard for the law among elite bureaucrats. Critics joked that the Obama nomination was a powerful new tool in the tax enforcement arsenal, but for hard-working taxpayers it was no joke.

---

15 Several months after the lien was filed, Killefer paid the delinquent taxes and had the lien extinguished. Associated Press. "White House: Performance Czar Nancy Killefer Withdraws Candidacy," FoxNews.com. http://www.foxnews.com/politics/2009/02/03/white-house-performance-czar-nancy-killefer-withdraws-candidacy/. Internet.

16 tax Caron, Charles L. "Daschle's Nomination for HHS Secretary Threatened by Failure to Pay $140k Taxes on Free Use of Limo and Chauffeur," Tax Prof Blog. http://taxprof.typepad.com/taxprof_blog/2009/01/groundhog-day-.html. Internet.

17 Freking, Kevin. "Obama: I will 'absolutely' stand by Daschle," NBC.NewYork.com. http://www.nbcnewyork.com/news/us_world/NATL-D.html. Internet.

18 Dickson, David M. and Sands, David R. "Taxes trip up another Obama nominee," WashingtonTimes.com. http://washingtontimes.com/news/2009/feb/06/tax-problems-trip-up-obama-again-with-nominee-for-/print/. Internet.

Further insulting hard-working taxpayers, the Department of Homeland Security (DHS) issued an unclassified report entitled "Rightwing Extremism: Current Economic and Political Environment Fueling Resurgence in Radicalization and Recruitment" eight days before the 2009 tax day tea parties; it warned, without naming specific groups or dangerous activity, of a surge in "rightwing extremism in the United States."

> Rightwing extremism in the United States can be broadly divided into those groups, movements, and adherents that are primarily hate-oriented (based on hatred of particular religious, racial or ethnic groups), and those that are mainly antigovernment, rejecting federal authority in favor of state or local authority, or rejecting government authority entirely. It may include groups and individuals that are dedicated to a single issue, such as opposition to abortion or immigration.[19]

The timing of the report, coupled with its lack of specificity, raised legitimate questions about DHS's intent. The government's assertion that citizens may be terrorists if they object to unparalleled government growth, bourgeoning debt, and the subversion of the rule of law was absurd.

Four days after the nationwide tea party protests, Senior White House adviser David Axelrod was asked on CBS's *Face the Nation* about the public disaffection with the Obama administration at the tea party rallies. "I think any time you have severe economic conditions there is always an element of disaffection that can mutate into something that's unhealthy," responded Axelrod.

Not only do the people not trust the government, but the government does not trust the people. When politicians, officials, and agencies react reflexively instead of actively listening, the trust deficit grows. The federal government will not restore citizens' trust by issuing unfounded reports warning of right-wing extremism.

President Obama's own "Organizing for America" website, mybarackobama.com commemorated Patriot Day (September 11) by asking supporters to "fight back against our own Right-Wing Domestic Terrorists who are subverting the American Democratic Process, whipped to a frenzy by their Fox Propaganda Network ceaselessly seizing power

---

19 Department of Homeland Security Office of Intelligence and Analysis. "Rightwing Extremism: Current Economic and Political Climate Fueling Resurgence in Radicalization and Recruitment," FAS.org. http://www.fas.org/irp/eprint/rightwing.pdf. Internet.

for their treacherous leaders."[20] But at the National Prayer Breakfast a few months later, Obama decried the lack of "serious and civil debate," adding that "this erosion of civility in the public square sows division and distrust among our citizens."[21] One can make a strong case that when it comes to division and distrust, Obama is sower-in-chief.

The trust deficit plaguing the political climate was not created overnight. It did not originate, as many on the Left like to pretend, with President George W. Bush, nor did it originate, as many on the Right like to pretend, with President Barack Obama. Americans have historically viewed government with a wary eye, not out of disdain for government, but based on the potential for unrestrained government to inflict harm.

Distrust of government is a natural response to a controlling and out-of-control bureaucracy. The motivation for protest and reform is not animosity towards government and its legitimate functions, but a love of America and a passionate desire to pass on to the next generation the innumerable blessings of liberty. Citizens are frightened by the government's relentless growth, unsustainable debt trajectory, culture of corruption and encroachment of individual rights. To sit idly by while government runs amuck is to abdicate one's duty as an American, so citizens voice their concerns in quintessentially American ways: peaceably assembling, discussing concerns with other citizens, running for public office, petitioning Congress, mobilizing voter support, studying American history, developing solutions, and spreading ideas for putting the country on the right track again. In 2009, citizens began gathering to protest uncontrolled government spending and the tea party movement was born.

I have never been, nor aspired to be, an activist. Before 2009, I had never participated in a political protest or activist gathering of any kind. But on April 15, 2009, I attended the Atlanta tea party with 15,000 other citizens who were frustrated with out-of-control governmental spending, unconstitutional power grabs, politically-correct national security failures, socialist policies, the threat to constitutional liberties, and corrupt politicians.

---

20   The Corner, by Jonah Goldberg, "Are You Ready for Patriot Day?" August 31, 2009 http://corner.nationalreview.com/post/?q=YWY5ZmYwNTkwMjE0MTMxYTk2ZjQyOTZhMmI0ZWQ3MzY=

21   "Obama at National Prayer Breakfast: The transcript," http://voices.washingtonpost.com/44/2010/02/obama-at-national-prayer-break.html

Critics of the tea party movement attempt to derail it with meritless charges of racism, extremism, bigotry, conspiracy, class-warfare, and malice. The claims are ridiculous. Tea party participants include members of every party, social class, ethnicity, age and gender; they hold varying views on a number of issues, but share a deep appreciation for the limited, constitutional government established by America's founders. They see Washington's profligate spending, imperious unaccountability, and reprobate political environment as symptoms of a federal government that recognizes no limitations on its power. They feel a civic responsibility to speak out and to work toward a return to constitutional governance and sound fiscal policy.

This is not a book about the tea party movement. It is a book about the political, economic and cultural upheavals fueling the movement: the insanely escalating national debt, the increasingly coercive and contemptuous political establishment, the arrogant failure of true political leadership, and the pervasive assault on the society-sustaining virtues of truth, trust, integrity, morality, freedom, and civility.

This is not a pro-Republican book. Both major political parties are sacrificing the economic security and constitutional freedom of Americans on the altars of power, status, and control. Certainly, Obama and the Democrats are leading the ignominious charge, but Republican politicians complicit in growing government, usurping constitutional freedoms, increasing the federal debt, and governing corruptly can also expect to face fierce opposition from tea party participants, as the 2010 primaries have already demonstrated.

This is not an anti-government book. It *is* an anti-unconstitutional, anti-out-of-control, and anti-corrupt government book. It is a pro-responsible, constitutionally-limited government book.

Finally, the sharp criticisms of the Obama administration herein are based solely on the policies, statements and actions of the administration. I have never met the president; by all accounts he is an intelligent, likeable man. As president of the United States of America, he is entitled to the respect that attends that high and honorable office. I simply disagree profoundly with his vision for the country.

America is not perfect, but the principles it was founded on, currently under attack, created a nation unique in its protection of individual freedoms and in its unparalleled contributions to the world. Every generation in American history has faced formidable threats. Every generation has grappled with and overcome inequities, problems and prejudices, leaving a better country for posterity. America's current problems are formidable, but not insurmountable.

Hopeful signs of an American rebirth are emerging. The political establishment's breach of trust has become so brazen that a critical mass of freshly engaged citizens is materializing. These citizens recognize the genius of the founders' vision: a limited government instituted to secure God-given rights, with powers derived from the consent of the governed. America rose to greatness as a nation that treasured individual freedom, secured by the rule of law. The tea party protesters simply want to chart a course to return America to the ideals that made her great.

PART 1

CRISIS OF INTEGRITY, DEFICIT OF TRUST

Saying What You Don't Mean

My family recently played an impromptu word game at the family dinner table that quickly had us all laughing so hard we almost choked on our food. The game was called Opposite World. In the game of Opposite World, there is only one rule: Say the opposite of what you really mean. I'll try to recreate a bit of the flavor of it:

Me: "Please don't pass the potatoes."
Son, age nine: "Not okay. Here you aren't!"
Me (upon receiving the potatoes): "You're welcome."
Son, to me: "You're not welcome, Mom!"
Me, to son: "Thank you, daughter."
Daughter, age seven: "You are all crazy! I mean not crazy! ... Whatever!"

We had to choose our words carefully at first, but I was surprised, and mildly alarmed, at how quickly my brain adjusted. It would not take much practice before I could convincingly communicate a message expressing the opposite of my true beliefs and intentions.

I expect that is one reason God endowed humans with a conscience. Of course, the conscience must be constantly exercised, developed, and purified; otherwise, it is vulnerable to the corrosive effects of rationalization. Our human capacity to self-justify and deceive ourselves and others is limitless.

Opposite World was a great dinner table game, but it was exhausting. Everything spoken had to be translated using the "opposite world" code. After a few minutes, we all were ready to return to "normal world."

Where did it go?

1

Opposite World

The real world is giving way to an opposite world where politicians operate like cat burglars, plundering the lexicon for personal gain; They distort facts, ignore inconvenient details, impugn motives, employ personal attacks, raise red herrings, and when all else fails, lie; not all politicians, but far too many.

Politicians have long had a well-earned reputation for twisting facts and bending the truth. Italian political philosopher Niccolò Machiavelli so epitomized the elevation of political expediency over morality that his name literally defines the practice.[22] Machiavelli wrote a short but influential treatise on government, *The Prince*,

Getting to Know Saul Alinsky

Saul Alinsky is commonly known as the founder of modern community organizing in America. He rejected mainstream liberalism as too passive and ineffectual. His book, *Rules for Radicals: A Pragmatic Primer for Realistic Radicals,* offered an aggressive approach for organizing mass power.

There are obvious comparisons between Alinsky's work and the most famous western work regarding power, Machiavelli's *The Prince*. Alinsky contrasts *Rules for Radicals* from *The Prince*, stating: "*The Prince* was written by Machiavelli for the Haves on how to hold power, *Rules for Radicals* is written for the Have-Nots on how to take it away."[1]

---

1   Alinsky, Saul. Rules for Radicals. London: Vintage Books (1989).

which lays out a strategy for gaining and maintaining political power. For Machiavelli, as for Saul Alinsky, the father of modern community organizing, the essential benchmark for success in politics is winning. Machiavelli considered ethics and morality ultimately relevant only to the extent they benefitted a politician. Cunning, scheming, and conniving, the successful politician, according to Machiavelli, is a master calculator who skillfully does or says whatever is most self-advantageous. We live

---

22   machiavellian. Dictionary.com. Dictionary.com Unabridged. Random House, Inc. http://dictionary.reference.com/browse/machiavellian. Internet.

in a Machiavellian age. Anyone familiar with the political culture in Washington D.C. might think the vast majority of elected officials today keep a copy of *The Prince* on their nightstands.

For example, in answering the question, "Should a prince be true to his word?" Machiavelli writes, "It's good to be true to your word, but you should lie whenever it advances your power or security – not only that, it's necessary."[23]

Most Americans over age thirty remember when Bill Clinton famously pointed his finger at the camera and emphatically told America, "I did not have sexual relations with that woman."[24] When "that woman" produced incontrovertible proof of the sexual nature of the relationship, America learned that their president had lied. Bill Clinton's legacy will always include his 1998 videotaped grand jury testimony, in which the president parsed the word "is" in what was surely the most existentially contrived rationalization in modern political history.[25] In order to avoid a perjury charge, Bill Clinton struck a deal at the end of his term in office, acknowledging that in giving his deposition in the Paula Jones case, "I tried to walk a fine line between acting lawfully and testifying falsely, but I now recognize that I did not fully accomplish that goal."[26] As part of the deal, he was barred from practicing law in Arkansas for five years. "Slick Willie" earned his nickname.

Politicians routinely attempt to walk that fine line; more and more Americans are ready to make them walk the plank instead. Voters are starving for principled leaders who say what they mean and mean what they say. The ascension of spin to an acceptable, even admirable, practice in politics creates a dangerous climate. Healthy debate is an essential component of a representative republic, and people who filter facts and ideas through differing worldviews sustain a healthy political environment with an informed electorate.

The informed exchange of ideas was critical to America's founding. After drafting and proposing the Constitution in September 1787, an intense debate on ratification ensued. James Madison, John Jay, and Alexander

---

23   Machiavelli, Niccolo. The Prince, translated by N.H. Thomson. Vol. XXXVI, Part 1. The Harvard Classics. New York: P.F. Collier & Son, 1909–14; Bartleby.com, 2001. www.bartleby.com/36/1/. (April 19, 2010).

24   "Bill Clinton Quotes." All Great Quotes. http://www.allgreatquotes.com/bill_clinton_quotes.shtml. Internet.

25   Noah, Timothy. "Bill Clinton and the Meaning of 'Is.'" September 13, 1998.http://www.slate.com/id/1000162/. Internet.

26   Pellegrini, Frank. "Well, There Goes the Country-Lawyer Gig." Time, January 19, 2001.

Hamilton laid out the arguments in favor of ratification in 85 Federalist Papers. Various anti-federalist authors, usually using pseudonyms, wrote articles opposing the proposed Constitution.[27]

Political debate in early America helped provide a check on the unbridled power of government:

> Debate flourished in the early days of this country because the country had to reestablish order after overthrowing one set of institutions for another... Where the colonists had remonstrated and pleaded without response from George III, here would be a system responsive to the voices of the aggrieved...The rhetoric of 'we, the people' and 'governments derive their just powers from the consent of the governed' was powerful stuff... Power would not transfer by bloodline but election. Power would be checked by power. At the heart of 'checks and balances' was a confidence in the ability of the best ideas to triumph if strongly presented by forceful advocates in a fair forum.[28]

As America evolved into the two-party system which has largely dominated the political landscape throughout its history, political debate took on a more structured form. In 1858, Abraham Lincoln and Stephen A. Douglas engaged in a series of seven debates while campaigning for the United States Senate. The debates focused heavily on the issue of slavery, particularly slavery's expansion into the territories. Douglas favored the doctrine of popular sovereignty, but Lincoln argued that popular sovereignty would nationalize and perpetuate slavery. Though Lincoln ultimately lost the Senate election to Douglas, the incumbent, the debates increased Lincoln's visibility among voters and helped him prepare for his successful presidential bid in 1860.

Obama mesmerized audiences on the campaign trail as he heralded a new day of hope and spoke of bringing "change we can believe in." He empathized with the struggles of hard-working Americans and persuaded audiences that they were joining him in making history; destiny beckoned,

---

27 Roland, Jon, Ed. "Anti-Federalist Papers." Constitution Society. http://www.constitution.org/afp/afp.htm. Internet. A prescient Patrick Henry noted, "A number of characters of the greatest eminence in this country object to this government for its consolidating tendency. This is not imaginary. It is a formidable reality." Jamieson, Kathleen Hall and Birdsell, David S. Presidential Debates: The Challenge of Creating an Informed Electorate. New York: Oxford University Press, 1988.

28 Jamieson, Kathleen Hall and Birdsell, David S. Presidential Debates: The Challenge of Creating an Informed Electorate. New York: Oxford University Press, 1988.

and, together, they would answer. With a broad brush, Obama painted a vague but inspiring image of the change brand and let his listener fill in the blanks about what that brand would encompass. Sandwiched between soaring elocution, the strategy worked wonders. Obama's Iowa Caucus victory speech is an excellent example of his oratory vagueness:

You know, they said this day would never come. They said our sights were set too high. They said this country was too divided; too disillusioned to ever come together around a common purpose. But on this January night – at this defining moment in history – you have done what the cynics said we couldn't do ... In lines that stretched around schools and churches; in small towns and big cities; you came together as Democrats, Republicans, and independents to stand up and say that we are one nation; we are one people; and our time for change has come.... Hope is that thing inside us that insists, despite all the evidence to the contrary, that something better awaits for us if we have the courage to reach for it, and to work for it, and

Brand Loyalty

Present day political debate is more like life in Shakespeare's *Macbeth*: "full of sound and fury, signifying nothing."[1] Instead of facts, politicians now rely on positioning to curry favor with the electorate. Political campaigns in recent years have borrowed aggressively from the marketing world's expertise in product positioning. Just as a brand manager attempts to carve out a unique image in customers' minds for a particular brand or product, a campaign team chooses a specific image to cultivate its candidate in voters' minds.

The Obama campaign strategy has already become a marketing classroom case study on how to effectively establish a brand.[2] The Obama brand could be reduced to one short word: change. The change brand resonated with a populace worried about the economy and tired of the war in Iraq. In the Democratic primary, Hillary Clinton's "experience" brand was no match for Obama's change. In the general election, Obama relentlessly pushed his brand deep into the minds of the voters while John McCain settled late in the election cycle on his "country first" brand.

Obama's effective branding campaign resulted in a decisive victory on Election Day. Every candidate seeks to present himself as an agent of change, but Obama owned the category in the voters' minds. In today's age of information overload, the simplicity of Obama's campaign was its genius.

1 Shakespeare, William. Macbeth. http://pd.sparknotes.com/shakespeare/macbeth. Internet.
2 Ries, Al. "What Marketers Can Learn From Obama." Advertising Age. http://www.ries.com/82/What-Marketers-Can-Learn-From-Obama percent27s-Campaign.html. Internet.

to fight for it....Hope is the bedrock of this nation; the belief that our destiny will not be written for us but by us, by all these men and women who are not content to settle for the world as it is; who have the courage to remake the world as it should be.... We are the United States of America; and at this moment, in this election, we are ready to believe again.[29]

Obama criticized his opposition without identifying the opposition and praised supporters for uniting behind a common purpose without identifying the purpose. The speech was shockingly vacuous, stunningly effective, and characteristic of many speeches to come. Obama's gifts for positioning and oratory were enough to win the White House. His ambiguous, eloquent words fell like manna on an American electorate starved after eight years of following President George W. Bush through an oratorical wasteland. In the midst of a crashing economy, with a fawning press, superior finances, and a floundering opponent, Obama rode "the gift" to victory.

Some administrations withstand the glaring light of scrutiny better than others. While President Richard Nixon's administration crumbled when his complicity in the Watergate cover-up was exposed and President George H. W. Bush helped secured his place as a one-term president when he reneged on his memorable "read my lips, no new taxes" promise, other presidents over the last 25 years have survived breaches of the public trust. Despite lying directly to the American public and in sworn testimony, Bill Clinton is remembered as one of the more popular modern presidents.[30] George W. Bush's administration parsed words in an attempt to divert attention from its many missteps in the

The Gift

I remember my surprise in March 2008 when discussing the upcoming presidential election with a sharp, socially conservative Christian businessman in his early forties who said he was tempted to vote for Obama. The reason? The gift.

"It would just be so refreshing," he said, particularly on the world stage, to have a president who "could complete a sentence without mangling it." He was mesmerized by Obama's oratory skills. It was the first time I considered that Obama had a realistic chance to become the next President of the United States.

---

29   Obama, Barack. "Barack Obama's Caucus Speech." New York Times. http://www.nytimes.com/2008/01/03/us/politics/03obama-transcript.html. Internet.

30   C-SPAN. "Survey of Presidential Leadership." C-SPAN.org. http://www.c-span.org/PresidentialSurvey/Overall-Ranking.aspx. Internet.

Iraq war. He won re-election, but, unlike Clinton, his polling numbers remained low throughout his second term.[31] Though the Patriot Act passed with bipartisan support in the wake of the terrorist attacks of September 11, 2001, the Republicans, as the majority party, were blamed for undermining critically important freedoms enshrined in the Bill of Rights.[32] Voters responded to the allegedly-fiscally-conservative, Republican-controlled Congress's spendthrift ways in 2006 by returning both chambers to Democratic control. When the financial crisis intensified and Bush, supposedly a free market proponent, proposed a $700 billion bailout, his already low job approval rating dropped four points to a new low of 27 percent. Only 28 percent of respondents approved of Bush's response to the financial crisis, while 68 percent disapproved.[33]

Misleading or lying to the public increases the trust deficit between citizens and government to a dangerous level. When national political leaders lie to their constituents, they do more than hurt their constituents; they damage the soul of the nation. Lying is more than a personal matter; more than a character flaw. The essence of lying is theoretically simple. *Webster's New World College Dictionary* defines the word "lie" as making "a statement that one knows is false, especially with intent to deceive."[34]

Intent is not always easy to discern. Words themselves have various shades of meaning, depending on the context. By carefully choosing words, a politician may communicate a message exactly opposite of the truth, even while making factual statements. Karl Rove's comments to CNN and ABC News during the Valerie Plame leak episode are but one example. In 2003, *Washington Post* columnist Robert Novak exposed Plame as a CIA operative. A subsequent investigation into who revealed Plame's identity as an undercover CIA operative put the spotlight on presidential advisor Karl Rove, among others. In *What Happened,* former White House Press Secretary Scott McClellan described how Rove narrowly focused on Plame's name as a way of denying his role in the leaking of her identity to the press:

---

31 Rasmussen Reports. "President Bush Job Approval." RasmussenReports.com. http://www.rasmussenreports.com/public_content/politics/political_updates/president_bush_job_approval. Internet.
32 Associated Press, "Sen. Clinton: Bush re-election would mean loss of freedoms." USA Today. 24 May 2004.
33 Gallup. "Bush's Approval Rating Drops to New Low of 27 percent." Gallup.com. http://www.gallup.com/poll/110806/bushs-approval-rating-drops-new-low-27.aspx. Internet.
34 Webster's New World Dictionary: Second College Edition. New York: New World Dictionaries/Simon and Schuster, 1984.

Rove was being too cute by half when he told CNN and later ABC News back in 2004, 'I did not know her name. I did not leak her name.' He did not have to know Plame's name to leak her identity, as he did to *Time* magazine White House correspondent Matt Cooper and as he confirmed for Bob Novak.[35]

When citizens have to dissect each word in search of the truth, they become frustrated and even angry. At that point, many simply disengage, turn a deaf ear to Washington, and focus on their own affairs; politicians anticipate this response to escape accountability.

In the hands of a skillful prevaricator, words and facts are like the magician's tools-in-trade: endlessly useful in creating a world of illusion. The adept dissembler mixes a bare thread of the truth into the fabric of a lie, just enough to weave a web of plausible deniability should the deception be uncovered. When politicians make promises, they take care to use ambiguous terms that leave plenty of room for back-pedaling later. Euphemisms provide cover for cold realities. A pork-infested government stimulus becomes a "jobs bill." Identifiable jobs-created data morph into a meaningless "jobs created or saved" propaganda mechanism.

A culture of dishonesty is a natural development in a society where truth is rejected. When nothing is objectively true, then the meaning of everything – words included – is subject to personal interpretation. Our tolerance for lying is an indictment of our own proclivity for deceiving both others and ourselves. When President Bill Clinton lied under oath to cover up his affair with an intern, Democrats gained traction with a host of unconscionable arguments:

- Lies about sex, even under oath, don't matter
- Character in our President is not important; competency is all that matters
- Since everybody lies, it is normal and acceptable for politicians to lie, too
- Adultery, (which inherently encompasses lying), is not a big deal.[36]

Someone who will lie to his family will lie to anyone. A habitual liar is, by definition, unfit for elected office in America for a very simple

35 McClellan, Scott. What Happened: Inside the Bush White house and Washington's Culture of Deception. New York: PublicAffairs, 2008.
36 Bennett, William J.. Death of Outrage: Bill Clinton and the Assault on American Ideals. New York: Free Press, 1998.

reason: he cannot be trusted to do the job voters elected him to do. We tolerate this corrupt species of politics because we too easily identify with it. Dishonesty is endemic in America today. The ends justify the means mentality that permeates politics is corrupting every American institution. In 2009, a North Carolina middle school principal actually decided it would be appropriate to raise money for the school by selling grade points. A parent advisory council came up with the cash-for-grades fundraiser and the school principal endorsed the plan. A student would receive twenty test points, ten points on two tests of the student's choosing, in exchange for a $20 donation to the school. That could raise a failing grade to a D, or a B to an A for each of the two tests. When a local newspaper raised concerns about the fundraiser, county administrators halted the program and announced that donations would be returned. Rather than admit the idea was wrong, or at least reflected poor judgment, the principal pointed out the expedient genius of the plan, "Last year they did chocolates, and it didn't generate anything" she said, adding that it was wrong to think "one particular grade could change the entire focus of nine weeks."[37]

Lying is wrong regardless of the reason for the lie. In politics, reasons will always be made to sound noble: saving the planet, providing universal health care, creating jobs, feeding children. Institutional integrity in American society must flow from individual integrity because institutions, whether political, religious, social or economic, are comprised of persons. Pursuit of the greater good cannot sanctify a lie.

Until more Americans make integrity a nonnegotiable core principle in their own lives and hold public officials accountable to the truth, liars will continue to lie.

Obama is by no means the first politician to mislead the public through positioning, misdirection, or lying. Politicians of every ideological persuasion lie. The difference is that Obama rose to power because he promised to end cynical, divisive politics. He forcefully argued for a government that is honest and ethical, open and transparent, unifying and inspiring, and worthy of the high ideals of America.

On the Senate floor, Obama advocated ethics reform, quoting at length the words of President Teddy Roosevelt:

> No republic can permanently endure when its politics are corrupt and base... we can afford to differ on the currency, the tariff, and foreign

---

37 Bonner, Lynn. "District nixes cash-for-grades fundraiser." The News & Observer. http://www.newsobserver.com/2009/11/11/v-print/185460/district-nixes-cash-for-grades.html. Internet.

policy, but we cannot afford to differ on the question of honesty... The nation will hopelessly blunt the popular conscience if it permits its public men continually to do acts which the nation in its heart of hearts knows are acts which cast discredit upon our whole public life.[38]

In Wisconsin, six weeks before the election, Obama again promised: "I'll make our government open and transparent so that anyone can ensure that our business is the people's business."[39]

Obama's pledge to restore America's faith in government was so central to his bid for president that he made it his campaign slogan: "Change You Can Believe In."

Obama entered office with high approval ratings. In his inaugural address, he spoke of the need to "restore the vital trust between a people and their government."[40] On his first full day in office, Obama signed a series of ethics-related directives, commenting that he hoped the new rules would help "restore

Sweet Little Lies?

What about the so-called "white lie"? This social palliative is not only tolerated but advocated as a means of smoothing out the bumps in interpersonal relationships.

A *Readers' Digest* advice columnist was asked how to deal with a repeated, but unwanted, social invitation from a business associate. The columnist responded: "You can keep declining and hope they get the hint. But here's a better option: Lie ... I don't like lying, but in this case, it's better than the brutal truth."[1]

One can debate the merits of the "white lie" told to spare another person's feelings, but the truth is most white lies are born of convenience, not of compassion. Once the barrier between truth and fiction is lowered, the allure of the lie in all walks of life becomes increasingly evident. Lies, after all, promise smaller tax liabilities, better grades, quicker advancement, more prestige, and less accountability or responsibility.

Politicians are, in a very real sense, products of the culture out of which they emerge. We too easily tolerate the politician who lies as a means to achieve an end of which we approve. We distinguish between character and competence as if the former is not a prerequisite for the latter. We are entertained by spin when we should be repulsed by its manipulative agenda. We reward the consummate politician adept at tickling the ears of whichever constituency he is addressing.

1   Laskas, Jeanne Marie. "Ask Laskas: Should I Risk My Marriage?." Reader's DIgest.

---

38   Obama , Barack. "Obama's Opening Statement - Floor Debate on Ethics Reform." ObamaSpeeches.com.   http://obamaspeeches.com/055-Debate-on-Ethics-Reform-Obama-Speech.htm. Internet.

39   "Obama at 100 Days – Assessments of Government Transparency and Regulatory Reform Efforts," April 28, 2009 http://www.ombwatch.org/obamaat100days

40   Obama, Barack. "Inaugural Address." ObamaSpeeches.com. http://obamaspeeches.com/. Internet.

trust" in the U.S. government.[41] In September 2009, 61 percent of Americans said they had "a great deal or fair amount of trust" in the executive branch of government, according to a Gallup poll, a double-digit improvement from the previous year's assessment of George W. Bush's administration. When Americans saw the Obama administration resort to politics-as-usual, however, the polling numbers went south. Trust in Congress plummeted to a record low of 45 percent in the 2009 poll. Trust in the "men and women in political life in this country who either hold or are running for public office" dropped to an all-time low of 49 percent, a drop of 17 percentage points from the middle of the 2008 presidential campaign.[42]

Lying: A Cultural Malaise

Aware of the prevalence of lying in our society, *Webster's Dictionary* includes a special synonym section that expounds on the intricacies of the disreputable art of lying:

> SYN. – lie is the simple direct word meaning to make a deliberately false statement; prevaricate strictly means to quibble or confuse the issue in order to evade the truth ...; equivocate implies the deliberate use of ambiguity in order to deceive or mislead; fabricate suggests the invention of a false story, excuse, etc. intended to deceive.[1]

Lying, prevaricating, equivocating, and fabricating are all epidemic in modern American politics. Americans are tired of being lied to by politicians who are willing to say or do anything to stay in office.

---

1 Webster's New World Dictionary: Second College Edition. New York: New World Dictionaries/Simon and Schuster, 1984.

---

41 "Obama promises." Earth Times. http://www.earthtimes.org/articles/show/251800,obama-promises-new-era-of-accountability-freezes-white-house-wages.html. Internet.

42 Newport, Frank. "Americans' Trust in Legislative Branch at Record Low Public places much more trust in the judicial and executive branches." Gallup.com. http://www.gallup.com/poll/122897/Americans-Trust-Legislative-Branch-Record-Low.aspx. Internet.

The Indispensable Work of Discernment

What works in campaigns does not always work in governance. At some point in the course of an administration, citizens demand that actions match words.

It is difficult not to look for the possible agenda lurking beneath the surface of each new White House initiative or congressional action when agendas are continually exposed after the fact:

- hidden bailouts to well-connected Wall Street firms[1]
- exorbitant new taxes disguised as energy reform[2]
- billions of dollars in Federal Reserve payments to foreign governments[3]
- mandated health insurance[4]
- Miranda rights for foreign terrorists in 2009; [5] efforts to limit Miranda rights even for American citizens in 2010.[6]
- huge bonuses to failed Fannie Mae and Freddie Mac executives[7]
- jobs created or saved statistics that collapse under scrutiny[8]
- billions of dollars in stimulus to phantom districts and pork projects[9]
- special backroom-negotiated health reform deals for unions and favored states[10]
- under-the-radar government takeover of the student loan program via the health reform legislation.[11]

The list seems endless.

1   Carney, Timothy P.. "Obama's hidden bailout of General Electric." The Examiner. 04 March 2009; Tavakoli, Janet. "Treasury Cover-Up of Goldman's Role in AIG Crisis?." The Huffington Post. http://www.huffingtonpost.com/janet-tavakoli/treasury-cover-up-of-gold_b_400300.html. Internet.
2   Loris, Nicolas. "Treasury Admits Cap and Trade is a Massive Tax." The Foundry. http://blog.heritage.org/2009/09/16/treasury-admits-cap-and-trade-is-a-massive-tax/. Internet.
3   Grim, Ryan. "U.S. Injecting Billions Into Foreign Central Banks." The Huffington Post. http://www.huffingtonpost.com/2009/03/17/us-injecting-billions-int_n_175454.html. Internet.
4   Seelye, Katharine Q.. "U.S. Has Right to Require Insurance, White House Says." New York Times. 30 October 2009
5   Hayes, Stephen F.. "Miranda Rights for Terrorists." The Weekly Standard. 10 June 2009
6   "President Obama's Administration Favors Limiting Miranda Rights for Terrorists," May 9, 2010 by Steven R. Hurst http://constitutioncenter.org/NewsWire.aspx?title=President+Obama's+Admi nistration+Favors+Limiting+Miranda+Rights+for+Terrorists
7   Hagerty, James R.. "Fannie, Freddie Bonuses Total About $210 Million." Wall Street Journal. 04 April 2009.
8   Freddoso, David, and Hemingway, Mark. "The Washington Examiner 'Bogus Stimulus Map'." The Examiner. 12 November 2009; Carroll, Conn. "Morning Bell: The Fake Jobs of Obama's Failed Stimulus." The Foundry. http://blog.heritage.org/2009/11/17/morning-bell-the-fake-jobs-of-obamas-failed-stimulus/. Internet.
9   "See No Earmarks: Defining spending deviancy down. "Wall Street Journal. 05 March 2009; "$6.4 Billion Stimulus Goes to Phantom Districts." Franklin Center for Government and Public Integrity. http://www.franklincenterhq.org/2009/11/17/6-4-billion-stimulus-goes-to-phantom-districts/. Internet.
10 Pear, Robert, and Greenhouse, Steven. "Accord Reached on Insurance Tax for Costly Plans." New York Times. 14 January 2010; Fox News. "The Price Is Right? Payoffs for Senators Typical in Health Care Bill." FoxNews.com. http://www.foxnews.com/politics/2009/12/21/price-right-payoffs-senators-typical-health-care/. Internet.
11 Baker, Peter and Herszenhorn, David M.. "Obama Signs Overhaul of Student Loan Program." New York Times. http://www.nytimes.com/2010/03/31/us/politics/31obama.html. Internet.

As Obama's first year in office wound down, his job approval ratings plunged. Rasmussen reported a new low of -21 on its December 22, 2009 "presidential approval index."[43] Gallup registered a new low of 47 percent approve, 47 percent disapprove on its three day rolling poll, January 20-22, 2010.[44] With the federal deficit skyrocketing, unemployment at 10 percent, and an expensive health care reform package clearing both chambers of Congress just before Christmas 2009, overall public trust in government was as low as it was when Obama took office.[45] After one year in office, the "change" brand that Obama touted on the campaign trail looked more like false advertising than real reform.

Obama's branding is an example of political positioning on the macro level. On the micro level, politicians posture on particular issues, mindful of the image they want to create in the minds of select groups of voters. Voters want, and deserve, politicians who clearly communicate what they believe and how they will respond on various issues. But when freed from the restraints of integrity and truthfulness, positioning quickly devolves to cynical manipulation of the electorate.

Obama uses rhetorical flair to create positions with maximum flexibility. Then he tailors the message to generate the most positive response from his audience, using nuance to appeal to both sides of an issue. "He's so good at having it both ways, so damn good," said a former Obama aide. "It's standard Barack procedure."[46]

The Jeremiah Wright mess is a case in point. When it became apparent that he could not casually dismiss the issue, Obama delivered his memorable speech on race. "That speech had it both ways: Keep Wright, make everybody happy," said the aide.[47] In the speech, Obama first condemned Wright's outrageous statements. Then he softened them by talking about Wright's long-time leadership of a church "that serves the community by doing God's work here on Earth... I can no more disown him than I can

---

43 "Obama Approval Index History." RasmussenReports.com. http://www.rasmussenreports. com/public_content/politics/obama_administration/obama_approval_index_history. Internet.

44 "Gallup Daily: Obama Job Approval." Gallup.com. http://www.gallup.com/poll/113980/ gallup-daily-obama-job-approval.aspx. Internet.

45 Enhanced Online News. "One Year Into Obama Presidency Trust in Government is Unchanged While Business Gains, According to Public Strategies Survey." EON. http:// eon.businesswire.com/portal/site/eon/permalink/?ndmViewId=news_view&newsId=20 100121005486&newsLang=en. Internet.

46 Schieber, Noam. "Is Obama's Cynicism Enough?" WAP.CBSNews.com. http://wap. cbsnews.com/site?sid=cbsnews&pid=sections.detail&catId=TOP&index=1&storyId=40 98647&viewFull=yes

47 Ibid.

disown the black community. I can no more disown him than I can my white grandmother."[48] Obama then attributed lingering disparities in the African-American community to inequalities passed on by the legacy of racial discrimination, in order to explain the deep-seated anger felt in the black community, especially by persons of Wright's generation.[49] Most of Obama's allies seem to see a genuine, deep-thinking politician willing to tackle the complexities of an issue. Critics see a calculating, disingenuous politician who advances a radical agenda through political expediency.

In *The Audacity of Hope*, Obama readily admits that positioning is more politically expedient than the truth.

> Today's politician understands... that there is no great reward in store for those who speak the truth, particularly when the truth may be complicated. The truth may cause consternation; the truth will be attacked; the media won't have the patience to sort out all the facts and so the public may not know the difference between truth and falsehood. What comes to matter then is positioning."[50]

In his book, Obama appeared to be lamenting the triumph of political positioning over speaking the truth. In the real world, Obama and his staff have fully embraced positioning.

Examples of Issue Positioning

NAFTA: During the 2008 Ohio Democratic primary debate, Obama attacked Senator Hillary Clinton for stating on the 2000 campaign trail that the North American Free Trade Agreement (NAFTA) had been good for America.[51] Though NAFTA is anathema to union members, an important

48 Obama, Barack. "Transcript of Obama's speech on race." CNN.com. http://www.cnn.com/2008/POLITICS/03/18/obama.transcript/. Internet.
49 In the weeks following the speech Wright continued to be a thorn in the side of Obama's campaign; in late April Obama did what he had said the previous month that he could not do – he disowned his pastor of 20 years. In the March speech, Obama's sincerity was burdened by the disconnect between his views and those of a large percentage of Americans. In the April flip-flop, his announced separation from Wright was burdened by the opportunism that sparked his 20-years-delayed sense of outrage.
50 Obama, Barack. The Audacity of Hope. New York: Crown, 2006.
51 CBS/Associated Press. Canadian NAFTA Remarks Rile Obama Campaign Senator's Senior Economic Advisor Says Diplomats Inaccurately Portrayed His Trade Stance." CBSNews.com. http://www.cbsnews.com/stories/2008/03/03/politics/main3898313.shtml percent20 percent20 percent20http://indigetnahole.blogspot.com/2008/03/barrack-obama-is-disingenuous.html. Internet.

Obama consituency, his criticism of NAFTA labor and environmental standards alarmed Canadian officials. Later, Austen Goolsbee, Obama's Senior Economic Policy Advisor, met with officials from the Canadian Consulate. Joseph DeMora, an employee of the consulate who attended the meeting, subsequently issued a memo, obtained by the Associated Press, which stated:

> Noting anxiety among many U.S. domestic audiences about the U.S. economic outlook, Goolsbee candidly acknowledged the protectionist sentiment that has emerged, particularly in the Midwest, during the primary campaign. He cautioned that this messaging should not be taken out of context and should be viewed as more about political positioning than a clear articulation of policy plans.

Goolsbee denied using the phrase "political positioning."[52]

Public campaign financing: In 2007, Obama positioned himself as a proponent of public campaign financing, a practice in which candidates agree to fund their campaigns with taxpayer dollars, capped by a spending limit set by the Federal Elections Commission (FEC). McCain agreed to accept public financing if the Democratic nominee also agreed. Obama spokesman Bill Burton responded, "If Senator Obama is the nominee, he will aggressively pursue an agreement with the Republican nominee to preserve a publicly financed general election."[53] Burton's statement was consistent with Obama's long-time positioning on the issue. As late as February 2008, Obama indicated that he would accept public financing: "I propose a meaningful agreement in good faith that results in real spending limits."[54] By March, Obama had repositioned: "What I've said is, at the point where I'm the nominee, at the point where it's appropriate, I will sit down with John McCain and make sure that we have a system that works for everybody."[55] Why the change? By that date, with campaign money pouring in to his coffers at a record-breaking rate, Obama knew what

---

52 Ibid.
53 Hollyfield, Amy. "Campaign finance: Deal or no deal?." Politifact.com. http://www.politifact.com/truth-o-meter/article/2008/mar/03/campaign-finance-deal-or-no-deal/. Internet.
54 Obama, Barack. "Opposing vie: Both sides must agree." USA Today. 20 February 2008
55 Hollyfield, Amy. "Campaign finance: Deal or no deal?." Politifact.com. http://www.politifact.com/truth-o-meter/article/2008/mar/03/campaign-finance-deal-or-no-deal/. Internet.

system would work best for him. It was no longer prudent to accept public financing, with its prescribed $84 million limit. On his campaign website, Obama laid blame on the financing system and on his opposition.

> The public financing of presidential elections as it exists today is broken, and we face opponents who've become masters at gaming this broken system. John McCain's campaign and the Republican National Committee are fueled by contributions from Washington lobbyists and special interest PACs.[56]

According to the Center for the Study of Elections and Democracy, the $730 million Obama spent on his presidential election campaign more than doubled that of rival McCain.[57] Obama would have voters believe the outlandish theory that little or none of his record campaign haul came from lobbyists and special interests. Obama, however, received mounds of cash from special interests, topping McCain's intake from fifteen of nineteen industry categories listed by the Center for Responsive Politics.[58] A few examples:

- Lawyers and Law Firms: Obama: $43 million, McCain $15.5 million[59]
- Education: Obama 22.9 million, McCain 4.4 million[60]
- Health Professionals: Obama $11.7 million, McCain $5.3 million[61]
- Securities and Investment: Obama $14.8 million, McCain $8.7 million[62]

---

56 Bentley, John. "McCain Accuses Obama of Flip-Flopping on Public Financing." CBSNews.com. http://www.cbsnews.com/8301-502443_162-4197553-502443.html. Internet.

57 Magleby, David. "Democrats Exploit Newfound Individual Donor Advantage and Superior Voter Mobilization Efforts as Part of a Dramatic Change Election." Center for the Study of Elections and Democracy. http://csed.byu.edu/Assets/Monograph percent20Executive percent20Summary percent202008_2.pdf. Internet.; Federal Election Commission. "Presidential Campaign Finance." FEC.gov. http://www.fec.gov/DisclosureSearch/ MapAppCandDetail.do?detailComeFrom=mapApp&cand_id=P80003338&cand_nm_ title=Obama, percent20 Barack. Internet.

58 Center for Responsive Politics. "Presidential Candidates: Selected Industry Totals, 2008 Cycle." OpenSecrets.org. http://www.opensecrets.org/pres08/select.php?ind=N07. Internet.

59 Center for Responsive Politics. "Presidential Candidates: Selected Industry Totals, 2008 Cycle." OpenSecrets.org. http://www.opensecrets.org/pres08/select.php?ind=K01. Internet.

60 OpenSecrets.org. http://www.opensecrets.org/pres08/select.php?ind=W04

61 Center for Responsive Politics. "Presidential Candidates: Selected Industry Totals, 2008 Cycle." OpenSecrets.org. http://www.opensecrets.org/pres08/select.php?ind=W04. Internet.

62 Center for Responsive Politics. "Presidential Candidates: Selected Industry Totals, 2008 Cycle." OpenSecrets.org. http://www.opensecrets.org/pres08/select.php?ind=F07. Internet.

- Computers/Internet: Obama $8.5 million, McCain $1.5 million[63]
- Hedge Funds/private equity: Obama $3.1 million, McCain $1.8 million[64]
- Goldman Sachs employees and executives gave $994,775 to Obama's campaign, four times as much as they gave to John McCain's campaign.[65]

Lobbyists: On the campaign trail, Obama repeatedly railed against the growing influence of more than 40,000 registered lobbyists, pointedly noting the lobbyists in McCain's campaign. "I have done more to take on lobbyists than any other candidate in this race. I don't take a dime of their money, and when I am president, they won't find a job in my White House."[66] A few days after his election he repositioned, saying through a spokesman that lobbyists would be allowed on his transition team as long as they worked on issues unrelated to lobbying work done in the previous two years. John Podesta, Obama's transition team co-chairman, heralded Obama's positioning as fulfilling his campaign pledge to change the Washington political machine by curbing the influence of lobbyists. "We are announcing rules that are the strictest, the most far-reaching ethics rules of any transition team in history."[67]

On his first full day in office, Obama announced limitations on the lobbyists joining his administration; lobbyists he had pledged wouldn't find a job in the White House. The rules included a gift ban and a requirement that lobbyists who join the administration not work on issues connected to their previous lobbying. Still, Obama played the part of reformer, musing: "We need to close the revolving door that lets lobbyists

63 Center for Responsive Politics. "Presidential Candidates: Selected Industry Totals, 2008 Cycle." OpenSecrets.org. http://www.opensecrets.org/pres08/select.php?ind=B12s.org/pres08/select.php?ind=F07. Internet.
64 Center for Responsive Politics. "Presidential Candidates: Selected Industry Totals, 2008 Cycle." OpenSecrets.org. http://www.opensecrets.org/pres08/select.php?ind=F27. Internet.
65 Center for Responsive Politics. "Candidate Comparison: Top Contributors 2008 Cycle." OpenSecrets.org. http://www.opensecrets.org/pres08/contriball.php?cycle=2008. Internet.
66 Kranish, Michael. "Obama softens ban on hiring lobbyists." Boston.com. http://www.boston.com/news/nation/articles/2008/11/12/obama_softens_ban_on_hiring_lobbyists/. Internet.
67 Kranish, Michael. "Obama softens ban on hiring lobbyists." Boston.com. http://www.boston.com/news/nation/articles/2008/11/12/obama_softens_ban_on_hiring_lobbyists/Internet.

come into government freely and lets them use their time in public service" to advance their own interests when they leave.[68]

Obama's announcement garnered headlines about the administration's tough new lobbying rules, but in Washington rules are made to be circumvented. The White House was forced to concede that the new lobbyist restrictions were not uniformly enforced after the Republican National Committee revealed that two of Obama's nominees - William Lynn, a defense contractor lobbyist nominated for deputy secretary of the Department of Defense, and William V. Corr, an anti-tobacco lobbyist nominated for deputy secretary of HHS – had previously lobbied the departments to which they were nominated.[69] A *National Journal* report, based on the public database of registered lobbyists, found that 267 persons appointed or nominated to various senior positions in the Obama administration were registered to lobby within the previous five years.[70]

Moving to the center: Obama needed the support of left-wing organizations to win the Democratic nomination. During the party primaries, he touted his support for the Association of Community Organizations for Reform Now (ACORN), Service Employees International Union (SEIU), pro-abortion policies, gay rights, and anti-war groups. Historically, left-leaning candidates move to the center for the general election campaign, and Obama was no exception. Moving to the center, of course, is a classic example of repositioning.

As the dust settled on his epic primary battle with Hillary Clinton, Obama began to espouse views that conflicted with his Democratic primary persona. In June 2008, he announced his support for the Foreign Intelligence Surveillance Act (FISA), after denouncing an earlier FISA bill as an attempt by President Bush to "put protections for special interests ahead of our security and our liberty."[71] He started giving speeches on

---

68 Runningen, Roger. "Obama Freezes Pay, Toughens Ethics and Lobbying Rules." Bloomberg.com. http://www.bloomberg.com/apps/news?pid=20601087&sid=azQJo_wu7f64. Internet.

69 Schlesinger, Robert. "No Lobbyist in the Obama Administration... Except When There Is One." U.S. News and World Report. http://www.usnews.com/blogs/robert-schlesinger/2009/01/22/no-lobbyist-in-the-obama-administration--except-when-there-is-one.html. Internet.

70 National Journal. "Obama's Lobbyists." NationalJournal.com. http://www.nationaljournal.com/njmagazine/sl_20090321_4967.php. Internet.

71 Kane, Paul. "Obama Supports FISA Legislation, Angering Left." WashingtonPost.com. http://blog.washingtonpost.com/44/2008/06/20/obama_supports_fisa_legislatio.html. Internet.

traditional issues like faith and patriotism.[72] He belatedly denounced Moveon.org months after it produced a disgraceful ad accusing General David Petraeus, a popular figure among conservatives and moderates, of betrayal.[73] He began wearing a flag lapel pin after previously decrying the flag pin as "a substitute for true patriotism." In October 2007 Obama explained that he had worn the pin after the 9/11 attacks, but had later decided, "I won't wear that pin on my chest. Instead, I'm going to try to tell the American people what I believe will make this country great."[74] Voters found his comments grating, and Obama was forced to reverse course on the pin decision to avoid alienating moderate swing voters.[75] Obama even embraced the Supreme Court's decision to overturn Washington D.C.'s absolute handgun ban, which prohibited citizens from possessing handguns in their homes for protection.[76] Politicians are notorious for gradually shifting their positions on critical issues to appeal to a broader spectrum of voters; it is not surprising that Obama utilized this tactic in his presidential bid. It is interesting, however, that Obama attacked Hillary Clinton's "political talk" for contributing to public cynicism about government when he regularly engages in political positioning.

> Senator Clinton and I were debating and she was asked about the bankruptcy law that she voted for in 2001 … During the debate she said, you know, 'I voted for it, but I hoped it wouldn't pass.' That was a quote on live TV. That kind of talk, I think it makes people not trust government.[77]

72   Associated Press. "Obama wants to expand faith-based programs," MSNBC.com. http://www.msnbc.msn.com/id/25473529/. Internet; Obama's Patriotism Speech Impresses Missourians," KCTV5.com. http://www.kctv5.com/politics/16738525/detail.html. Internet.

73   Hurt, Charles and Campanile, Carl. "Barack Blasts Moveon,"New York Post. http://www.nypost.com/p/news/national/item_UneUs2FGMq2j60XEV4tIlL;jsessionid=20A4D992CFBADADED066029ECAE3AC31

74   Malcolm, Andrew. "Breaking News: Obama caves! Flag pin returns to his coat lapel," LATimes.com. http://latimesblogs.latimes.com/washington/2008/04/obamaflagpinlap.html. Internet.

75   Wright, David and Miller, Sunlen. "Obama Dropped Flag Pin in War Statement," ABCNews.com. http://abcnews.go.com/Politics/story?id=3690000&page=1. Internet.

76   An exception in the law allowed possession in the home of unlocked or disassembled handguns registered before 1975 or owned by active or retired law officers. Lott, John R. Jr. "John Lott: Reaction to D.C. Gun Ban Decision," FoxNews.com. http://www.foxnews.com/story/0,2933,373663,00.html. Internet.

77   Politifact.com. "That's not the actual quote." Politifact.com. http://www.politifact.com/truth-o-meter/statements/2008/feb/11/barack-obama/thats-not-the-actual-quote/. Internet.

Obama's criticism would have been valid, except Hillary Clinton never made the statement.[78] The Pulitzer Prize-winning, political fact-checking website, Politifact.com, rated Obama's charge against Hillary Clinton as "false." Ironically, Obama misrepresented Hillary Clinton's remarks while arguing that the American public wants to engage in "straight talk" on the issues.[79]

Americans are indeed looking for straight talk, but they rarely get it from Obama – or any other politician. Instead of reforming the world of political positioning, Obama has consistently proven he is more interested in refining the art. Political positioning is critical to Obama's success because his worldview differs dramatically from that of mainstream America. When Obama is forthright about his opinions, the incongruity is apparent.[80] For example, Obama has apologized to foreign leaders, described Midwestern, small town Americans as bitter citizens who "cling to guns or religion or antipathy toward people who aren't like them," made rash assumptions in a police matter, ridiculed tea party participants, slammed entire industries, strongly supported ACORN, advocated redistributionist policies, and mocked those concerned about the expanding power of government.[81]

Obama uses words and phrases that resonate with the American public, but his speeches should not be taken at face value. When Obama uses phrases like "social justice" or "economic justice," for instance, he deliberately appeals to America's historic commitment to due process, individual rights and equal opportunity. He also mines the nation's Judeo-Christian heritage, referencing Jesus' directive to feed the hungry, care for the sick, help the poor, and defend the defenseless, but, despite blatant rhetorical references to history and faith, Obama's understanding of social justice is framed by his socialistic worldview, not by the Constitution, (which he views as fundamentally flawed), or the

---

78　"Obama is referring to a Jan. 15, 2008, Democratic debate in Las Vegas when Clinton was asked by moderator Tim Russert if she regretted her vote in favor of the 2001 bankruptcy bill. Here's what Clinton said: 'Sure I do, but it never became law, as you know. It got tied up. It was a bill that had some things I agreed with and other things I didn't agree with, and I was happy that it never became law. I opposed the 2005 bill as well.'" Politifact. com. "That's not the actual quote." Politifact.com. http://www.politifact.com/truth-o-meter/statements/2008/feb/11/barack-obama/thats-not-the-actual-quote/. Internet.

79　Politifact.com. "That's not the actual quote." Politifact.com. http://www.politifact.com/truth-o-meter/statements/2008/feb/11/barack-obama/thats-not-the-actual-quote/. Internet.

80　In a September 2001 interview on Chicago public radio, Obama said that the Constitution "reflected the fundamental flaw of this country that continues to this day." "Reagan and Obama," by Jean Kaufman, October 7, 2009 http://www.weeklystandard.com/Content/Public/Articles/000/000/017/049ykkgx.asp?pg=1

81　Halperin, Mark. "Transcipt of Obama's Remarks at San Francisco Fundraise Sunday," Time. http://thepage.time.com/transcript-of-obamas-remarks-at-san-francisco-fundraiser-sunday/.

Judeo-Christian ethic, which he rejects in favor of reason and science.[82] He misappropriates the Judeo-Christian ethic, which advocates compassionate personal outreach to the needy, and uses it as a moral injunction for advocating big government entitlements and wealth redistribution.

Obama strips words of their context and uses generalities. Reduced to campaign slogans and platitudes, words and phrases like 'hope,' 'change,' 'fair play,' and 'a level playing field,' are meaningless. Generalities like 'a better brand of politics,' and 'a new era of responsibility,' must be borne out in the real world of governmental policymaking, day-to-day administration, and the legislative process.

---

82   Patten, David A. "Obama: Constitution is 'Deeply Flawed'," Newsmax.com. http:// newsmax.com/InsideCover/obama-constitution/2008/10/27/id/326165.

Obama's Inaugural Address

Obama's inauguration was a moving moment in American history, and his inaugural address was rich in symbolism, expertly-crafted, and well-delivered. Many of Obama's actions as president, however, have been inconsistent with key themes of the speech.

Obama opened by calling on Americans to remain "faithful to the ideals of our forbearers, and true to our founding documents."[1] No honest student of American history can say that Obama's policies accurately reflect the founders' ideals or the intentions of the Constitution.

He said America has "chosen hope over fear, unity of purpose over conflict and discord."[2] Less than halfway into Obama's presidency, partisan acrimony has arguably never been more pronounced in Washington, and millions of Americans deeply fear for the future of the country for the first time in their lives.

He proclaimed "an end to the petty grievances and false promises, the recriminations and worn out dogmas," yet the Obama administration has escalated, rather than ended, these political ailments.[3]

Obama quoted the Apostle Paul's admonition to "set aside childish things," but Paul's context was the body of Christ, not the bloated bureaucracy. Next, he lauded hard work, productivity, inventiveness, and risk-taking, though his policies typically punish these attributes.[4]

Obama continued, "We will restore science to its rightful place, and wield technology's wonders to raise health care's quality and lower its cost." It is difficult to pack so much disinformation into one sentence. Obama implied that George W. Bush's administration somehow sequestered science, and that his own policies would restore its unfettered advancement, yet Obama ignores or politicizes science, depending on the context.[5] His science czar, John Holdren, has a history of dangerously conflating politics with ideologically-driven science. As for advancing technology in the area of health care, America has long led the world in new medical technologies. In awarding the federal government more control over the private health sector, the new health care bill threatens to stifle technological innovation by making it unprofitable.

"The question we ask today is not whether our government is too big or too small, but whether it works,"[6] Obama asserted in the speech, as if the mammoth size, power and reach of the ever-expanding federal government is unrelated to its proper functioning. It is an indisputable maxim that the bigger the federal bureaucracy grows, the less effective it becomes.

Obama claimed, "We will not apologize for our way of life," but he apologizes for America on his overseas trips and many of his advisors and political appointees, including Van Jones, Andy Stern, Ron Bloom, Mark Lloyd, Jim Wallis, and Jeremiah Wright, are frequent critics of America's free-market based system.

1   Obama, Barack. "Obama Inaugural Address." ObamaSpeeches.com. http://obamaspeeches.com. Internet.
2   Ibid.
3   Ibid.
4   Ibid.
5   Cohen, Eric, and George, Robert P.. "The President Politicizes Stem-Cell Research." Wall Street Journal. http://online.wsj.com/article/SB123664280083277765.html. Internet.
6   Obama, Barack. "Obama Inaugural Address." ObamaSpeeches.com. http://obama speeches.com. Internet.

2

Spiraling Down:
From Universal Truth to Raw Power

Obama sailed into office in 2008 aboard the S.S. Fluff. Most of his speeches consisted of rhetoric. While it was annoying to watch voters swoon over his empty themes of hope and change, Obama's vague speeches were less threatening to personal liberty than his substantive speeches. Far too often, Obama's substantive speeches have been part of a general misinformation campaign designed to undermine religious conservatives.

Religious conservatives tout Judeo-Christian values as the root of the social conscience in America. This is not to suggest that every American shares a certain set of religious beliefs; instead, it recognizes that, historically, a majority of Americans come from Judeo-Christian backgrounds. While some Americans today would decline to describe themselves as followers of a particular faith, Judeo-Christian precepts have shaped the country's moral conscience since its founding. For example, the Ten Commandments dictate that stealing and lying are wrong; these beliefs continue to be part of the social conscience even among those who no longer adhere to religion. Though history clearly records America's Judeo-Christian roots, Obama is determined to dismiss - in the name of diversity – the very historical underpinnings that enabled diversity to flourish in America.[83]

> I think that the United States and the West generally, we have to educate ourselves more effectively on Islam. And one of the points I want to make is... that if you actually took the number of Muslim Americans, we'd be one of the largest Muslim countries

---

83 Jackson, Brooks. "Q: Did Obama say we "are no longer a Christian nation"?." FactCheck.org. http://www.factcheck.org/askfactcheck/did_obama_say_we_are_no_longer.html.   Internet. America's diversity has always been, and can continue to be, a strength. Today's diversity in no way makes America's historical roots irrelevant.

in the world. And so there's got to be a better dialogue and a better understanding between the two peoples.[84]

The remark was one of a host of erroneous, misleading and unsubstantiated claims in the speech. In 2007, the Pew Research Center estimated the number of Muslim Americans in the United States at 2.35 million.[85] Notwithstanding a generous estimate of 4.14 million Muslim Americans, Nationmaster.com lists 40 countries with a larger Muslim population. To fully appreciate the absurdity of Obama's claim, consider that the four actual largest Muslim populated countries (Indonesia, Pakistan, India, and Bangladesh) have a combined 635.15 million Muslims.[86] While these facts are readily available to anyone with Internet access, President Obama nevertheless claimed that America, by the numbers, is "one of the largest Muslim countries in the world." Even if one used Obama's grossly inflated estimate of seven million Muslim Americans, the United States would rank thirty-third on Nationmaster.com's list.[87]

Unfortunately, Obama is on a religious misinformation crusade. In 2006, Obama said, "Whatever we once were, we are no longer a Christian nation – at least not just. We are also a Jewish nation, a Muslim nation, a Buddhist nation, and a Hindu nation, and a nation of unbelievers."[88] He repeated the claim to CBN news in 2007.[89] On his first trip to the Middle East as president, Obama announced at a news conference:

One of the great strengths of the United States is, although as I mentioned, we have a very large Christian population, we do not consider ourselves a Christian nation or a Jewish nation, or a

84 Sargent, Greg. "Yikes! Did Obama Really Call America A Muslim Country? Nope.." WhoRunsGov.com. http://theplumline.whorunsgov.com/political-media/yikes-did-obama-really-call-america-a-muslim-country-nope/. Internet.

85 Pew based the estimate on data from a nationwide, random sample survey of Muslim Americans, which included 55,000 interviews, along with available Census Bureau data on immigrants nativity and nationality. "Muslim Americans: Middle Class and Mostly Mainstream." Pew Research Center (22 May 2007)

86 "Religion Statistics: Islam - Population (most recent) by country." Nationmaster.com. http://www.nationmaster.com/graph/rel_isl_pop-religion-islam-population. Internet.

87 "Religion Statistics: Islam - Population (most recent) by country." Nationmaster.com. http://www.nationmaster.com/graph/rel_isl_pop-religion-islam-population. Internet.

88 Jackson, Brooks. "Q: Did Obama say we "are no longer a Christian nation"?." FactCheck.org. http://www.factcheck.org/askfactcheck/did_obama_say_we_are_no_longer.html. Internet.

89 Brody, David. "Obama to CBN News: We're no Longer Just a Christian Nation." CBN.com. http://www.cbn.com/CBNnews/204016.aspx. Internet.

Muslim nation. We consider ourselves a nation of citizens who are bound by our ideals and a set of values.[90]

It may be more sensitive to say that we are a nation predominantly populated by Christians than to say that we are a "Christian nation," but Obama is seeking to detach America from its historic Judeo-Christian roots. Even as America's religious diversity explodes, 76 percent of Americans continue to identify themselves as Christians.[91]

Though Obama acknowledges the impact of the Judeo-Christian tradition on our system of law and counts himself as a Christian believer, he ushers Christians to the sidelines by labeling religious values unfit for public debate, unless first translated into secular terminology:

> To say that people should not inject their personal morality into public debates is a practical absurdity; our law is, by definition a codification of morality, much of it grounded in the Judeo-Christian tradition. What our deliberative, pluralistic democracy demands is that the religiously motivated translate their concerns into universal, rather than religion-specific values; their proposals must be subject to argument and amenable to reason. Faith and reason operate in different domains and involve different paths to discerning truth. Reason involves the accumulation of knowledge based on realities that we can apprehend. Religion, by contrast, is based on truths that are not provable through ordinary human understanding – the "belief in things not seen."[92]

The founders would have scoffed at Obama's contrivance that religious values must be "translated," or secularized, before being admitted into the marketplace of ideas. In a ten-year study begun in the 1970s, a group of political scientists analyzed more than 15,000 political writings from 1760-1805 in order to isolate the sources most cited during America's founding period. The two individuals quoted most often by the founders, Charles Montesquieu and William Blackstone, each grounded human law upon God's transcendent law. Further, according to the study, the Bible

---

90 The White House: Office of the Press Secretary. "JOINT PRESS AVAILABILITY WITH PRESIDENT OBAMA AND PRESIDENT GUL OF TURKEY." WhiteHouse.gov. http://www.whitehouse.gov/the_press_office/Joint-Press-Availability-With-President-Obama-And-President-Gul-Of-Turkey/. Internet.

91 U.S. Census Bureau. "The 2010 Statistical Abstract." Census.gov. , http://www.census.gov/compendia/statab/cats/population.html. Internet.

92 Obama, Barack. The Audacity of Hope. New York: Crown, 2006.

accounted for 34 percent of the 3,154 quotes referenced by the founders, four times more than either Montesquieu or Blackstone.[93]

Far from relegating religion to the sidelines, the founders held that religion and morality were foundational to sound government. John Adams, Samuel Adams, John Hancock, Gouverneur Morris, Benjamin Rush, and a host of other founders cited religion and morality, or virtue, as necessary to ordered liberty. Thomas Jefferson spoke of the "obligation of the moral precepts of Jesus." Benjamin Franklin said that "only a virtuous people are capable of freedom." George Washington perhaps said it best in his farewell address: "Of all the dispositions and habits which lead to political prosperity, religion and morality are indispensable supports. In vain would that man claim the tribute of patriotism who should labor to subvert these great pillars of human happiness."[94]

According to Obama, religion is based on truths that are not "provable through ordinary human understanding."[95] By arguing that reason "involves the accumulation of knowledge based on realities that we can apprehend," Obama implies that science is more authoritative than religion. He purports to retain the propriety of faith's role in political debate but strips it of any moral authority. Faith is reduced to a wellspring of imagery detached from its biblical context and misappropriated at will by the administration to support policy initiatives which, more often than not, fly in the face of scriptural imperatives. Obama has set up a false dichotomy between faith and reason: science is reasonable, faith is irrational.

Science is a wonderful discipline and a valuable methodology for advancing human understanding, but it is not the only tool; science does not have a monopoly on reason. Modern science has little or nothing to say about what is morally reasonable or true. The truths of Christian principles are borne not out of scientific proof, but in the human heart and in human experience. Further, modern science, like all of society, is subject to corruption by disreputable scientists and agenda-driven politicians, as the global warming scandal dubbed "Climategate" illustrated.

When Obama's Supreme Court nominee, Elena Kagan, served as a deputy assistant to President Clinton for domestic policy, she brazenly distorted science by rewriting the critical language of a draft report on the partial-birth abortion procedure by a panel of the American College

93 Barton, David. Original Intent: The Courts, the Constitution, and Religion. Aledo: Wallbuilder Press, 2000.
94 Barton, David. Original Intent: The Courts, the Constitution, and Religion. Aledo: Wallbuilder Press, 2000.
95 Ibid.

of Obstetricians and Gynecologists (ACOG), an allegedly nonpartisan organization. The ACOG panel had originally concluded that it "could identify no circumstances under which this procedure ... would be the only option to save the life or preserve the health of the woman."

Kagan received a copy of the draft and noted in an internal memorandum that ACOG's conclusions "would be a disaster." So Kagan proposed that ACOG include the following language: "An intact D&X [the medical term for the procedure], however, may be the best or most appropriate procedure in a particular circumstance to save the life or preserve the health of a woman." The ACOG executive board incorporated Kagan's exact language into its final report, providing evidentiary ammunition to those seeking to overturn the federal ban on partial-birth abortion.[96]

Like the vast majority of founders, George Washington viewed faith in God as critical to America's early development:

> I am sure that never was a people, who had more reason to acknowledge a Divine interposition in their affairs, than those of the United States: and I should be pained to believe that they have forgotten that agency, that was so often manifested during our Revolution, or that they failed to consider the omnipotence of that God who is alone able to protect them.[97]

America benefitted greatly in its founding and first 150 years from Judeo-Christian principles such as integrity, personal responsibility, the reality of sin, the sanctity of human life, a strong work ethic, the covenant of marriage, the gift of family, and the God-given nature of unalienable, individual rights. In straying from these ideals, America finds itself adrift. In contrast to America's rich religious heritage, Obama's way of defining the boundaries of political argument pushes biblical Christianity to the sidelines; the reasoned moral arguments of practicing Christians are labeled as the biased ranting of the religiously motivated.

Science, by its nature, is morally neutral. It stakes no moral claim and its efforts can be used for good or evil, as history amply demonstrates. Likewise reason, set adrift from the natural constraint of moral absolutes, leads only to moral confusion. This functional acquiescence to materialism in the realm of political debate is strange coming from one who writes of

---

96   "Kagan's Abortion Distortion," by Shannen W. Coffin, June 29, 2010 http://article. nationalreview.com/437296/kagans-abortion-distortion/shannen-w-coffin

97   Washington, George. "George Washington Society: Our Mission." George Washington Society. org. http://www.georgewashingtonsociety.org/Mission.html. Internet.

the "audacity of hope." Can science or reason prove the value of hope? Of unconditional love? Of human dignity? Of any of the values that make us truly human? In Obama's mind, are science and reason truly the only avenues of discerning truth that are "accessible to all"? Of course not.

Reason is not the enemy of faith, unless it seeks the de facto elimination of faith's role in shaping our understanding of morality. Christians believe that humans are made in the image of God, with a soul and a conscience as well as the ability to reason; the more a person uses his intellect in search of truth, the closer he comes to God.

Obama frames the debate in a way that makes the views of Bible-believing Christians inherently suspect and exclusionary and makes secular views appear enlightened and inclusive. His appeal to reason, however, is just another façade: he elevates reason above faith only to diminish the influence of biblical Christianity and its adherents in the political process. Obama does not govern by appealing to reason or to values held by all reasonable people – or even to values held by a majority of Americans. He epitomizes the condescending "we-know-best" attitude rampant in America's ruling class today, which sets itself apart from all other citizens by its blind arrogance. Obama governs against the views of the majority on issue after issue, from passing the health care bill to siding with Mexico against Arizona on border security and illegal immigration, to endlessly expanding the size, power, and debt of the federal government.

Obama cannot build momentum for major policy initiatives by appealing to reason because *his values* are light-years apart from those of mainstream America, on the proper roles of government and the free market, on the source and scope of individual rights, on social issues, on the character of the Constitution, and even on the character of the nation itself. In the health care debate, for example, Obama failed to convince Americans that a massive government overhaul would increase competition, lower costs, maintain individuals' choice of doctors and insurance, avoid rationing of health care, or improve medical care. He could not make the case because both reason and history were against him on every point. Thus, Obama resorted to scare tactics, demonization of opponents, creative accounting, deceptive promises, and back-room power politics.

One problem with Obama's dissection of the relationship between faith, religion, and politics is how he substitutes *universal values* for *universal truth*. A universal value, at least as used by Obama, is little more than a populist-sounding political talking point. Truth is "the true or actual state of a matter," or "conformity with fact or reality."[98] A universal truth is a truth that is applicable everywhere or in all cases.[99] "Value," refers to "relative worth, merit, or importance."[100] Value, by definition, is relative. One person's treasure is another person's trash; the saying is usually applied to material goods, but it also describes the way the word value is used in a spiritual or moral framework.

Universal truths are grounded in objective reality, fixed, and unalterable. Universal values are personality-based, subjective, and change as they are applied to evolving facts, situations, and perspectives. Universal truths apply to everyone. Universal values apply only to those who choose to apply them. Finally, universal truths are self-evident. Universal values are evident only to those who accept the values as right for them.

Obama dismisses universal truth as too ideological, rigid and inflexible.[101] When he speaks of universal values, he is really talking about "common ground," another of his oft-repeated slippery phrases. Obama has observed that, "democracy must be more than what the majority insists on … No one is exempt from the call to find common ground."[102] At best, Obama believes that universal values are merely the theoretical common ground a society reaches when empathetically applying the facts before it. In practice, common ground is a euphemism for "government knows best," as the health care legislation which Obama signed into law against the will of the American people amply illustrates.

Actually, the ingenious constitutional system of checks and balances and separation of powers is rooted in the biblical understanding of humanity's propensity for evil. Obama's universal values twist in the wind of unfettered moral relativism. "Common ground" is an ephemeral mist because it is not grounded to any objective reality. Obama demonstrated the moral confusion inherent in his perspective when he defined sin as

---

98   truth. Dictionary.com. Online Etymology Dictionary. Douglas Harper, Historian. http://dictionary.reference.com/browse/truth (accessed: April 21, 2010).

99   universal. Dictionary.com. The American Heritage® Dictionary of the English Language, Fourth Edition. Houghton Mifflin Company, 2004. http://dictionary.reference.com/browse/universal (accessed: April 21, 2010).

100 value. Dictionary.com. Dictionary.com Unabridged. Random House, Inc. http://dictionary.reference.com/browse/value (accessed: April 21, 2010).

101 Obama, Barack. The Audacity of Hope. New York: Crown, 2006.

102 Obama, Barack. The Audacity of Hope. New York: Crown, 2006.

"being out of alignment with my values."[103] Obama's answer never rises above the ceiling of his own self-importance. If sin is being out of alignment with your own values, then Jeffrey Dahmer, Charles Manson, and Bernie Madoff are vindicated by their own standards. Instead of defining sin, Obama inadvertently defined self-righteousness.

The founders explicitly tied the colonies' right to break free from Great Britain to certain self-evident truths; Obama nonetheless claims that the founding fathers rejected the concept of absolute truth:

> Implicit in [the Constitution's] structure, in the very idea of ordered liberty, was a rejection of absolute truth, the infallibility of any idea or theology.... The rejection of absolutism implicit in our constitutional structure ... has encouraged the very process ... that allows us to make better, if not perfect choices, not only about the means to our ends, but also about the ends themselves.[104]

Obama's universal values are a ruse; the term is an empty, albeit useful, phrase that creates a void to be filled through the exercise of raw power. Simply put, those holding political power determine which values are universal and therefore true.[105] Once he has successfully de-legitimized the truths emanating from Christian principles, Obama is free to introduce his own "truths" in support of his policies and decisions. Since he has successfully cast himself, at least for now, as the unbiased voice of reason, he need not actually provide reasoned support for his assertions. Usually, these so-called truths sound similar to the principles posited by persons of faith, only once Obama has control of how and when they are utilized, he can seamlessly blend in new values, as he did in his inaugural address:

---

103 "Barack Obama: The 2004 "God Factor" Interview Transcript." Audacity of Hypocrisy. http://www.audacityofhypocrisy.com/2008/06/06/barack-obama-the-2004-god-factor-interview-transcript/. Internet. The interviewer, Cathleen Falsani, also asked Obama, "Do you pray?" Though it would be unfair to read too much into Obama's answer, it too seems self-bound: "Uh, yeah, I guess I do. It's not formal, me getting on my knees. I think I have an ongoing conversation with God. I think throughout the day, I'm constantly asking myself questions about what I'm doing, why I'm doing it..."
104 Obama, Barack. The Audacity of Hope. New York: Crown, 2006.
105 Jonah Goldberg, editor-at-large of National Review Online and author of Liberal Fascism, makes the case that Obama is a postmodern: "'PoMos' hold that there is no such thing as capital-T 'Truth.' There are only lower-case 'truths.'... In the PoMo's telling, reality is 'socially constructed.' And so the PoMos seek to tear down everything that 'privileges' the powerful over the powerless and to replace it with new truths more to their liking. Hence the deep dishonesty of postmodernism. It claims to liberate society from fixed meanings and rigid categories, but it is invariably used to impose new ones, usually in the form of political correctness." Goldberg, Jonah. "Obama, the postmodernist." USAToday.com. http://blogs.usatoday.com/oped/2008/08/obama-the-postm.html. Internet.

Our challenges may be new. The instruments with which we meet them may be new. But those values upon which our success depends - honesty and hard work, courage and fair play, tolerance and curiosity, loyalty and patriotism - these things are old. These things are true. They have been the quiet force of progress throughout our history. What is demanded then is a return to these truths.[106]

Following his demand that "the religiously motivated translate their concerns into universal, rather than religion-specific values" Obama gives a single example:

If I am opposed to abortion for religious reasons and seek to pass a law banning the practice, I cannot simply point to the teachings of my church or invoke God's will and expect that argument to carry the day. If I want others to listen to me, then I have to explain why abortion violates some principle that is accessible to people of all faiths, including those with no faith at all.[107]

The example betrays his weak position. One must first deal with Obama's assertion that only a religious person would oppose abortion and the only support a religious person would give for that position is religion itself. Obama implies that this stereotype of the Christian right, so ingrained that his disdain is palpable, is the norm, and he uses it to relegate the views of Christians to second-class status in political affairs. With rare exception, Christians and Christian-based organizations do not rely solely on religion when seeking to shape social policy in America. Christians understand that reason and experience are indispensably valuable tools in advancing true morality, and they use both in their arguments.

Obama is exploiting the popular myth that Christianity is anti-science, which is particularly offensive since many early scientists were Christians.[108] In contrast to the cyclical-centered cosmology of non-Christian cultures that looked to astrology, magic or fatalism for understanding the world around them, the Christian perception of a God who created and gave

---

106 Obama, Barack. "Obama Inaugural Address." ObamaSpeeches.com. http://obamaspeeches. com. Internet.
107 Obama, Barack. The Audacity of Hope. New York: Crown, 2006.
108 Early scientists, including Blaise Pascal, Isaac Newton, Charles Babbage, Louis Aggasiz, Georges Cuvier, Ambrose Fleming, Robert Boyle, William Thomson Kelvin, Carolus Linnaeus, Johannes Kepler, and Louis Pasteur, took a keen interest in theology. Gregor Mendel, the father of genetics, was a monk. Bumbulis, Michael. "Christianity and the Birth of Science." Lambert Dolphin's Library. http://ldolphin.org/bumbulis/. Internet.

order to the universe provided an impetus to search for causal relationships in the world. The same God who created moral laws was understood to have created laws of nature. The same God who embodies Truth created a physical world ordered by certain observable, objective truths. Several aspects of Christian theology, such as belief in a personal, rational, transcendent God who created an ordered universe ex nihilo, were contributing factors to the birth of modern science. Francis Bacon, a Christian who is credited with establishing the scientific method, viewed science as an apologetic and evangelistic tool for the Church.

> A plea for the faith can be effectively made through this science, not by arguments but by works, which is the more effective way. For the man who denies the truth of the faith because he cannot understand it I shall state the mutual attraction of things in nature.[109]

Bacon's early observation of the "mutual attraction" of things in nature and spiritual truth holds true today. While there are a few ultraconservative Christian sects that take an adversarial stance to certain scientific findings and a larger body of Christians who take issue with the extreme, anti-supernatural stances of many scientists and scientific bodies, most Christian organizations recognize that arguments based solely on Scripture are likely to be dismissed in today's secular society. Like Bacon, Christians understand that reason and science are valuable to the Christian worldview, and use the truths they reveal to undergird their positions. The Family Research Council (FRC), the American Center for Law and Justice (ACLJ), and the Alliance Defense Fund (ADF) are just three of many Christian-based organizations that formulate policy positions using sound legal, sociological, and scientific understandings. ACLJ and ADF have used reason, not religion, to win numerous legal cases at the Supreme Court. Christian views should not be disregarded solely because they are consistent with biblical teaching.

Obama's implication that the pro-life position is inextricably tied to religion is unfounded. Numerous pro-life organizations are explicitly non-religious, including Secularprolife.org and the Atheist and Agnostic Pro-life League. Pro-life advocates, regardless of their religious perspective, are indebted to modern science's understanding that human life begins at conception. Christian and secular crisis pregnancy centers alike utilize ultrasound technologies to help pregnant women have the information they

---

109 Ibid. Christianity and the Birth of Science." Lambert Dolphin's Library. http://ldolphin. org/bumbulis/. Internet.

need to make sound decisions.[110] In October 2009, LifeSiteNews.com, a website that "emphasizes the social worth of traditional Judeo-Christian principles…," hailed the release of handheld ultrasound machines for their potential use in pro-life counseling, noting, "For pro-lifers on the front lines, the new gadget could hugely improve abortion-bound women's access to ultrasounds, which have been highly effective in helping mothers choose life for their baby."[111] The Church has a biblical mandate to care for the poor and to speak up for the weakest and most vulnerable members of society, but Obama's argument that the "religiously motivated translate their concerns into universal, rather than religion-specific values" undermines the validity of contributions Christians organizations have made to the political arena.

The Tebow Effect

When the media reported that former University of Florida quarterback Tim Tebow and his mother, Pam Tebow, would be featured in a pro-life commercial during the 2010 Super Bowl, the visceral reaction was immediate; several pro-abortion groups urged CBS to drop the ad before the commercial was even released for screening. The story behind the ad, which was only vaguely alluded to in the actual commercial, is that while pregnant with her fifth child, Pam Tebow developed complications. Doctors recommended she have an abortion, but she and her husband, serving as missionaries in the Philippines at the time, chose to give birth to their son Tim, an outspoken Christian who won the 2007 Heisman trophy and led the Florida Gators to two BCS championships.

In the ad, placed by the well-known conservative Christian group Focus on the Family as part of their "Celebrate Life, Celebrate Family" campaign, Pam Tebow says of her son, "I call him my miracle baby. He almost didn't make it into this world. I can remember so many times when I almost lost him. It was so hard. Well he's all grown up now, and I still worry about his health. You know, with all our family's been through, you have to be tough." The ad concludes with son Tim tackling his mom, apologizing, and asking if she still worries about him. Pam Tebow responds, "Well, yeah, you're not nearly as tough as I am."[1]

ChoiceUSA spokesperson Kierra Johnson slammed Focus on the Family, calling it an "Anti-American" and "Anti-Woman" group and calling the ad an

---

1   Ertelt, Steven. "Focus on the Family Pro-Life Tim Tebow Super Bowl Commercials." LifeNews. com. http://www.lifenews.com/timtebow.html. Internet.; Stuever, Hank, and Yahr, Emily. "Super Bowl ad featuring quarterback Tebow, mother riles abortion rights groups." WashingtonPost.com. http://www.washingtonpost.com/wp-dyn/content/article/2010/01/26/AR2010012603739.html. Internet.

---

110   New, Michael J. "The Case for Pro-Life Optimism." National Review. January 22, 2009.

111   "About LifeSiteNews.com." LifeSiteNews.com. http://www.lifesitenews.com/aboutlifesite/index.html. Internet.; Gilbert, Kathleen. "Handheld Ultrasound: A Peek at the Future of the Pro-Life Movement?." LifeSiteNews.com. http://www.lifesitenews.com/ldn/2009/oct/09102312.html. Internet.

"un-American message of "hate."[2] In a letter of protest, the Women's Media Center labeled Focus on the Family an "anti-equality, anti-choice, homophobic organization." Terry O'Neill, president of the National Organization for Women (N.O.W.) condemned the 30 second spot as "extraordinarily offensive and demeaning." None of the commentators had even seen the ad at the time.[3]

---

2   Winder, John G. "PRO-ABORTION GROUPS PLAY THE "H" CARD OVER TEBOW SUPER BOWL AD." The Cypress Times. http://www.thecypresstimes.com/article/News/Opinion_Editorial/PROABORTION_GROUPS_PLAY_THE_H_CARD_OVER_TEBOW_SUPER_BOWL_AD/27299. Internet.
3   Associated Press. "Women's groups urge CBS to drop Tebow Super Bowl ad." Fox Sports. http://msn.foxsports.com/nfl/story/Womens-groups-urge-CBS-to-drop-Tebow-Super-Bowl-ad-012510. Internet.

Even when restricted to Obama's preferred debate fodder of universal values, the Christian position on abortion would remain constant. If there is any universal value that all people can agree on, surely it is the inherent value of every human life. This principle is accessible to everyone; after all, every person is a member of the human race – even Keith Olbermann.[112]

The American public is divided on the abortion issue, yet an increasing majority of Americans favor common-sense restrictions on the right to abortion. Nonetheless, Obama fights to protect abortion-on-demand through all nine months of pregnancy. His views are among the most radical of any elected official in America, even further left than the pro-choice advocacy group NARAL. As an Illinois state senator, Obama made the irrational argument that an abortionist - the one attempting to kill the unborn child - can be trusted to provide medical care in the event that his attempt to abort the baby accidentally results in a live birth.[113]

As a U.S. senator, Obama issued a statement highlighting his pro-choice credentials on the 35th anniversary of the *Roe v. Wade* decision: "Throughout my career, I've been a consistent and strong supporter of reproductive justice, and have consistently had a 100 percent pro-choice rating with Planned Parenthood and NARAL Pro-Choice America ...

---

112 Bloggers debate the human credentials of Olbermann. Diogenes2008: "The real truth is that Keith is an alien. Not an illegal alien, an outer-space alien. He is currently working on his plan to take over the whole world. I know because I'm one of his sneaky little cohorts…" "JW, in Dallas: "Are you sitting down? I have some difficult news for you: Keith Olbermann is human. I know it's hard to accept, so take all the time you need to process it. I struggled with this myself, but the news was broken to me by someone I trust…" "Keith Olbermann "Hiking the Appalachian Trail?"." Daily Kos. http://www.dailykos.com/story/2009/7/24/757176/-Keith-Olbermann-Hiking-the-Appalachian-Trail. Internet.
113 Carpenter, Amanda B. "Obama more pro-choice than NARAL." Human Events. http://www.humanevents.com/article.php?id=18647. Internet.

And I will continue to defend this right by passing the Freedom of Choice Act (FOCA) as president."[114]

FOCA enshrines abortion on demand as a fundamental right and would invalidate state legislative attempts to enforce or enact widely supported restrictions, including parental notice, informed consent, and partial-birth abortion.[115] As president, Obama overturned the Mexico City policy that prohibited the use of taxpayer money to promote or perform overseas abortions, signed an executive order forcing taxpayer funding of new lines of embryonic stem cell research, and released a new budget that allows the Legal Services Corporation to use tax dollars for pro-abortion litigation.[116]

Obama's abortion record reveals a person ideologically attached to abortion-on-demand with just the kind of unreasonable religious fervor he attacks. His appeals to reason in support of his extreme position are unconvincing. Obama even thinks it is reasonable for pro-life advocates to respect the value system of women for whom abortion is a sacrament:

> Our democracy might work a bit better if we recognized that all of us possess values that are worthy of respect: if liberals at least acknowledged that the recreational hunter feels the same way about his gun as they feel about their library books, and if conservatives recognized that most women feel as protective of their right to reproductive freedom as evangelicals do of their right to worship.[117]

In a 2003 study funded by the pro-abortion Center for the Advancement of Women, 51 percent of women held pro-life beliefs; seventeen percent favored outlawing abortion completely, while 34 percent favored outlawing abortion except in cases of rape, incest, or to save the life of the mother. Since 2003, the pro-life position has generally gained favor among Americans. In 2009, 41 percent of Americans favored more restrictions on abortion, up six points in just two years. Only eight percent of liberal

---

114 Obama, Barack. "Obama Statement on 35th Anniversary of Roe v. Wade Decision." BarackObama.com. http://www.barackobama.com/2008/01/22/obama_statement_on_35th_ annive.php. Internet.

115 "S.1173 - Freedom of Choice Act." Open Congress. http://www.opencongress.org/ bill/110-s1173/text. Internet.

116 Cuttie, Heather. "A Chronology Of Obama Pro-Abortion on Demand Policies And Nominations." A Constitutional Conservative Catholic Mom's Blog. http://heathercuttie. wordpress.com/2009/12/22/a-chronology-of-obama-pro-abortion-on-demand-policies-and-nominations/. Internet.

117 Obama, Barack. The Audacity of Hope. New York: Crown, 2006.

Democrats in 2009 consider abortion a critical issue, down 26 points since 2006. While the law may protect a woman's right to choose an abortion, statistics contradict Obama's assertion that reproductive rights rise to the level of a universal value, much less a universal truth.[118]

The founders set a firm moral foundation for America by anchoring our freedom to the universal truths that all persons are created equal and entitled to life, liberty, and the pursuit of happiness. When leaders substitute their own truths for self-evident truth, they crack that foundation. Universal truth is our common ground, not because we chose it, but because it defines reality.

118 Ertelt, Steven. "Pro-Abortion Poll Shows Majority of Women Are Pro-Life." LifeNews. com. http://www.lifenews.com/nat13.html. Internet.; "Support for Abortion Slips." PewForum.org. http://pewforum.org/docs/?DocID=441. Internet.

3

Closing the Door on Openness and Transparency

Transparent government and a free press are essential to a constitutional republic. Together they provide a critical safeguard against fraud, waste, and abuse of power. The need for transparency should only be outweighed by concerns for national security and individual privacy.

On the campaign trail, Obama promised to "make our government open and transparent so that anyone can ensure that our business is the people's business."[119] On his first day in office, Obama promised "a new era of openness in our country" and said, "Transparency and the rule of law will be the touchstones of this presidency."[120] Based on the Obama administration's actions so far, nothing could be further from the truth. Instead, the administration's actions have exhibited the same evasiveness as the Obama campaign, the most tightly-controlled presidential campaign in history. White House Communications Director Anita Dunn described the campaign's media strategy, explaining, "Very rarely did we communicate through the press anything that we didn't absolutely control."[121]"A huge part of our press strategy was focused on making the media cover what Obama was actually saying as opposed to, you know, why the campaign was saying it, what the tactic was."[122] The Obama administration has attempted to maintain the same tight control of its public persona, offering the media severely limited access to the president for informal question and

119 Pittman, Mark, Bob Ivry and Alison Fitzgerald. "Fed Defies Transparency Aim in Refusal to Disclose." Bloomberg.com. http://www.bloomberg.com/apps/news?pid=20601087&sid=aatlky_cH.tY. Internet.

120 "Vowing transparency, Obama OKs ethics guidelines." CNN.com. http://www.cnn.com/2009/POLITICS/01/21/obama.business/index.html. Internet.

121 FoxNews.com. "Top White House Official Says Obama Team 'Controlled' Media Coverage During Campaign." FoxNews.com. http://www.foxnews.com/politics/2009/10/19/white-house-official-says-obama-team-controlled-media-coverage-campaign/. Internet.

122 Media Matters. "UPDATED: Beck, Drudge, WND, Fox Nation falsely accuse Dunn of admitting White House "control" over news media." MediaMatters.org. http://mediamatters.org/mobile/research/200910190025. Internet.

answer sessions as compared to his two predecessors in office. The White House has also established a practice of barring photojournalists from some events and instead releasing its own pictures.[123]

Evasiveness on the Campaign Trail

Here is a sampling of issues about which Obama and his campaign staff were less than forthcoming.

- The extent of Obama's association with unrepentant Weather Underground terrorist Bill Ayers and his terrorist wife Bernadine Dohrn, whose leftist-fringe organization was responsible for the bombings of dozens of facilities in the early 1970's, including several federal buildings.[1]

  Obama held one of the first meetings of his political career in 1995 in Ayers' home and worked with Ayers on controversial education-related projects in Chicago. Ayers fought to have the $50 million Annenberg Challenge Project brought to Chicago, and Barack Obama was recruited to be its Chair. In that position, Obama helped funnel hundreds of thousands of dollars to Ayers Small Schools Project and millions to an assortment of leftist organizations[2]. The blog Verum Serum charged – and presented a paper trail to document – that Ayers and Obama even shared the same Chicago office building on the same floor for at least three years.[3]

  The Obama campaign attempted to portray Ayers as simply someone who happened to live in the same neighborhood as Obama, though by 1995 "Barack Obama had known Bill Ayers at least eight years since their shared involvement in The Alliance for Better Chicago Schools, if not longer."[4] CNN investigative correspondent Drew Griffin reported that despite the spin from the Obama campaign, "the relationship between Obama and Ayers went much deeper, ran much longer, and was much more political than Obama said."[5] When interviewed by the New York Times on September 11, 2001, Ayers said, "I don't regret setting bombs. I feel we didn't do enough."[6]

---

1   Owens, Bob. "Ayers-Dohrn-Obama Tie Shouldn't Be Dismissed." Pajamas Media. http://pajamasmedia.com/blog/ayers-dohrn-obama-tie-shouldnt-be-dismissed/. Internet.
2   Transcipt: "Anderson Cooper 360 Degrees," October 6, 2008 http://transcripts.cnn.com/TRANSCRIPTS/0810/06/acd.01.html
3   "Crossing Paths Daily: Obama and Ayers Shared an Office (Update: For Three Years)," October 16, 2008 http://www.verumserum.com/?p=2907
4   Ibid.
5   Transcipt: "Anderson Cooper 360 Degrees," October 6, 2008 http://transcripts.cnn.com/TRANSCRIPTS/0810/06/acd.01.html
6   Smith, Dinitia. "No Regrets for a Love Of Explosives; In a Memoir of Sorts, a War Protester Talks of Life With the Weathermen." New York TImes. 11 September 2001

---

123 "White House video blog offers an inside view," by Paul Farhi, May 15, 2010 http://www.washingtonpost.com/wp-dyn/content/article/2010/05/14/AR2010051401316.html?hpid=topnews

- The questionable source of many of Obama's campaign contributions. In October 2008, Newsmax.com reported, "more than 37,000 Obama donations appear to be conversions of foreign currency ... potential foreign currency donations could range anywhere from $12.8 million to a stunning $63 million in all. With the addition of $150 million raised in September, this amount could be much more"[7]
- The extent of Obama's association with convicted financier Tony Rezko, convicted Illinois governor Rod Blagojevich, anti-Israel terror apologist (and alleged Obama friend) Rashid Khalidi, and controversial Father Michael Pfleger (an Obama spiritual advisor)[8]
- Obama's birth records, medical records, passport records, Hawaii college prep school records, Harvard records, Columbia college records, Occidental College records, and legislative records[9]
- The nature and extent of Muslim influence and teaching in Obama's childhood[10]
- Obama's schizophrenic pro-Second Amendment, anti-handgun statements[11]
- Increased tax burdens embedded in Obama's political positions (cap and trade, health care reform, etc.)
- Obama's position that the Supreme Court "didn't break free from the essential constraints that were placed by the founding fathers in the Constitution" during the Civil Rights Movement, as well as his desire to "put together actual coalitions of power through which you bring about redistributive change."[12]

---

7   Timmerman, Ken. "Obama's Secret Campaign Cash: Has $63 Million Flowed from Foreign Sources?." NewsMax.com. http://newsmax.com/InsideCover/obama-illegal-donations/2009/ 12/12/id/341673. Internet.; Isikoff, Michael. "Obama's 'Good Will' Hunting." Newsweek. 13 October 2008

8   Associated Press. "Questionable Associations of Obama." Newsvine.com. http://www.newsvine.com/_news/2008/12/10/2197204-questionable-associations-of-obama Source 2. Internet.; McCarthy, Andrew C. "The L.A. Times Suppresses Obama's Khalidi Bash Tape." National Review. 27 October 2008; Falsani, Cathleen. "Obama: I have a deep faith Barack Obama credits his multicultural upbringing for his theological point of view." Chicago Sun-Times. http://www.suntimes.com/news/falsani/726619,obamafalsani040504.article. Internet.

9   Baldwin, Steve. "The Mystery of Barack Obama Continues." Western Journalism. http://www.westernjournalism.com/?page_id=3255. Internet.

10 Tapper, Jake and Miller, Sunlen. "The Emergence of President Obama's Muslim Roots." ABCNews.com. http://blogs.abcnews.com/politicalpunch/2009/06/abc-news-jake-tapper-and-sunlen-miller-report-the-other-day-we-heard-a-comment-from-a-white-house-aide-that-neverwould-have.html. Internet.

11 "Barack Obama on Gun Control." OnTheIssues.org. http://www.ontheissues.org/domestic/Barack_Obama_Gun_Control.htm. Internet.

12 Whittle, Bill. "Shame, Cubed." National Review. http://article.nationalreview.com/376519/shame-cubed/bill-whittle. Internet.

During and after his presidential campaign for president, Obama pointedly promised a more open and transparent government. He criticized George W. Bush's administration for being too secretive and pledged to reverse this practice. The Obama transition team website stated:

> The Bush administration has been one of the most secretive, closed administrations in American history. Our nation's progress has been stifled by a system corrupted... An Obama presidency will use cutting-edge technologies to reverse this dynamic, creating a new level of transparency, accountability and participation for America's citizens.[124]

Upon taking office in January 2009, Obama issued a "Memorandum for the Heads of Executive Departments and Agencies: Transparency and Open Government," in which he issued the following pledge:

> My Administration is committed to creating an unprecedented level of openness in Government. We will work together to ensure the public trust and establish a system of transparency, public participation, and collaboration. Openness will strengthen our democracy and promote efficiency and effectiveness in Government. Government should be transparent. Transparency promotes accountability and provides information for citizens about what their Government is doing.[125]

The Obama campaign's promise of open government came as a relief to many Americans who felt disenfranchised by the previous administration's lack of transparency and candor, especially in regard to the justifications for, and the conduct of, the Iraq war. The George W. Bush-era government's secret wiretapping program, warrantless searches and obfuscation about the progress of the Iraq war all evidenced a disturbing pattern of government opacity and intrusion.[126]

Despite the government's need for confidentiality in matters of national security and the heightened threat so violently demonstrated by the 9/11 attacks, some of the George W. Bush administration's actions have been rightly scrutinized. According to *Judicial Watch*, a report issued by watchdog groups concluded that the Bush administration restricted public access to

124 "Technology." BarackObama.com. http://www.barackobama.com/issues/technology/index_campaign.php. Internet.
125 "Transparency and Open Government." WhiteHouse.gov. http://www.whitehouse.gov/the_press_office/TransparencyandOpenGovernment/. Internet.
126 Taylor, Kathleen. "Abuse of power must be challenged." Seattle Times. http://community.seattletimes.nwsource.com/archive/?date=20060323&slug=kathleentaylor23. Internet.

information at unprecedented levels by asserting executive powers and national security state secrets privileges in court.[127] Obama's transparency pledge would seemingly reverse the Bush administration's opacity, but the directive crafted by Obama administration lawyers to implement his new transparency policy created various loopholes that render it "astonishingly weaker" than the policy set by Democratic predecessor Bill Clinton's attorney general, Janet Reno. For example, the directive holds that the new transparency standard applies "if practicable" for cases involving pending litigation.[128]

The Left is incensed that Obama is continuing to exert the same executive power and privileges claims that George W. Bush frequently used to prevent the release of information.[129] Left-wing icon Daniel Ellsberg, who leaked the Pentagon Papers in 1971, charges, "Obama, in ... matters related to secrecy and whistleblowing, is doing worse than Bush. His violation of civil liberties and the White House's excessive use of executive secrecy privilege is [sic] inexcusable. .... His actions are totally uncoupled from his public statements anymore."[130] The current administration's actions are a far cry from Obama's 2006 criticism of Vice President Dick Cheney's secret energy meetings at the White House:

---

127 "Obama Promises Transparency, Openness." Corruption Chronicles: A Judicial Watch Blog. http://www.judicialwatch.org/blog/2008/nov/obama-promises-transparency-openness. Internet.

128 Isikoff, Michael. "Obama Closes Doors on Openness." Newsweek. 29 June 2009

129 Glen Greenwald, writing at salon.com, quotes fourteen separate news reports that detail a pattern of retreat from Obama's transparency and openness promises. Half of the quotes described a continuation of Bush policies; others dealt with secrecy regarding new situations. A sampling follows:
"In a closely watched case involving rendition and torture [Mohamed v. Jeppesen Data], a lawyer for the Obama administration seemed to surprise a panel of federal appeals judges on Monday by pressing ahead with an argument for preserving state secrets originally developed by the Bush administration." -- New York Times, February 9, 2009
"The Obama administration, siding with former President George W. Bush, is trying to kill a lawsuit that seeks to recover what could be millions of missing White House e-mails." -Huffington Post, February 21, 2009
"A federal judge on Friday threatened to severely sanction the Obama Administration for withholding a top secret document he ordered given to lawyers suing the government over its warrantless wiretapping program..." San Francisco Chronicle, May 22, 2009
"The Obama administration has decided to keep secret the locations of nearly four dozen coal ash storage sites that pose a threat to people living nearby. The Environmental Protection Agency classified the 44 sites as potential hazards to communities while investigating storage of coal ash waste after a spill at a Tennessee power plant in December." - Associated Press, June 12, 2009"
"President Obama has embraced Bush administration justifications for denying public access to White House visitor logs..." --Washington Post, June 17, 2009

130 "Obama Deceives the Public," Spiegel Online, June 9, 2010 www.spiegel.de/international/world/0,1518,druck-699677,00.html

What's truly offensive about these scandals is that they don't just lead to morally offensive conduct on the part of politicians; they lead to morally offensive legislation that hurts hardworking Americans. Because when big oil companies are invited into the White House for secret energy meetings, it's no wonder they end up with billions in tax breaks while Americans still struggle to fill up their gas tanks and heat their homes. [131]

Interestingly, Citizens for Responsibility and Ethics in Washington (CREW) filed a Freedom of Information Act (FOIA) lawsuit on June 16, 2009, based on the Secret Service's refusal to provide access to the Obama administration's White House visitor logs detailing visits by top coal executives.[132] The following month CREW filed another lawsuit over the Obama administration's refusal to release records of White House visits by health care executives.[133] In both cases, Obama's stance mirrors the George W. Bush policy in claiming that that the records were presidential records protected by the presidential communications privilege.

As a candidate in September 2007, Obama unveiled his plan to make the federal government more transparent. He promised "national broadband town hall meetings," which he called "21st Century Fireside Chats,"

131 Obama, Barack. "LOBBYING REFORM SUMMIT." ObamaSpeeches.com. http:// obamaspeeches.com/047-Lobbying-Reform-Summit-National-Press-Club-Obama-Speech.htm. Internet. Obama's concern for Americans struggling with rising energy costs rings hollow, given his subsequent statements. In January 2008 he told the San Francisco Chronicle in a videotaped interview, "Under my plan of a cap-and-trade system, electricity rates would necessarily skyrocket." "Pence claims that Obama said energy costs will skyrocket with a cap-and-trade plan." Politifact.com. http://www.politifact.com/truth-o-meter/statements/2009/jun/11/mike-pence/pence-claims-obama-said-energy-costs-will-skyrocke/. Internet. In February 2008 Obama said, "What we ought to tax is dirty energy, like coal and, to a lesser extent, natural gas." "Q&A with Sen. Barack Obama." MySanAntonio.com. http://www.mysanantonio.com/news/MYSA021908_ObamaQnA_e-n_c1d9803_html19832.html. Internet. When CNBC's John Harwood asked Obama in June 2008 if high gas prices (which averaged over $4/gallon at the time) could help America shift to alternative energy sources, Obama replied, "I think I would have preferred a gradual adjustment." Dauble, Jennifer. "CNBC Exclusive: CNBC's Chief Washington Correspondent John Harwood Sits Down with Presidential Candidate Senator Barack Obama (Transcript Included)." CNBC.com. http://www.cnbc.com/id/25084346/CNBC_Exclusive_CNBC_s_Chief_Washington_Correspondent_John_Harwood_Sits_Down_with_Presidential_Candidate_Senator_Barack_Obama_Transcript_Included. Internet.
132 "CREW V. U.S. DEPARTMENT OF HOMELAND SECURITY (WHITE HOUSE VISITOR LOGS - COAL EXECS)." CitizensforEthics.org. http://www.citizensforethics.org/node/40129. Internet.
133 "Obama asked about turning down CREW's request for records of White House visits by health care execs." CitizensforEthics.org. http://www.citizensforethics.org/taxonomy/term/1509?page=1. Internet.

Gibbs v. the Press

Every administration covets positive press coverage, but few have worked so actively to control as much as possible of the media's reporting. Throughout the campaign and the first 100 days of his administration, Obama had no real need to exert control over the mainstream media; they were willing accomplices in promulgating his message on virtually every topic. But one thing most media still will not stand for is covert attempts by government to control the reporting process.

Veteran White House Correspondent Helen Thomas has covered the news of every administration since John F. Kennedy. During a July 1, 2009 White House briefing conducted by Press Secretary Robert Gibbs, she interrupted a testy exchange between Gibbs and Chip Reid, the White House correspondent for CBS news. Reid was challenging the administration's practice of pre-selecting both questions and questioners at President Obama's scheduled events, including a town hall meeting to be held later that day.

Reid: This is an open forum for the public to ask questions, but it's not really open.
Gibbs: (over Reid) I couldn't agree more.
Reid: But it's not open.
Gibbs: Based on what?
Reid: Based on the information that your staff gave us on how the audience and the questions are being selected.

A few moments later, Thomas entered the fray and quickly made her opinion known:

Thomas: I'm amazed -- I'm amazed at you people who call for openness and transparency and-
Gibbs: Helen, you haven't even heard the questions.
Reid: It doesn't matter. It's the process.
Thomas: You have left open –
Reid: Even if there's a tough question, it's a question coming from somebody who was invited or was screened, or the question was screened.
Thomas: It's shocking. It's really shocking.[1]

---

1   Montopoli, Brian. "CBS' Chip Reid, Gibbs Spar Over "Town Hall"." CBSNews.com. http://www.cbsnews.com/blogs/2009/07/02/politics/politicalhotsheet/entry5129482.s html?tag=contentMain;contentBody. Internet.

between himself, his cabinet, and the American people.[134] The term "town hall meetings" connects to a simpler time in American history and evokes an environment in which ordinary Americans can get straightforward answers from government officials, including the president.

---

134 "Ethics." BarackObama.com. http://www.barackobama.com/issues/ethics/index_campaign. php. Internet.

The press rightly recognized that town hall meetings conducted by the Obama administration are a sham; the meetings are tightly controlled in every respect. The people in attendance are carefully screened to ensure they are administration cheerleaders. Of course, the press only protested the administration's lack of transparency when the White House attempted to control even the media's questions.[135] Media events, however, are not the only victims of the Obama transparency lie.

Obama Non-transparency Examples

TARP Money Shell Game: The Emergency Economic Stabilization Act of 2008 (EESA), enacted on October 3, 2008, authorized the Treasury Department to establish the Troubled Asset Relief Program (TARP). Hurriedly passed amidst dire warnings of impending financial meltdown absent immediate action, TARP authorized the Treasury Department to purchase or insure up to $700 billion of "troubled assets," consisting of residential or commercial mortgages and related securities, in order to promote stability in the financial markets.[136]

TARP has been a widely unpopular program from the start, with little oversight and even less transparency. The original TARP plan, developed by then-Treasury Secretary Hank Paulson, called for the U.S. Treasury to purchase devalued mortgage assets through a reverse auction, with banks bidding to sell them to the government for pennies on the dollar. In theory, banks would get the bad assets off their books and taxpayers would get a bargain, but the plan would have forced many banks into insolvency by forcing them to write down the value of the assets. "It would have been a financial holocaust," said Bill Black, a former regulator at the Office of Thrift Supervision (OTS).[137]

Realizing the plan's eminent downfall, Paulson quickly changed his strategy away from a focus on mortgage-backed security purchases. On

135 Montopoli, Brian. "CBS' Chip Reid, Gibbs Spar Over "Town Hall"." CBSNews.com. http://www.cbsnews.com/blogs/2009/07/02/politics/politicalhotsheet/entry5129482.shtml?tag=contentMain;contentBody. Internet.
136 "The Troubled Asset Relief Program: Report on Transactions through June 17, 2009." http://docs.google.com/viewer?a=v&q=cache:cuLREcvHoGwJ:www.cbo.gov/ftpdocs/100xx/doc10056/06-29-TARP.pdf+ percent22cbo+report percent22+ percent22troubled+asset+relief+program percent22+ percent22transactions percent22&hl=en&gl=us&pid=bl&srcid=ADGEESi3lQVu2zKZbyfPlUy322psBC_6K5uuBM3A8L81hHvWG0O13tWQkb3aI-bGmrYcEV7Urs605O2O0paTDBI6E4YwRueQ2dd0eKqa_0UVNN0Oj0et6WaFF3T2BR2e_FXfp-6Mpm5I&sig=AHIEtbQSeZ26lM5ehIM52ydQ2qqFSPwqmQ. Internet.
137 Phillips, Matthew. "TARP: One Year Later." Newsweek. 12 November 2009.

November 12, 2008, Paulson announced that buying mortgage-related assets is "not the most effective way to use TARP funds." According to his new plan, Paulson said TARP funds "may also be used to support new commercial and residential mortgage-backed securities lending."[138] Instead of buying existing toxic assets from banks for pennies on the dollar, the Treasury decided to provide cash to distressed financial institutions in exchange for preferred stock. At the time of the announcement, Paulson had already spent a large share of the TARP I funds, including $115 billion forced on the nine largest U.S. banks and $40 billion used to rescue AIG.[139] By July 2009, the Treasury and the Federal Reserve had funneled a mind-boggling $182 billion dollars to AIG.[140] In return, the government took a 78 percent stake in the company.[141]

Even after the biggest bailout in history, critics charged that AIG's filings with state insurance regulators revealed continued financial weakness. The AIG umbrella of insurance companies includes more than 4000 units in more than 100 countries, including 71 American insurers, spread among nineteen state insurance commissions.

W.O. Myrick, a retired chief insurance examiner for Louisiana, saw red flags in his review of many state filings. He said that because AIG has engaged in extensive risk-spreading between its companies, largely through "reinsurance" practices, a conglomerate like AIG "can keep moving assets around to clean up one company" when it is being examined.[142] Myrick contended that only a coordinated, multistate examination of all AIG's insurance companies could properly assess the true financial condition of the company, and warned that if incoming premiums shrink, "the whole thing's going to collapse in on itself."

Thomas D. Gober, a former insurance examiner who currently operates a forensic accounting firm that specializes in insurance fraud, echoed Myrick's concerns: "Eventually, there's going to be a battle between the

---

138 Shenn, Jody. "Mortgage Bonds Fall to New Lows as Paulson Scraps U.S. Buying." Bloomberg. http://www.bloomberg.com/apps/news?pid=20601087&sid=aoO72tY0wjK 4&refer=home (accessed April 21, 2010).

139 Ibid.

140 Walsh, Mary Williams. "After Rescue, New Weakness Seen at A.I.G.." New York Times. 30 July 2009.

141 Cohan, Peter. "After $182 Taxpayer Rescue, is AIG on the Verge of Collapse?." Daily Finance. http://www.dailyfinance.com/story/company-news/after-182-billion-taxpayer-rescue-is-aig-on-the-verge-of-colla/19115352/. Internet.

142 Walsh, Mary Williams. "After Rescue, New Weakness Seen at A.I.G.." New York Times. 30 July 2009.

policyholders and the feds. The Fed is going to say, 'We want our money back,' but the law says, 'Policyholders come first.' It's going to be ugly."[143]

AIG's ill-conceived business strategy involved selling insurance policies, called credit default swaps (CDSs), on hundreds of billions of dollars' worth of bonds, subprime mortgages and other assets. By purchasing CDSs, big-hitters like JP Morgan and Goldman Sachs could wipe risk from their books and free up reserves.[144] But AIG failed to establish adequate reserves to cover claims.

> Even after the insurance conglomerate negotiated for steeply lower prices, $62 billion of the TARP money that went to AIG ended up going to its counterparties, which were paid 100 cents on the dollar for credit-default swaps they'd bought from AIG. Among the largest counterparties were firms like Goldman Sachs.[145]

Paulson's original reverse-auction strategy was doomed from the outset, but his "audible" opened gigantic government coffers of cash to many of the very firms that had engaged in, and profited immensely from, excessive risk taking. The Treasury asked for too little in return, and failed to provide the public with transparency regarding how the TARP funds were distributed.

> TARP has been administered with a transparency that is at best opaque. Tracking the funds over the last year, figuring out who got what from where, has been like following laundered money, leading to a situation rife with conspiracy theories and potential conflicts of interest.[146]

Well-known American finance expert and author John R. Talbott was even sharper in his criticism of Paulson and TARP:

> It turns out that Hank Paulson and TARP did not buy a single underwater mortgage security. They promptly took the money that was directed to that program and used it in a vast giveaway scheme in which over $300 billion was given to the commercial banks and investment banks, most of them good friends of Hank Paulson... Paulson used TARP like his own private piggy bank...

---

143 Ibid.
144 Phillips, Matthew. "The Monster that ate Wall Street." Newsweek. 06 October 2008
145 Phillips, Matthew. "TARP: One Year Later." Newsweek. http://www.newsweek.com/id/222321. Internet.
146 Ibid.

There is no rhyme or reason to who receives funds and who does not. We have wasted $350 billion plus of our hard-earned taxpayer money and we have nothing to show for it.[147]

The fact that the first half of the $700 billion bailout program lacked basic accountability and transparency, and that panic in financial markets had abated, did not prompt Congress to rescind its authority for the expenditure of the second half of TARP. At President-Elect Obama's request, George W. Bush asked Congress to release the second $350 billion of the TARP funding.[148] Obama allegedly warned in an off-the-record meeting that he would veto any bill passed by Congress that held up the funds.[149] Though Congress objected to the George W. Bush administration's handling of TARP I, they downplayed the need for TARP reform legislation, signaling a willingness to trust the Obama administration to spend the money wisely.[150]

In February 2009, newly-appointed Treasury Secretary Geithner announced details of the new, already congressionally-approved TARP II program. He specifically promised "new, higher standards for transparency and accountability" in the financial system, and promised to make spending details available on a new government website, FinancialStability.gov.[151] In July 2009, Special Inspector General for TARP Neil Barofsky issued a report revealing a continued and deliberate lack of transparency on the part of the Treasury. Barofsky said that Treasury had rejected several recommendations for providing more transparency, including a basic requirement that all bailout recipients explain what they were doing with their government funds. Barofsky also criticized the Federal Reserve for a lack of transparency regarding TARP expenditures.

In response, the Obama administration argued that accounting for TARP expenditures was impossible. Barofsky quickly disproved

147 Talbott, John R. *The 86 Biggest Lies on Wall Street.* New York: Seven Stories Press, 2009.
148 Lillis, Mike. "Congress Dems Prepare to Defer to Obama: Leaders Say TARP Reform Legislation Not Necessary Under New White House." *Washington Independent.* http://washingtonindependent.com/25516/democrats-in-congress-prepared-to-defer-to-obama. Internet.
149 Grim, Ryan. "Obama Issues First Veto Threat." *The Huffington Post.* http://www.huffingtonpost.com/2009/01/13/obama-issues-first-veto-t_n_157585.html. Internet.
150 Lillis, Mike. "Congress Dems Prepare to Defer to Obama." *Washington Independent.* http://washingtonindependent.com/25516/democrats-in-congress-prepared-to-defer-to-obama. Internet.
151 "Geithner: TARP II to Assist Homeowners, Be More Transparent, and Less Risky to Taxpayer." FoxBusiness.com. http://wheresmymoney.blogs.foxbusiness.com/2009/02/10/geithner-tarp-ii-to-assist-homeowners-be-more-transparent-and-less-risky-to-taxpayer/". Internet.

the administration's contention by taking a voluntary survey of banks receiving TARP money, which showed that the funds could be tracked.[152] Barofsky's report showed that 43 percent of banks used TARP to shore up their balance sheets, 4 percent used the funds to complete acquisitions and 25 percent of banks used the money to invest in mortgage-backed securities affiliated with federal housing agencies. Though the stated purpose of TARP was to free up money for new loans, less than half of 364 banks surveyed indicated that they used the funds to support residential mortgage loans or other types of consumer loans.[153]

The lack of transparency is even more disturbing in light of the amount of taxpayer money at risk; Barofsky estimates the government's potential exposure to programs in place to solve the financial crisis at $23.7 trillion or approximately $80,000 per American. [154]

In an attempt to stifle Barofsky's independent oversight, the White House sought a Justice Department ruling that would make Barofsky's office subject to the supervision and authority of the Treasury Secretary.[155] The move was a blatant attempt to evade transparency and accountability; Congress established the office of Inspector General to provide independent oversight in critical areas of governmental action. It would be impossible for Barofsky to assure accountability in the execution of TARP while reporting to Geithner, who oversees TARP. In September 2009, the Treasury Department retreated from its attempt to exert control over Barofksy, withdrawing its request for a Justice Department legal opinion.[156]

---

152 "SIGTARP Survey Demonstrates that Banks Can Provide Meaningful Information on Their Use of TARP Funds." Office of the Special Inspector General for the Troubled Asset Relief Program. http://www.sigtarp.gov/reports/audit/2009/SIGTARP_Survey_ Demonstrates_That_Banks_Can_Provide_Meaningfu_ percent20Information_On_ Their_Use_Of_TARP_Funds.pdf. Internet.

153 "SIGTARP Survey Demonstrates that Banks Can Provide Meaningful Information on Their Use of TARP Funds." Office of the Special Inspector General for the Troubled Asset Relief Program. http://www.sigtarp.gov/reports/audit/2009/SIGTARP_Survey_ Demonstrates_That_Banks_Can_Provide_Meaningfu_percent20Information_On_ Their_Use_Of_TARP_Funds.pdf. Internet.

154 Associated Press. "Watchdog sees huge U.S. bill for banks bailout."MSNBC.com. http:// www.msnbc.msn.com/id/32010841. Internet.

155 Barofsky said that the Treasury Department told him that the agency has legal authority over his office. O'Keefe, Ed and Paley, Amit R. "In Letter, Barofsky Explains Concerns."Washington Post. http://voices.washingtonpost.com/federal-eye/2009/06/bailout_inspector_general_resp.html. Internet.

156 Perez, Evan and Solomon, Deborah. "Treasury Retreats From Standoff With TARP Watchdog." Wall Street Journal. 03 September 2009.

The Stimulus Package: On his first full day in office, Obama declared "For a long time now there's been too much secrecy in this city ... That era is now over."[157] In February 2009, he celebrated Congress' passage of the American Recovery and Reinvestment Act of 2009 (ARRA) during his weekly radio address, while acknowledging the skepticism of those who feared the federal government's ability to effectively implement the gargantuan $787 billion stimulus plan. "Washington hasn't set a very good example in recent years. And with so much on the line, it's time to begin doing things differently. That's why our goal must be to spend these precious dollars with unprecedented accountability, responsibility, and transparency."[158]

Obama announced that stimulus spending would be tracked through a new, publicly-accessible government website, Recovery.gov. According to the website, citizens would be able to track stimulus expenditures not only to states, but to congressional districts and even to specific federal contractors.[159] ARRA allocated $84 million in annual funding to create the Recovery Accountability and Transparency Board, charged with overseeing ARRA spending and managing the Recovery.gov website.[160]

Three months after the bill was signed, the *Washington Post* reported that Recovery.gov offered "little beyond news releases, general breakdowns of spending, and acronym-laden spreadsheets and timelines."[161] The *Post* specifically took issue with Obama's promise to provide street level scrutiny of the money flow. Instead, the paper noted, "reporting rules for the money extend only to two levels, often stopping short of the contractors." For example, if a state receives stimulus money and subsequently awards money to a city, two levels have been reached and the tracking stops – far short of street level.[162] ABC News followed with reports that the officially- sanctioned government

---

157 Jackson, David, et al. "Starting with diplomacy, Obama sets new course."USA Today. 22 January 2009

158 Phillips, Macon. "The Recovery Act: A Major Milestone."WhiteHouse.gov. http://www. whitehouse.gov/blog/09/02/14/a-major-milestone. Internet.

159 Albanesius, Chloe. "Obama Signs Stimulus Bill, Launches Recovery.gov." PCMag.com. http://www.pcmag.com/article2/0,2817,2341236,00.asp. Internet.

160 According to Recovery.gov, "the Board shall establish and maintain...a user-friendly, public-facing website to foster greater accountability and transparency in the use of covered funds. The website...shall be a portal or gateway to key information relating to the Act and provide connections to other government websites with related information." In July 2009 the General Services Administration announced it had contracted with a Maryland firm for an $18 million redesign of Recovery.gov. Klein, Rick. "$18M Being Spent to Redesign Recovery.gov Web Site."ABCNews.com. http://blogs.abcnews.com/ thenote/2009/07/18m-being-spent-to-redesign-recoverygov-web-site.html. Internet.

161 MacGillis,Alec. "TrackingStimulusSpendingMayNotBeasEasyasPromised."Washington Post. 21 May 2009.

162 Ibid.

website was "riddled with errors," documenting millions of dollars spent to create hundreds of jobs in nonexistent districts, including"[163]

- In Oklahoma, $19 million spent, 15 jobs "created"
- In Iowa, $10.6 million spent, 39 jobs "created"
- In Connecticut, $0 spent, 25 jobs "created"
- In the U.S. Virgin Islands, $8.4 million spent, 40.3 jobs "created"
- In Puerto Rico, $47.7 million spent, 291 jobs "created" Arizona, $761,420 spent, 30 jobs "saved" or "created."

The White House trumpeted Recovery.gov's figures, claiming in November 2009 that the stimulus had created or saved more than 640,000 jobs. The figure, however, was based on White House economic models that purported to calculate the "buckshot" effect of the stimulus. Based on computer modeling, White House economic advisor Jared Bernstein had projected near the beginning of the year that the stimulus would keep the unemployment rate under 8 percent,[164] but the *New York Times* reported that the economy shed 8 million jobs from the beginning of the recession in December 2007 through September 2009.[165] Three months later, the Department of Labor's monthly unemployment report came in at 10 percent, and Obama commented, "So overall this is the best jobs report that we've seen since 2007."[166] The annual average unemployment rate in 2007 was 4.6; prior to 2009, the nation had not suffered annual average double-digit inflation in more than 60 years. In January 2010, the Department of Labor updated the recession's job toll, estimating the figure at 8.4 million jobs lost.[167]

Even the White House's concept of jobs "saved" is nothing more than a cynical ruse. The government does not keep statistics on jobs saved; there is no practical way to calculate or track such a statistic, which frees the White House to create its own method in search of a high number.

163 Karl, Jonathan. "White House Vows to Correct Stimulus Reports Officials Tell ABC News So Far, They Found 700 Mistaken Congressional Districts Out of More Than 130,000 Stimulus Grants." ABCNews.com. http://abcnews.go.com/WN/white-house-stimulus-website-riddled-errors/story?id=9110298. Internet.

164 Carroll, Conn. "White House: 3.6 Million Jobs Lost is "Quite Positive"."The Foundry. http://blog.heritage.org/2009/10/15/white-house-36-million-jobs-lost-is-quite-positive/. Internet.

165 Norris, Floyd. "The Jobs News Gets Worse." New York Times. 03 October 2009.

166 Source: "Obama's Jobs Speech in Pennsylvania," December 4, 2009 http://www.nytimes.com/2009/12/05/business/economy/05obama.text.html

167 Reuters. "Economy Sheds 20,000 Jobs But Rate Drops to 9.7 Percent."CNBC.com. http://www.cnbc.com/id/35254420. Internet.

In November 2009, just four days before ABC News broke the Recovery.gov scandal, Obama boasted, "Through the Recovery Act, we've ... created and saved more than a million jobs."[168] Ed Pound, Communications Director for the Recovery Board, initially seemed unconcerned by ABC's report: "We expected all along that recipients would make mistakes on their congressional districts, on jobs numbers, on award amounts, and so on. Human beings make mistakes."[169] David Obey (D-WI), Chair of the House Appropriations Committee, was less charitable after learning that a sewer project in his district reported creating 100 jobs when the real number was five. Obey demanded that the website be corrected, saying "The inaccuracies on Recovery.gov that have come to light are outrageous and the Administration owes itself, the Congress, and every American a commitment to work night and day to correct the ludicrous mistakes."[170]

Officials acknowledged to ABC News that the administration had found 700 mistakenly credited congressional districts.[171] In theory, Recovery.gov could be a good idea if operated independently of the White House; in its current form, it is a cynical smoke-and-mirrors game of distraction and a clearinghouse for propagandist disinformation.

Further proving that the White House's transparency efforts are critically flawed, fraud prevention expert David Williams, who runs Deloitte Financial Services Advisory, warned in June 2009 that up to $50 billion dollars of stimulus money could be siphoned off by fraud.[172] Vice President Joe Biden, to whom Obama gave oversight responsibility

---

168 Obama, Barack. "Remarks by the President on the Economy."WhiteHouse.gov. http:// www.whitehouse.gov/the-press-office/remarks-president-economy-jobs-forum. Internet.

169 Karl, Jonathan. "Exclusive: Jobs 'Saved or Created' in Congressional Districts That Don't Exist Human Error Blamed for Crediting New Stimulus Jobs to Nonexistent Places." ABCNews.com. http://abcnews.go.com/Politics/jobs-saved-created-congressional-districts-exist/story?id=9097853. Internet.

170 Karl, Jonathan. "White House Vows to Correct Stimulus Reports Officials Tell ABC News So Far, They Found 700 Mistaken Congressional Districts Out of More Than 130,000 Stimulus Grants." ABCNews.com. http://abcnews.go.com/WN/white-house-stimulus-website-riddled-errors/story?id=9110298. Internet.

171 Ibid. In many cases, the numbers reported bore no resemblance to reality:
Moore's shoes in Campbellsville, Kentucky reported nine jobs created from an $890 grant for nine pairs of work boots for the Army Corp of Engineers.Head Start of Augusta, Georgia, used a $790,000 grant to give a raise to its 317 employees. It reported 317 jobs created. Chris Whitley, a fiscal officer for the organization which administers the Augusta Head Start program, pointed the finger back to the Administration's stimulus help line. "It wasn't illegal, immoral or unethical. And they told me to do it, so I did it," said Whitley.

172 Williams's comments echoed those of FBI Director Robert Mueller, who also warned of a potential crime wave of corruption and fraud related to the stimulus.

regarding implementation of the stimulus, acknowledged that some stimulus-related scams had already occurred.[173]

One could fill a book detailing transparency concerns related to governmental activities on a host of issues; the administration's nexus to two organizations in particular demonstrates the far-reaching consequences of transparency, of the lack thereof, in both private and public institutions.

ACORN: The Association of Community Organizations for Reform Now, better known as ACORN, is a tangled web of 361 affiliated organizations that pursue self-described social justice causes by demonstrating, "negotiating," and lobbying Congress for power and money.[174] ACORN bills itself as a "non-profit, non-partisan social justice organization." It is "the nation's largest grassroots community organization of low-and-moderate-income people with over 400,000 member families organized into more than 1,200 neighborhood chapters in about 75 cities across the country."[175]

ACORN grew out of the National Welfare Rights Organization (NWRO) of the 1960s, which mobilized tens of thousands of single minority mothers to force a restructuring of America's capitalist system through protests and demonstrations at welfare offices.[176] The campaign yielded results: "From 1965 to 1974, the number of single-parent households on welfare soared from 4.3 million to 10.8 million, despite mostly flush economic times. By the early 1970s, one person was on the welfare rolls in New York city for every two working in the city's private economy."[177] The anti-capitalist campaign failed to spark the desired restructuring, instead facilitating a rampant culture of family breakdown and dependency, punctuated by illegitimacy, crime, school failure, drug abuse, joblessness, and poverty.

In 1970, NRWO founder George Wiley tapped Wade Rathke to launch a new community organizing group that became known as

---

173 Morcroft, Greg. "Fraudsters eye huge stimulus pie, consultant says Companies will face extra requirements to prevent problems."MarketWatch.com. http://www.marketwatch.com/story/stimulus-fraud-could-hit-50-billion?siteid=rss&rss=1#mod=BOL_hps_BOL2MW. Internet.

174 Murdock, Deroy. "ACORN: Tax cheat." NYPost.com. http://www.nypost.com/p/news/opinion/opedcolumnists/item_rGElUcHk82b5We97CU80KI. Internet.

175 ACORN. "Who is ACORN?." ACORN.org. http://www.Acorn.org/index.php?id=12342. Internet.

176 Stern, Sol. "ACORN's Nutty Regime for Cities." City Journal. http://www.city-journal.org/html/13_2_Acorns_nutty_regime.html. Internet.

177 Ibid.

Arkansas Community Organizations for Reform Now. "Arkansas" was later changed to "Association of" and a modern-day movement was born. ACORN grew quickly, becoming infamous for its in-your-face intimidation tactics.[178]

In 2008, Pittsburgh attorney Heather Heidelbaugh filed a lawsuit accusing ACORN of corruption and seeking injunctive relief against it for fraudulent voter registration activities. In the suit, Heidelbaugh alleged that ACORN and Project Vote performed fundraising and get-out-the-vote (GOTV) services for Obama during the 2008 campaign. As federally tax-exempt organizations, both ACORN and Project Vote are prohibited from engaging in partisan political activity.[179]

As part of her legal investigation, Heidelbaugh questioned Anita Moncrief, a fired ACORN worker who later was employed by Project Vote. In her testimony, Moncrief explained that Project Vote is part of ACORN.

> Honestly, there really isn't a difference between Project Vote and ACORN except for the fact that one is a 501(c)(3) and one is not … Project Vote is basically considered Acorn political operations… There was active cooperation between ACORN's political wing and Project Vote … [They] basically had the same staff. … All of the organizations and the entities worked together. We shared the same space … there's no real separation between the organizations for real.[180]

Moncrief testified that part of her job while working for ACORN and Project Vote included soliciting donations for ACORN from major Obama contributors who had already contributed the maximum amount allowed by federal election law to the Obama campaign. According to Moncrief, the Obama campaign sent ACORN its maxed-out donor list.[181]

Moncrief also alleged that ACORN's issues campaigns are really an extortion scheme, better known as "muscle for money." Though known as a GOTV operation, Moncrief said the muscle for money program engaged in mob style intimidation to collect "protection" money from targets for ACORN, sometimes at the behest of the SEIU.

---

178 Ibid.
179 Miller, S.A. "Conyers suggests probe of ACORN." WashingtonTimes.com. http://www.washingtontimes.com/news/2009/mar/20/conyers-suggests-probe-of-Acorn/. Internet.
180 "Testimony of Heather S. Heidelbaugh, Esquire." Judiciary.House.Gov. http://judiciary.house.gov/hearings/pdf/Heidelbaugh090319.pdf. Internet.
181 "Testimony of Heather S. Heidelbaugh, Esquire." Judiciary.House.Gov. http://judiciary.house.gov/hearings/pdf/Heidelbaugh090319.pdf. Internet.

It was always referred to as 'Muscle for the Money' because they would go out there, intimidate these people, protest. They did it in front of Sherwin Williams. They did it at H&R Block, where H&R Block was a target for years. And instead of, you know, reforming the way [H&R Block] did the rapid anticipation loans, [H&R Block] ended up giving money to the ACORN tax sites, which paid for new computers and money to run these tax filing sites around the country ... The protesting was used to get companies to negotiate. The companies would pay money to get the protesting to stop. In addition to calling this activity, 'Muscle for the Money,' the insiders at ACORN called it 'protection.'[182]

ACORN and its affiliates are the target of numerous lawsuits related to voter fraud, including a suit filed by former ACORN employees under the Racketeer Influenced and Corrupt Organizations Act (RICO), a law typically reserved for prosecuting the mob.[183] Seventeen states investigated ACORN for voter registration fraud in the 2008 election.[184] Even ACORN employees suspect the organization is involved in criminal activity. A 2008 internal report by ACORN attorney Elizabeth Kingsley identified concerns about the organization's "improper use of charitable dollars for political purposes; money transfers among the affiliates; and potential conflicts created by employees working for multiple affiliates."[185] Most of the criminal conduct charges lodged against ACORN and its affiliates stem from voter registration fraud.[186]

In May 2009, Nevada officials charged ACORN, its regional director and its Las Vegas director with submitting thousands of fraudulent voter registration forms for the 2008 election. According to Larry Lomax, the

---

182 "Testimony of Heather S. Heidelbaugh, Esquire." Judiciary.House.Gov. http://judiciary. house.gov/hearings/pdf/Heidelbaugh090319.pdf. Internet.

183 Conery, Ben. "ACORN files lawsuit on voter registration," WashingtonTimes.com. http://www.washingtontimes.com/news/2009/jul/23/Acorn-files-lawsuit-on-voter-registration/. Internet.

184 Fund, John. "More Acorn Voter Fraud Comes to Light," Wall Street Journal. http://online.wsj.com/article/SB124182750646102435.html. Internet.

185 Strom, Stephanie. "Acorn Report Raises Issues of Legality," New York Times. 21 October 2008.

186 In addition to the fraud allegations and internal speculation of illegal activity, ACORN failed to pay social security, Medicare, and unemployment taxes on its employees. Louisiana tax officials, along with the IRS, had nearly $2 million in tax liens against ACORN in 2009. Though ACORN is a non-profit and exempt from federal income taxes, it does have to pay social security, Medicare, and unemployment taxes on its employees. Murdock, Deroy. "ACORN: Tax cheat." NYPost.com. http://www.nypost.com/p/news/opinion/opedcolumnists/item_rGElUcHk82b5We97CU80KI. Internet.

registrar of voters in Las Vegas, almost half of ACORN's forms "are clearly fraudulent."[187] Cortex Masto, Nevada's Attorney General, said that ACORN's training manuals "clearly detail, condone and … require illegal acts…"[188] The same week, Pittsburg prosecutors charged seven ACORN employees with submitting hundreds of fraudulent voter registrations before the 2008 general election. Complaints against ACORN's practice of filing fraudulent registrations echoed in Missouri and in Washington state, where several ACORN employees were convicted of voter registration fraud in 2007.

In July 2009 Congressman Darrell Issa (R-CA), Ranking Member on the House Committee on Oversight and Government Reform, released a scathing report alleging that ACORN was engaged in massive fraud and corruption and calling for a criminal investigation into ACORN. The report charged that ACORN "has repeatedly and deliberately engaged in systemic fraud," including evading taxes, racketeering, obstructing justice, violating the civil rights of whistleblower employees known as the "ACORN 8", money laundering, and defrauding the United States.

ACORN has received over $53 million in federal funds since 1994 despite the organization's documented disregard for the law.[189] Even as the lawsuits multiplied, the U.S. Census Bureau enlisted ACORN in February 2009 to assist with the recruitment of 1.4 million temporary workers needed for the 2010 census.[190] The Census Bureau finally severed ties with ACORN in September 2009 in response to public outcry stemming from an undercover video depicting ACORN workers allegedly instructing a couple posing as a pimp and prostitute in ways to subvert the law.[191] The move was largely symbolic, given that it contained a December 12, 2009

---

187 Choate, Alan. "ACORN voter registration drive nets charges." Las Vegas Review-Journal. 04 May 2009

188 According to Heidelbaugh, Moncrief also testified that ACORN used a quota system that required voter registration canvassers to secure at least 20 registrations per day or be fired. Such a system is illegal in several states. "Testimony of Heather S. Heidelbaugh, Esquire." Judiciary.House.Gov. http://judiciary.house.gov/hearings/pdf/Heidelbaugh090319.pdf. Internet.

189 Oliphant, James. "House and Senate take action against ACORN," LATimes.com. http://articles.latimes.com/2009/sep/18/nation/na-Acorn18. Internet.

190 The census plays a critical role in determining the number of Congressional representatives states are allotted, how Congressional districts are drawn, and how federal funds are allocated. Corbin, Cristina. "ACORN to Play Role in 2010 Census." FoxNews.comm. http://www.foxnews.com/politics/2009/03/18/Acorn-play-role-census/. Internet.

191 Waters, Clay. "New York Times Jumps on Arrest of ACORN 'Pimp' – Yet Waited 6 Days to Report ACORN Revelations," Wall Street Journal. 29 January 2010. "Census Bureau Severs Ties with ACORN," FoxNews.com. http://www.foxnews.com/politics/2009/09/11/census-bureau-severs-ties-Acorn/. Internet.

built-in expiration date.[192] Thus, unless Congress takes further action, ACORN will remain eligible to compete for up to $3.99 billion in federal funding included in Obama's 2011 blueprint budget.[193]

In March 2009, House Judiciary Committee Chairman John Conyers called the ACORN accusations "a pretty serious matter" and suggested a congressional probe of the allegations. Three months later he reversed course, saying, "The powers that be decided against it."[194] Obama boldly promised an open and transparent government, so why hasn't he opposed future ACORN funding? Why doesn't he support an ACORN probe?

Obama's ties to ACORN and Project Vote go back decades. ACORN first noticed Obama when he was working the south side of Chicago as a community organizer for the Developing Communities Project.[195] In 1992, Obama directed Project Vote, the most successful grass-roots voter-registration campaign in recent city history.[196] According to Phil Kerpen, Director of Policy for Americans for Prosperity, Obama actually served as ACORN's chief national trainer.[197] As a board member for the Woods Fund and Joyce Foundation, Obama helped direct tens of millions of

192 Vadum, Matthew. "Enabling ACORN's Comeback," American Spectator. http://spectator.org/archives/2009/12/10/enabling-Acorns-comeback. Internet.
193 Vadum, Matthew. "Show ACORN the Money," American Spectator. http://spectator.org/archives/2010/02/02/show-Acorn-the-money. Internet.
194 Miller, S.A. "Conyers suggests probe of ACORN," Washington Times. 20 March 2009; Miller, S.A. "Conyers abandons plan to probe ACORN," Washington Times. 25 June 2009.
195 Moberg, David. "Obama's Community Roots," The Nation. April 16, 2007. Social Policy magazine, which shares the same New Orleans street address as ACORN and Project Vote, published a case study by Chicago ACORN leader Toni Foulkes on the Barack Obama U.S. Senate campaign that detailed the Obama-ACORN-Project Vote connection.
"He was a very good organizer. When he returned from law school, we asked him to help us with a lawsuit to challenge the state of Illinois' refusal to abide by the National Voting Rights Act, also known as motor voter. ... Obama then went on to run a voter registration project with Project VOTE in 1992 that made it possible for Carol Mosely Braun to win the Senate that year. ....
Since then, we have invited Obama to our leadership training sessions each year to run the session on power every year, and, as a result, many of our newly developed leaders got to know him before he ever ran for office. Thus, it was natural for many of us to be active volunteers in his first campaign for State Senate and then his failed bid for U.S. Congress in 1996 [actually, 2000]. By the time he ran for U.S. Senate, we were old friends." Foulkes, Toni. "Case Study: Chicago: The Barack Obama Campaign." Social Policy 34 no. 2 (Winter 2003); Foulkes, Toni. "Case Study: Chicago: The Barack Obama Campaign." Social Policy 34 no. 3 (Spring 2004).
196 "RNC: Obama & Acorn fact sheet," PR News Wire. http://www2.prnewswire.com/cgi-bin/stories.pl?ACCT=104&STORY=/www/story/10-04-2008/0004897846&EDATE=. Internet.
197 Fox News. "Linking Social Justice to 'Green' Jobs," FoxNews.com. http://www.foxnews.com/story/0,2933,535284,00.html. Internet.

dollars in grants to liberal organizations, including the Chicago branch of ACORN, which endorsed Obama's Illinois senate race.[198]

Despite proof from multiple sources of Obama's longstanding work with, and for, ACORN, the Obama campaign explicitly disavowed the connection. It set up a website, Fightthesmears.com, which lists as "facts" that "Barack was never an ACORN community organizer" and that "ACORN never hired Obama as a trainer, organizer, or any type of employee."[199] As the ACORN voter-fraud scandal grew in the month before the election, Obama denied ACORN's involvement in his campaign and claimed that his only direct involvement with ACORN was as an attorney representing ACORN in a lawsuit to enforce the Illinois motor-voter law.[200] Obama's denial regarding ACORN's involvement in his campaign was particularly suspicious since his campaign hired ACORN for get-out the-vote work.

> Citizens Consulting Inc., the umbrella group controlling ACORN, was paid $832,000 by the Obama campaign for get-out-the-vote efforts in key primary states. In filings with the Federal Election Commission, the campaign listed the payments as "staging, sound, lighting," only correcting them after reporters from the Pittsburgh Tribune-Review revealed their true nature.[201]

Over a year after Obama took office, Congressman Daryl Issa (R-CA) exposed a video interview Obama did with ACORN during the presidential campaign, in which he wooed the organization with promises of an Obama administration – ACORN partnership.

> And I definitely welcome ACORN's input. You don't have to ask me about that. I'm going to call you even if you didn't ask me.... When I ran Project Vote, voter registration drive in Illinois, you know, ACORN was smack dab in the middle of it....Once I was elected, there wasn't a campaign that ACORN worked on down in Springfield that I wasn't right there with you. ...Since I've been in

198 Kurtz, Stanley. "Inside Obama's Acorn," National Review Online. http://article. nationalreview.com/358910/inside-obamas-Acorn/stanley-kurtz. Internet.
199 "Barack Obama Never Organized with ACORN," Fightthesmears.org. http:// fightthesmears.com/articles/20/Acornrumor. Internet.
200 Hemingway, Mark. "New video: Obama didn't tell the truth about his relationship to ACORN,"SFExaminer.com. http://www.sfexaminer.com/opinion/blogs/beltway-confidential/Obama-didnt-tell-the-truth-about-his-relationship-to-ACORN-84845947. html. Internet.
201 Fund, John. "More ACORN voter fraud comes to light," Wall Street Journal. 09 May 2009.

the United States Senate I've been always a partner with ACORN as well. ...I've been fighting with ACORN, alongside ACORN, on issues you care about, my entire career.[202]

Given his close historic ties to ACORN, the charge of ACORN illegally aiding the Obama campaign, and ACORN'S continued partnership with the radical agenda of the Democratic party, it is no surprise that the powers that be crushed Conyers' calls for an ACORN investigation.

The Federal Reserve: The 1913 Federal Reserve Act established the Federal Reserve System, comprised of a Board of Governors, the Federal Open Market Committee, twelve regional Federal Reserve Banks, and over 5500 private member commercial banks throughout the United States.[203] Congress passed the Act largely in response to prior financial panics, especially the Panic of 1907.[204] The purpose of the Federal Reserve Act was to establish a decentralized central bank to provide the United States with "a safer, more flexible, and more stable monetary and financial system."[205]

The Federal Reserve is "a bank for individual banks and their lender of last resort."[206] Originally the Federal Reserve's control of discount loans to member banks was its lone tool for steering U.S. monetary policy. In the 1920s, the Federal Reserve began using open market operations as a monetary policy tool.

From 1930 to 1933 nearly 10,000 banks failed, and by March 1933 newly inaugurated President Franklin Delano Roosevelt declared a bank holiday, while government officials grappled with ways to remedy the nation's economic woes. Many people blamed the Fed for failing to stem speculative lending that led to the crash, and some also argued that inadequate understanding of monetary economics kept the Fed from pursuing policies that could have lessened the depth of the Depression... In reaction to the Great Depression, Congress passed the Banking Act of 1933,

202 "Did Obama Lie About Relationship with ACORN?" Tuesday, February 23, 2010 http://www.foxnews.com/story/0,2933,587239,00.html
203 Little, Jeffrey B. and Rhodes, Lucien. Understanding Wall Street. New York: McGraw-Hill, 2004.
204 "Fed 101 - History." FederalReserveEducation.org. http://www.federalreserveeducation.org/fed101/history/. Internet.
205 "Federal Reserve System: Purposes and Functions." FederalReserve.gov. http://federalreserve.gov/pf/pdf/pf_1.pdf. Internet.
206 Little, Jeffrey B. and Rhodes, Lucien. Understanding Wall Street. New York: McGraw-Hill, 2004.

better known as the Glass-Steagall Act [which] established the Federal Deposit Insurance Corp. (FDIC), placed open market operations under the Fed and required bank holding companies to be examined by the Fed … Also, as part of the massive reforms taking place, Roosevelt recalled all gold and silver certificates, effectively ending the gold and any other metallic standard.[207]

Both liberals and conservatives are concerned that the Federal Reserve exerts significant control over U.S. monetary policy with virtually no accountability or transparency. Obama wants to increase the already-mammoth power of this secretive group of unelected central bankers, giving it more oversight over financial firms, including the authority to determine which firms are "too big to fail."[208]

President Obama has promised to run an administration of unprecedented openness.… But in the most important area of all, the financial rescue, the administration is making trillion dollar decisions relying on the Federal Reserve and a small Wall Street club of advisors, with no transparency or public accountability… The administration is now using the Federal Reserve as an unlegislated, all-purpose slush fund. Because the Fed's operations are largely beyond the reach of Congressional appropriations or scrutiny, the Fed can do whatever it wishes with the money. What we have is something perilously close to a dictatorship of the Fed and the Treasury, acting in the interests of Wall Street.[209]

Fortune once described the Federal Reserve as "secretive by nature, suspicious of outsiders, and possessed of an esprit de corps that borders on fanaticism."[210] Judge Andrew Napolitano noted: "We know more about the CIA than we do about the Federal Reserve."[211] The power and secrecy of the Federal Reserve is not in dispute; its effectiveness and constitutionality is. Though Chairman Ben Bernanke predictably disagrees,

207 "Fed 101 - History." FederalReserveEducation.org. http://www.federalreserveeducation.org/fed101/history/. Internet.
208 Appelbaum, Binyamin and Cho, David. "Obama Blueprint Deepens Federal Role in Markets," Washington Post. 17 June 2009.
209 Kuttner, Robert. "Obama's Banking Rescue: O for Opaque," HuffingtonPost.com. http://www.huffingtonpost.com/robert-kuttner/obamas-banking-rescue-o-f_b_180529.html. Internet.
210 "A Brief Analysis of the History of the Federal Reserve System from 1967 to 1997," LotsofEssays.com. http://www.lotsofessays.com/viewpaper/1706944.html. Internet.
211 Ibid.

conservative economists blame the Federal Reserve's easy money policies for contributing to the housing bubble and consequent economic crisis.[212] The few, unelected members of the Federal Reserve, acting without any congressional oversight or accountability, have continued to take secretive, unprecedented and controversial steps in response to the crisis. In an attempt to promote credit flow, the Federal Reserve has held interest rates down and pumped trillions of dollars into not only the United States economy, but into foreign banks.[213]

Congressional calls for more Federal Reserve transparency grew louder in the wake of the outrage sparked by the $700 billion bailout in October 2008. In November 2008, the Federal Reserve refused to identify the recipients of nearly $2 trillion of emergency loans it issued or the troubled assets it was accepting as collateral. [214]

Former Republican presidential candidate and Texas Representative Ron Paul has introduced legislation that would require the Comptroller General to complete an audit of the Board of Governors of the Federal Reserve System and of the Federal Reserve banks by the end of 2010 and submit a detailed report to Congress. The Federal Reserve Transparency Act of 2009, also known as H.R. 1207, had gained 319 cosponsors as of April 22, 2010.[215]

H.R. 1207 was introduced to the Committee on Banking, Housing, and Urban Affairs on March 16, 2009, where it has stalled.[216] Bernie Sanders (I- VT) introduced a companion bill, S. 604, the "Federal Reserve Sunshine Act of 2009, in the Senate, which had 32 sponsors as of April 2010.[217]

Promises of transparency and accountability are but meaningless words that rub raw the disaffection and disenfranchisement citizens feel when they see credible charges and evidence of wrongdoing repeatedly swept under the rug. To rebuild trust, the Obama administration must

---

212 Weisberg, Jacob. "What Caused the Economic Crisis," Slate.com. http://www.slate.com/id/2240858/. Internet. Economists Debate Roots of Financial Crisis," Cato Policy Report, January/February 2009. https://www.cato.org/pubs/policy_report/v31n1/cpr31n1-3.html. Internet.

213 Goldman, David. "CNNMoney.com's bailout tracker," CNNMoney.com. http://money.cnn.com/news/storysupplement/economy/bailouttracker/index.html. Internet.

214 Pittman, Mark, Ivry, et al. "Fed defies transparency aim in refusal to disclose," Bloomberg.com. http://www.bloomberg.com/apps/news?pid=20601087&sid=aatlky_cH.tY. Internet.

215 "H.R. 1207," Thomas.loc.gov. http://thomas.loc.gov/cgi-bin/bdquery/z?d111:h1207. Internet.

216 Ibid. The majority of bills never make it out of committee. While strong support from co-sponsors appears to give the bill a veto-proof majority in the House, but the bill would likely be attached to other legislation before being considered for a full House vote, which would provide cover for legislators who may have co-sponsored the bill only as a populist move.

217 "S. 106," Thomas.loc.gov. http://thomas.loc.gov/cgi-bin/thomas. Internet.

Transparency Bayou

Like Obama, Governor Bobby Jindal (R-LA) hails from a state infamous for its political chicanery. "Corruption in Illinois is mainly pedestrian and shameful. In Louisiana, it's flamboyant and shameless."[1] In 2007, Corporate Crime Reporter named Louisiana the most corrupt state in America, based on its analysis of the Justice Department's Public Integrity Section's 2006 report.[2] Jindal tapped into the public's hunger for an end to his state's longstanding culture of political corruption by making ethics reform a central tenet of his 2007 campaign for governor.

The first bills Jindal signed as governor set sweeping new ethics standards for elected officials and lobbyists, including: mandating new financial disclosure rules for elected officials, banning elected officials from contract work with the state, requiring annual ethics training for all public servants and lobbyists, establishing contribution limits for gubernatorial transition teams, expanding whistleblower protection, increasing penalties for bribery, creating/defining the crime of "abuse of office," increasing lobbyist transparency, and tightening conflict-of-interest restrictions.[3]

Jindal's commitment, in both word and deed, to creating a more responsible and accountable political environment in Louisiana is already having an effect in restoring the public's trust in that state's government. The Center for Public Integrity advanced Louisiana from forty-fourth place among states to first place in its legislative financial disclosure index. Similarly, Louisiana's ranking on the Better Government's Association's Integrity Index improved from number forty-six to number five.[4]

---

1 Weisberg, Jacob. "A Battle for the Basement," Newsweek. December 22, 2008.
2 "Louisiana Most Corrupt State in the Nation, Mississippi Second, Illinois Sixth, New Jersey Ninth," CorporateCrimeReporter.com. http://corporatecrimereporter.com/corrupt100807.htm. Internet. Louisiana had a rate of 7.67 federal corruption convictions per 100,000 residents from 1997-2006. Mississippi, which placed second, had a 6.66 rate.
3 "Jindal Signs Ethics Bills into Law," State of Louisiana Office of the Governor. http://gov.louisiana.gov/index.cfm?md=newsroom&tmp=detail&articleID=93.   Internet;   "Governor Bobby Jindal Signs Additional Ethics Bills into Law," State of Louisiana Office of the Governor. http://gov.louisiana.gov/index.cfm?md=newsroom&tmp=detail&articleID=100.   Internet; "Governor Bobby Jindal Signs Additional Ethics Bills into Law," State of Louisiana Office of the Governor. http://gov.louisiana.gov/index.cfm?md=newsroom&tmp=detail&articleID=101. Internet; "Governor Bobby Jindal Signs Additional Ethics Bills into Law," State of Louisiana Office of the Governor. http://gov.louisiana.gov/index.cfm?md=newsroom&tmp=detail&article ID=108. Internet; Kornick, Cheryl. "Jindal signs ethics laws," Energy Law Blog. http://www.theenergylawblog.com/2008/03/articles/industry-news/jindal-signs-ethics-laws/. Internet.
4 Alford, Jeremy."Man in the middle," 1012Corridor.com. http://1012corridor.com/news/2009/nov/01/man-middle/. Internet. Not everyone has championed Jindal's reforms. The Chairman of the Louisiana Board of Ethics charged that the new laws "crippled" Louisiana's ethics system. Board chairman Frank Simoneaux was particularly unhappy with a law that transferred judicial power from the board to administrative law judges. Shuler, Marsha."Law gives judges board's power," The Advocate. November 3, 2009.

do more than mouth empty promises; it must follow words with authentic and tangible action.

The national trust deficit, like the federal deficit and cumulative debt, continues to soar. According to a February 2010 Rasmussen poll, 75 percent of likely voters say they are at least somewhat angry at the federal government's policies.[218]

Obama promised an end to politics-as-usual. He pledged to restore the public's trust in government, but trust cannot be built with disingenuous platitudes and broken promises.

218 "75 percent Are Angry At Government's Current Policies," RasmussenReports.com. http:// www.rasmussenreports.com/public_content/politics/general_politics/february_2010/75_ are_angry_at_government_s_current_policies. Internet.

4

Rising Taxes, Reckless Spending

Santelli's Tea Party

Speaking from the floor of the Chicago Mercantile Exchange on CNBC's *Squawk Box* February 19, 2009, Rick Santelli joined a discussion about the Obama Administration's $75 billion mortgage bailout plans for people with upside down mortgages, including those who took risky, undercapitalized loans.

The government is promoting bad behavior. How about this, President and new Administration? Why don't you put up a web site to have people vote on the Internet as a referendum to see if we really want to subsidize the losers' mortgages, or would we like to at least buy cars and houses in foreclosure and give them to people that might actually have a chance to prosper down the road and reward people who can carry the water instead of drink the water?[1]

Santelli's comments served as a rallying cry for Americans frustrated by the federal government's reckless tax-and-spend, ever-expansive federal government policies. Across the country, tax day tea party plans sprang up rapidly. Hundreds of thousands attended tea parties across the nation.

---

1   "Santelli's Tea Party," CNBC.com. http://www.cnbc.com/id/15840232?video=1039849853. Internet.

Raising taxes has been raised to an art form by our government. In addition to explicit taxes, the government levies fees, surcharges, offset charges, and other tricks that ultimately empty citizens' pockets. David Walker, former U.S. Comptroller, foresees higher future taxes as the inevitable consequence of the government's addiction to spending:

There's not a party of fiscal responsibility right now. ... We've lost our way. We think we're too big to fail, and we have huge and growing legacy costs as well. We need to get back to basics. Government has overpromised, under-delivered. You can't tax your way out of this problem although taxes will go up. They will go up.[219]

---

219   "How high would taxes have to go to cover U.S. debt?" FoxNews.com. http://www.foxnews.com/story/0,2933,515618,00.html. Internet.

Democrats have long campaigned on the promise of middle-class tax cuts only to raise taxes on the middle-class once in office. Bill Clinton repeatedly promised a middle-class tax cut in 1992, but promptly raised taxes on the middle class after elected. Clinton famously told the crowd at a 1995 Houston fundraiser, "Probably there are people in this room still mad at me at that [1993] budget because you think I raised your taxes too much. It might surprise you to know that I think I raised them too much too."[220]

Similarly, Obama promised a tax cut to any family that earned less than $250,000 a year, estimating that 95 percent of Americans would enjoy a tax cut.[221] Obama's plan included a child care credit, an expansion of the earned-income tax credit, a savings tax credit, a college tuition tax credit, and the "make work pay" credit worth $500 for individuals and $1000 for families, all of which were payable even if a person owed no income taxes. The Heritage Foundation's Center for Data Analysis projected that, under the Obama plan, an additional ten million filers would pay no taxes while receiving a check from the IRS.[222]

The $787 billion stimulus plan that Obama forced through Congress after being sworn in fell short of the tax-cutting hype. The bill, better known as the American Recovery and Reinvestment Act, (ARRA), did not lower the effective tax rate. Rather, it provided a tax credit, or rebate, for 2009 and 2010 only.[223] Americans familiar with congressional tax tactics feared that any small income tax cuts would soon be offset by new taxes, resulting in a net tax increase. As a candidate, Obama emphatically denied that this would happen.

Less than two years into his presidency, Obama has proposed almost $1 trillion dollars in new taxes to be levied over a ten year period beginning in fiscal year 2011, $636 billion of which would target individuals earning more than $250,000. Another $353 billion would be imposed on businesses through

---

220 "Clinton Quotes," Trettel.com. http://www.trettel.com/ccrc/quotes/quotesClinton.html. Internet.

221 Politifact.com rated Obama's claim "half-true," citing a detailed analysis by the nonpartisan Tax Policy Center, which found that only 81 percent of tax filers would pay slightly less taxes in 2009 and 2010 under the Obama plan. "Under Obama's tax plan, '95 percent of you will get a tax cut,'" Politifact.com. http://www.politifact.com/truth-o-meter/statements/2008/sep/27/barack-obama/many-will-get-tax-cuts-but-not-that-many/. Internet; "Barack Obama pledges tax cut for 95 percent of Americans in Eau Claire, Wis., speech," Suntimes.com. http://www.suntimes.com/news/politics/obama/1124081,tax082408.article. Internet.

222 "Obama's 95 percent illusion," Wall Street Journal. http://online.wsj.com/article/SB122385651698727257.html; Internet.

223 In 2009 and 2010, the Making Work Pay provision of the American Recovery and Reinvestment Act will provide a refundable tax credit of up to $400 for working individuals and up to $800 for married taxpayers filing joint returns. This tax credit will be calculated at a rate of 6.2 percent of earned income and will phase out for taxpayers with modified adjusted gross income in excess of $75,000, or $150,000 for married couples filing jointly. "The Making Work Pay Tax Credit," IRS.gov. http://www.irs.gov/newsroom/article/0,,id=204447,00.html; Internet.

various repeals of existing deductions, changes in the tax rules for international profits, and other changes to the tax code.[224]

It is worth noting that the Constitution ratified by the founders denied Congress the power to levy any direct tax "unless in Proportion to the Census or enumeration herein before directed to be taken."[225] In 1862 Congress passed an income tax to pay for the war, but the tax was repealed a decade later. In 1894 Congress again passed an income tax, but the next year the Supreme Court ruled it unconstitutional. Article 1, Section 9 was modified by the Sixteenth Amendment to the Constitution: "The Congress shall have power to lay and collect taxes on incomes, from whatever source derived, without apportionment among the several States, and without regard to any census or enumeration." The first income tax levied a one percent tax on net personal income above $3,000 and a surtax of six percent on incomes exceeding $500,000.[226]

Overwhelming the System

On May 2, 1966, Richard Cloward and Frances Fox Piven published a provocative article in The *Nation*, entitled "The Weight of the Poor: A Strategy to End Poverty." The authors articulated a scheme for overwhelming America's existing bureaucratic system and social safety net through "a convergence of civil rights organizations, militant anti-poverty groups and the poor." Through "a series of welfare drives in large cities," the groups would place as many persons on public welfare programs as possible, thus causing "bureaucratic disruption in welfare agencies and fiscal disruption in local and state governments."

According to what has become known as the Cloward-Piven strategy, these disruptions would pressure the political establishment to "eliminate poverty by the outright redistribution of income." To be effective, the authors added, the federal government's eventual redistributive plan must include an unconditional, individual right to a "guaranteed annual income," set high enough to supposedly assure every poor person's escape from poverty.[1]

The National Welfare Rights Organization (NWRO), a progenitor of ACORN, and other activist organizations implemented the strategy in the late sixties and early seventies, precipitating a major financial crisis in New York City. As the welfare state continues to expand, so does the sense that the scheme is rapidly gaining momentum in the new millennium.

1   "The Weight of the Poor: A Strategy to End Poverty," by Frances Fox Piven and Richard Cloward, March 8, 2010 (article appeared in the May 2, 1966 issue of *The Nation*). http://www.thenation.com/article/weight-poor-strategy-end-poverty

224 Tapper, Jake. "Obama's Budget: Almost $1 Trillion in New Taxes Over Next 10 yrs, Starting 2012," ABCNews.com. http://blogs.abcnews.com/politicalpunch/2009/02/obamas-budget-a.html. Internet.
225 U.S. Constitution, Article 1 Section 9
226 Constitution of the United States, http://www.archives.gov/exhibits/charters/constitution_amendments_11-27.html#16 ADD ENDNOTE: "Brief History of IRS," http://www.irs.gov/irs/article/0,,id=149200,00.html

Every citizen, or at least the members of the shrinking tax base, can sympathize with the Herculean task of navigating the impossibly complicated tax code, and nearly everyone agrees that it is broken. The current tax code is largely incomprehensible for the average American and full of loopholes, exclusions, social engineering regulations, and special interest provisions. The IRS estimates that the average individual tax return will require 17.3 hours to prepare and cost the filer $225. Business 1040 forms will take an average of 31.9 hours to prepare, at a cost of $434. Since 1993, the percentage of taxpayers preparing their own returns dropped from nearly 40 percent to less than 10 percent in 2006.[227] The instruction booklet that accompanies the 1040 long form is 172 pages.[228] Obama himself has referred to the current tax code, over 40,000 pages of regulations and myriad loopholes, as a broken system, and appointed a task force to reform the code.[229]

> Let's begin with a simple premise: nobody likes paying taxes, particularly in times of economic stress. But most Americans meet their responsibilities because they understand that it's an obligation of citizenship necessary to pay the costs of our common defense and our mutual well-being.[230]

It would be wonderful if Obama actually believed that paying taxes is an obligation of citizenship, but the stimulus bill he guided through Congress significantly increased the already escalating percentage of persons who avoid tax liability and receive a tax welfare check. According to the nonpartisan Tax Foundation, of the nearly 142 million Americans who filed a tax return in 2008, a record 51.6 million, (more than 36 percent) had no income tax obligation. Twenty-five million tax filers received a total of $51.6 billion dollars in earned-income tax credits, which are payable to eligible filers even if they did not have to pay income taxes during the year.[231]

227 "DIY or CPA," BankofAmerica.com. http://smallbusinessonlinecommunity.bankofamerica.com/blogs/Taxes/2010/01/29/diy-or-cpa. Internet.
228 "Tax code grows like kudzu as another April 15 approaches," USAToday.com. http://www.usatoday.com/news/opinion/editorials/2010-04-07-editorial07_ST_N.htm. Internet.
229 Runningen, Roger and Donmoyer, Ryan J. "Obama asks Volcker to lead panel on tax-code overhaul," Bloomberg.com. http://www.bloomberg.com/apps/news?sid=a8yCQsJfpb24&pid=20601087; accesed 22 April 2010.
230 "Remarks by the President on International Tax Policy Reform," WhiteHouse.gov. http://www.whitehouse.gov/the_press_office/Remarks-By-The-President-On-International-Tax-Policy-Reform; accessed 18 April 2010.
231 "Record Numbers of People Paying No Income Tax; Over 50 Million 'Nonpayers' include Families Making over $50,000," by Scott A. Hodge, March 10, 2010 http://www.taxfoundation.org/publications/show/25962.html

The income level at which a typical family of four owes no income taxes has increased rapidly, hitting $51,000 in 2008.[232] The Tax Policy Center, a joint research venture of the Urban Institute and Brookings Institute, estimated that approximately 47 percent of Americans did not have to pay federal income taxes in 2010.[233] Thus, Obama's promise of a tax cut for 95 percent of Americans was disingenuous. In Obama-speak, however, a tax cut is not limited to a reduction in taxes owed on earned income; it includes government handouts, disguised as tax credits, to those who owe no income taxes.

In a joint session of Congress on February 24, 2009, Obama could not have been more emphatic in reiterating his pledge: "If your family earns less than $250,000 a year, a quarter million dollars a year, you will not see your taxes increased a single dime. I repeat: Not one single dime. In fact – not a dime..."[234] The pledge was disturbing in light of Obama's reckless spending proposals.

If government spending continues to spiral out-of-control, and 95 percent of families are not subject to tax hikes, the remaining 5 percent of taxpayers are left to pay for all new government expenditures. Obama pits American families that earn more than $250,000 a year against those earning less, suggesting that the former can, and should, carry the entire government budget for the latter. History, human nature, and common sense suggest that the risk-takers and innovators who are stuck with the tax burden will change their behaviors when redistributive taxes become oppressive. They will stop expanding their businesses and starting new ones. They will move their operations and families overseas. They will work less or retire early. Excessive taxation acts as a powerful disincentive to the innovators and moneymakers who create jobs and opportunities for millions of Americans. Obama's pledge is not only discouraging to higher wage earners, but to all who aspire to a better standard of living. His pledge symbolically – if not literally – caps the American dream at $250,000, minus local, state, and federal taxes and fees.

Though Obama has not proposed a direct increase in the baseline (tax table) income tax rate for families earning under $250,000 annually, his

232 Hodge, Scott. "Fiscal Facts," TaxFoundation.org. http://www.taxfoundation.org/publications/show/25962.html. Internet.

233 Ohlemcacher, Stephen. "Nearly half of US households escape fed income tax," USAToday.com. http://www.usatoday.com/money/perfi/taxes/2010-04-07-income-taxes_N.htm. Internet.

234 "Address Before a Joint Session of Congress: February 24, 2009," The American Presidency Project. http://www.presidency.ucsb.edu/ws/index.php?pid=85753&st=&st1=. Internet.

tax policies are indirectly hurting families. For example, Obama's proposed 2010 budget included a $646 billion cap-and-trade bill.[235] Proponents cast the legislation as an effective method for achieving reduced emissions of pollutants that would be critical to the fight against global warming. Under the bill, the government would set a limit on a company's emissions by issuing tradable allowances called "credits." A company's total emissions could not exceed its credits. Companies that needed to exceed their emission allowance would be required to buy or trade more credits.

If a cap-and-trade bill were to become law, the new system would significantly increase the cost of business, especially for manufacturers. Companies, in turn, would pass the increased cost through to consumers, including those who earn less than $250,000 a year. While some companies would actually stand to gain from the massive legislation, other companies and industries would be forced to pay for extra emissions credits in order to run their basic operations. The cap-and-trade bill amounts to perhaps the largest income redistribution scheme ever devised and promises to be a magnet for massive fraud.[236] Additionally, the scheme would be subject to manipulation from the outset, given that there is no reliable method even to accurately determine a company's total level of CO_2 emissions.

The cap-and-trade bill is also one of the largest proposed tax increases in U.S. history. Even Democrats recognize that cap-and-trade is a tax by a different name. Senator John Dingell notes, "Nobody in this country realizes that cap-and-trade is a tax. And it's a great big one."[237]

The House of Representatives passed the cap-and-trade bill, labeled the American Clean Energy and Security Act (by a vote of 219-212 on June 26, 2009. The legislation stalled in the Senate,[238] but Senators John Kerry (D-Mass) and Joe Lieberman (I-Conn.) reintroduced a new version of the

235 Riedl, Brian. "The Obama Budget: Spending, Taxes, and Doubling the National Debt," The Heritage Foundation. http://www.heritage.org/Research/Reports/2009/03/The-Obama-Budget-Spending-Taxes-and-Doubling-the-National-Debt. Internet.
236 Radio and television personality Glenn Beck has traced a labyrinth of suspicious organizations and persons positioning themselves to profit from the new multi-trillion market in emissions credits, and has charged that the administration is complicit. See "Crime, Inc.," by Glenn Beck, April 29, 2010 http://www.foxnews.com/story/0,2933,591790,00.html
237 "Dem Congressman: 'Nobody in this country realizes that cap-and-trade is a tax,'" CSPAN. http://www.breitbart.tv/html/325633.html; Internet.
238 "H.R. 2454 – American Clean Energy And Security Act of 2009," OpenCongress. org. http://www.opencongress.org/bill/111-h2454/actions_votes; Internet. Obama subsequently dropped cap-and-trade from his budget proposal. Bull, Alister and Mason, Jeff. "Obama's 2010 budget: deficit soars amid job spending," Reuters. http://www.reuters.com/article/idUSTRE60U00220100201; Internet.

bill on May 12, 2010 and Obama issued a statement indicating his intention to pass a cap-and-trade bill by the end of the year.[239]

The health care legislation Obama signed into law in March 2010 also levies a multitude of new taxes that the congressional Joint Committee on Taxation (JCT), a nonpartisan agency, estimates will generate $409.2 billion in revenue by 2019. The bill applies a first-ever 3.8 percent Medicare tax to capital gains, dividends, rents, and royalties; higher Medicare taxes for individuals earning more than $200,000 and families with income exceeding $250,000 beginning in 2012; a 40 percent excise tax on high-end employer-provided insurance beginning in 2018; an increase in the threshold for deductibility of medical expenses from 7.5 percent of income to 10 percent of income; new restrictions on use of health savings accounts; a new $2500 cap on contributions to employer-sponsored flexible spending accounts; a 10 percent excise tax on tanning salon patrons; and a $2000 fee per employee for employers with more than 50 workers if the employer does not offer health insurance.[240]

> ### Smokers' Sticker Shock
> On April 1, 2009, Obama signed legislation that raised the federal tax on each pack of cigarettes roughly 160 percent, from 39 cents per pack to $1.01 per pack. The tax on chewing tobacco rose to 50 cents per pound from 19.5 cents. Some smokers tried to circumvent the new tax by rolling their own cigarettes and cigars. Congress cut them off at the pass by increasing the per pound tax on tobacco purchases from $1.09 to $24.78.[1]
>
> ---
> 1 Schiller, Brad. "Obama's Poor Tax: Why raising the tobacco levy will hurt the states," Wall Street Journal. http://online.wsj.com/article/SB123854056373275583.html. Internet.

Hidden in the new law are still more taxes: a tax on cosmetic surgery and fees for drug makers, medical device makers, and health insurance companies totaling more than $100 billion in anticipated additional tax revenues.[241] Whether through cap-and-trade or excise taxes, Obama is indirectly taxing the struggling American families that his policies purport to help.

---

239 "Kerry, Lieberman Unveil Bill to 'Change the Face of American Energy," by Stephanie Condon, May 12, 2010 http://www.cbsnews.com/8301-503544_162-20004830-503544.html

240 Donmoyer, Ryan J. "New Health-Care Taxes Help Obama 'Spread the Wealth'", Bloomberg.com. http://www.bloomberg.com/apps/news?pid=20601103&sid=ake7tOWwUT6E. Internet.

241 Goldstein, Jacob. "Listing the New Taxes in the Senate Health-Care Bill," Wall Street Journal. http://blogs.wsj.com/health/2009/11/19/listing-the-new-taxes-in-the-senate-health-care-bill/tab/article/. Internet.

In 2008, Obama promised, "When I'm President I will go line by line to make sure that we are not spending unwisely."[242] Obama's "line by line" line was laughable, given the sheer size of appropriations bills, which often contain thousands of pages.

Once in office, Obama allowed congressional leaders to take the lead in crafting the stimulus legislation, assuring a plethora of pork. Earmarks are all about wasteful, special interest spending commonly called "pork" or "pork barrel spending." Obama vowed in January 2009, that the stimulus plan would not contain any earmarks. As the bill moved through Congress he assured the public, "This bill does not have a single earmark in it." Upon passage of the $787 bill (ARRA), he declared, "I'm proud that we passed a recovery plan free of earmarks."[243]

Obama's claim of an earmark-free stimulus bill was an attempt to stand firmly on a technicality; the legislation was free of earmarks, but loaded with pork barrel spending. Critics recognized that the administration was playing word games; the *Wall Street Journal* defined it as "defining spending deviancy down."

> Not so long ago – before President Obama's inauguration – "earmarks" referred to the special appropriations that bypass the normal budget process to cater to special interests and protect the incumbents who inserted them. The difference now is that the politicians have gotten much better at disguising their handiwork. Under the cover of emergency spending, the projects have also grown much larger.[244]

For example, the bill included a spending item for "one or more near zero emissions power plants(s)." Despite the general description, the only plant that meets the criteria is the FutureGen project in Obama's home state of Illinois; Senator Dick Durbin ensured that ARRA included $1 billion for the project.[245]

---

242 "Transcript of first presidential debate," CNN.com. http://www.cnn.com/2008/POLITICS/09/26/debate.mississippi.transcript/. Internet.

243 "Address to Joint Session of Congress: Tuesday, February 24, 2009." WhiteHouse.gov. http://www.whitehouse.gov/the_press_office/remarks-of-president-barack-obama-address-to-joint-session-of-congress/. Internet.

244 Source: online.wsj.com/article/SB123621360683535103.html "See No Earmarks" March 5, 2009)

245 Source: online.wsj.com/article/SB123621360683535103.html "See No Earmarks" March 5, 2009)

Even appropriations divided on a "competitive basis", such as the last-minute $8 billion dollar appropriation for high-speed rail projects, were suspect.[246] In business, the company offering the best value on a given contract wins the job. In a corrupt congressional culture buzzing with back-room deals, pressure tactics, and vote-trading, it is still a matter of who you know.

In theory and publicity, the package was "earmark free," but it contains dozens of narrowly defined programs that send money to specific areas or cater to special interests, despite President Barack Obama's pledge to pass "an economic recovery plan that is free from earmarks and pet projects."[247] Perhaps stung by the mocking over the dubious "no earmarks" claim with ARRA, the administration dropped the pretense for the next massive spending legislation.

After signing the $787 billion ARRA bill in February, (on the heels of George W. Bush's $800 billion TARP bill), Obama signed a $410 billion omnibus spending bill into law in March 2009. The bill included 9278 partisan earmarks totaling at least $7.7 billion (over $12 billion, according to the non-partisan Sunlight Foundation).[248] As usual, both Democrats and Republicans were complicit. The top eight Republican ear-markers held their own against the top twelve Democrat ear-markers, with each group accounting for approximately half a billion of the $7.7 billion total. The total of earmarks for fiscal year 2009 spending was $14.8 billion, compared to $14.3 billion in 2008.[249]

Dubbed "Porkulus" by critics, the omnibus was passed under the pressure and pretense of impending disaster. Obama's name was even attached to one earmark for a vocational training program for Native Americans in North Dakota and New Mexico.[250] Not to be outdone,

---

246 Source: online.wsj.com/article/SB123621360683535103.html "See No Earmarks" March 5, 2009)

247 MSNBC February 5, 2009 http://www.msnbc.msn.com/id/29025047/ (Heading: In stimulus bill, earmarks by any other name. Exclusive by Michael Grabell and Christopher Weaver of Propublica)

248 Watzman, Nancy. "Read the Bill: Spending Bills Rushed," SunlightFoundation.org. http://blog.sunlightfoundation.com/2009/03/12/read-the-bill-spending-bills-rushed/. Internet. Even that amount excluded earmarks sponsored by both parties. "$7.7 billion in earmarks in 2009 omnibus spending bill," Taxpayers for Common Sense. http://www. taxpayer.net/resources.php?category=&type=Project&proj_id=1961&action=Headlines percent20By percent20TCS. Internet.

249 These figures represent only "disclosed earmarks" – those with a Senator's name attached. Taxpayers for Common Sense found another 3.5 billion in "disguised earmarks" – undisclosed items embedded in the spending bills that failed the earmark smell test.

250 Tapper, Jake. "President Obama to Sign Pork-Laden Omnibus Spending Bill," ABCNews. com. http://blogs.abcnews.com/politicalpunch/2009/03/president-obama.html. Internet.

Biden's name was attached to multiple earmarks totaling $94.9 million in the bill.[251] "I'm signing an imperfect … bill," Obama said, "because it's necessary for the ongoing functions of government, and we have a lot more work to do."[252] Nevertheless, Obama remained firmly in favor of reforming earmarks … some other time. "Let there be no doubt, this piece of legislation must mark an end to the old way of doing business and the beginning of a new era of responsibility and accountability."[253]

If Washington D.C. is to begin to rebuild trust with the American people, politicians must say what they mean and mean what they say. Promises made must become promises kept.

Hypocrisy feeds distrust; Washington's penchant for misleading, spinning, misdirecting, covering up, obfuscating, and plain old lying has given disbelieving Americans plenty to chew on.

251 Ham, Mary Katherine. "Oops: Obama Breaks Campaign No-Earmarks Pledge in Ominbus Spending Bill," Weekly Standard. http://www.weeklystandard.com/weblogs/TWSFP/2009/02/oops_obama_breaks_campaign_noe.asp. Internet.
252 Ruggeri, Amanda. "Obama pledges to reform earmarks ahead of signing spending bill full of them," US News and World Report. http://www.usnews.com/articles/news/obama/2009/03/11/obama-pledges-to-reform-earmarks-ahead-of-signing-spending-bill-full-of-them.html. Internet.
253 Ibid.

The Trouble with Earmarks

Anyone unfamiliar with the impact earmarks can have on a bill should consider Senator John McCain's floor statement on earmarks contained in the 2009 omnibus bill.

> Here we are, with a Statement of Managers that totals 1844 pages, including 775 pages identifying over 9,000 members' earmark requests that are expected to be funded, although most of them are not contained in the bill text. And, because they are conveniently not listed in the bill text, members who question the merits of specific earmarks are unable to offer an amendment to specifically strike them... The Army Corps of Engineers has the distinction of having the largest number of individual earmarks imposed among all of the federal agencies funded in this legislation, with an amazing 1,849 ....(E)very agency is chock full of earmarks...If this bill isn't proof that we need earmark reform...then I don't know what is. Examples include: [Earmarks under $1.5 million edited out]
> - $3.8 million for a Sun Grant Initiative in SD
> - $1.7 million for pig odor research in Iowa
> - $2.0 million for the promotion of astronomy in Hawaii
> - $6.6 million for termite research in New Orleans
> - $2.1 million for the Center for Grape Genetics in New York
> - $1.7 million "for a honey bee factory" in Weslaco, TX
> - $7.1 million for the conservation and recovery of endangered Hawaiian sea turtle populations.
> - Earmarks by Division:
> - Division C - Energy and Water Development and Related Agencies Appropriations (164 pages of earmarks) - Total: 2,402 earmarks
> - Division F – Departments of Labor, Health and Human Services, and Education, and Related Agencies: (211 pages of earmarks) - Total: 2125 earmarks
> - Department of Education – Total: 700 earmarks
> - Department of Health and Human Services – Total: 1223 earmarks
> - Health Resources and Services Administration – Total: 924 earmarks
> - Division I - Transportation, Housing and Urban Development, and Related Agencies (114 pages of earmarks) – Total: 1,858 earmarks[1]

---

1 "List of Earmarks in Latest Spending Bill," Rightbias.com. http://rightbias.com/News/031709pig.aspx. Internet.

5

A Framework for
Unaccountability and Irresponsibility

The Declaration of Independence eloquently affirms that government is inherently accountable to the people. Two weeks before taking office, Obama promised that he would bring "a long overdue sense of responsibility and accountability to Washington." He told reporters that his stimulus package would set "a new higher standard of accountability, transparency and oversight." "I want you to hold our government accountable," Obama said. "I want you to hold me accountable."[254] He returned to the theme again in early March, promising that in his administration government will be "more efficient, more accountable, and more responsible."[255] Yet the pattern of his presidency is unmistakable: blame the former administration, make undeliverable promises, and take credit where it is not due.

Obama claims victory whenever the economy shows a glimmer of hope, but he attributes every dismal detail to "the failed policies" of the George W. Bush administration.[256] Biden hails improvements in Iraq as one of Obama's "greatest achievements," though, as a candidate, Obama opposed both the war and the surge, which increased stability in the region.[257] At the Fiscal Responsibility Summit in February 2009, Obama repeated his familiar "we inherited" finger-pointing toward the deficit: "My administration came into office one month ago in the depths of an economic crisis unlike any that we've seen in generations. .... This

---

254 Associated Press. "Obama bans earmarks from economic package," MSNBC.com. http://www.msnbc.msn.com/id/28525113/. Internet.

255 Beesley, Shadra. "Obama pledges to cut wasteful spending, be accountable," Personal Money Store. http://personalmoneystore.com/moneyblog/2009/03/04/obama-pledges-cut-wasteful-spending/. Internet.

256 Soraghan, Mike. "Obama takes credit for economic turnaround," The Hill. http://thehill.com/homenews/administration/65699-obama-takes-credit-for-economic-turnaround. Internet.

257 "Joe Biden update: Iraq One of Obama's 'Greatest Achievements,'" Los Angeles Times. http://latimesblogs.latimes.com/washington/2010/02/joe-biden-update-larry-king-iraq-obama-sarah-palin.html. Internet.

administration has inherited a $1.3 trillion dollar deficit, the largest in our nation's history.[258] A year later Obama was beating the same Congress-and-Bush-bashing drum:

> Over the course of the past 10 years, the previous administration and previous Congress created an expensive new drug program, passed massive tax cuts for the wealthy and funded two wars without paying for any of it, all of which was compounded by recession and by rising health care costs. As a result, when I first walked through the door, the deficit stood at $1.3 trillion, with projected deficits of $8 trillion over the next decade.[259]

Obama's depiction of the deficit picture is self-serving at best, and his criticism of George W. Bush rings hollow in the face of his own ten year budget estimates, which project annual average deficits in excess of $850 billion dollars.[260]

The $1.3 trillion deficit Obama pins on George W. Bush is misleading. The federal fiscal year runs through September each year. George W. Bush's 2008 record budget deficit totaled $454.8 billion dollars.[261] The economic crisis in the fall of 2008 led George W. Bush and Congress to pass the $700 billion dollar TARP bailout, which Obama supported. That, coupled with increased recession-related spending and plummeting revenues, pushed the deficit to the $1.3 trillion figure that Obama claims for his predecessor.

For all of TARP's many problems, even Obama admits that it did not add $700 billion dollars to the deficit on George W. Bush's watch. "It turns out, actually, TARP – as wildly unpopular as it has been – has been much cheaper than any of us anticipated," Obama said in December 2009.[262] Bernanke echoed the observation, saying he believed that, in the end, TARP would come close to breaking even.[263]

258 "Opening Remarks at Fiscal Responsibility Summit," New York Times. http://www.nytimes.com/2009/02/23/us/politics/23text-summit.html?pagewanted=5. Internet.
259 Thomma, Steven. "Obama's budget deficits to rise from wars, recession," Miami Herald. http://www.miamiherald.com/news/politics/AP/story/1457649.html?storylink=mirelated. Internet.
260 Ibid.
261 Associated Press. "2008 federal budget deficit was a record 454.8 billion," Tuscaloosa News. http://news.google.com/newspapers?nid=1817&dat=20081015&id=xlspAAAAI BAJ&sjid=Nr0EAAAAIBAJ&pg=3064,6201228. Internet.
262 "Banks have repaid half of TARP funds already," NJ.com. http://www.nj.com/business/index.ssf/2009/12/banks_have_repaid_half_of_tarp.html. Internet.
263 Ibid.

<u>"We Just Need a Government that Will Trust in Us"</u>

*The American people want to trust in our government again -- we just need
a government that will trust in us.*[1]
-- Barack Obama, September 4, 2007

On the campaign trail, Obama touted the need for the government to trust the
people, but his administration has proven that it is unwilling to make the leap
of faith. Under the Obama regime, the American people cannot be trusted to
choose their own light bulbs, cars, or kitchen appliances. Americans are unable
to engage in free-market capitalism or create jobs without the guiding hand of
Big Brother. Americans are not qualified to make moral choices, remain true to
their individual beliefs, or contribute to causes in which they believe. Americans
cannot be trusted with their own money, their own property, their own food
choices, or their own children.

Thanks to Representative Brian Baird, (D-WA), help may be on the way. In July
2009, Baird introduced H.R. 3247, which would establish a social and behavioral
sciences research program at the Department of Energy. The program would
study factors that influence energy consumption and use the research results to
"help" consumers make better decisions in the development and application of
energy technologies.[2]

1   Helman, Scott. "Obama to reignite fireside chats," Boston.com. http://www.boston.com/
    news/politics/politicalintelligence/2007/09/obama_to_reigni.html. Internet.
2   "H.R. 3247: To establish a social and behavioral sciences research program at the Department
    of Energy, and...," Govtrack.us. http://www.govtrack.us/congress/bill.xpd?bill=h111-
    3247&tab=summary. Internet.

At the end of Obama's first year in office, $545 billion in total TARP
funds had been spent, of which $165 billion had been repaid. In January
2010, $320 billion remained in the TARP till.[264] The TARP program was
scheduled to end at the end of 2009, but Geithner extended the program
until October 3, 2010. Senator John Thune (R-SD) introduced a bill to
end TARP and to use the $320 billion to reduce the deficit. Fifty-three
senators, including all of the Republican members of the Senate, supported
the measure, but the bill fell short of the 60 votes needed to cut off
debate.[265] Thune charged that TARP, unless reigned in, would become a
permanent Democratic slush fund. Though the TARP program stipulates
that all repaid funds be used to reduce the federal debt, Obama proposed
in his 2010 State of the Union Address that $30 billion in repaid bailout

264 Montgomery, David. "Thune fails in another effort to end TARP," NJ.com.y http://
    www.capjournal.com/articles/2010/01/22/news/doc4b59521d39118950111885.txt.
    Internet.
265 Ibid.

funds be allocated for small business lending.[266] Obama repeated the proposal a few days later, but later backtracked, saying the funds would come from the unspent portion of TARP.[267]

George W. Bush and Obama share responsibility for the 2009 deficit, but when Obama uses the $1.3 trillion figure as a basis of comparison to his future projected deficits, he is speeding the country's road to financial bankruptcy. The country was indeed mired in a fiscal mess when Obama took office. Under George W. Bush, the nation's deficit grew at an unprecedented rate. In January 2007, George W. Bush was outlining a path to eliminate the deficit by 2012, but abandoned the plan when the economy started to falter.[268] The federal government spent money at an unsustainable pace under Bush and the voters punished the Republican-led Congress at the polls in 2006 for bankrolling the federal government's spending spree.[269]

But if federal spending from 2000-2008 was irresponsible, government spending in 2009 under Obama was utterly indefensible, between the spending spree stimulus and the pork-filled omnibus bill. Michael Boskin, professor of economics at Stanford University and a senior fellow at the Hoover Institution, put the magnitude of Obama's spending orgy in historical perspective:

> Mr. Obama's $3.6 trillion budget blueprint, by his own admission, redefines the role of government in our economy and society. The budget more than doubles the national debt held by the public, adding more to the debt than all previous presidents — from George Washington to George W. Bush — combined. It reduces defense spending to a level not sustained since the dangerous days before World War II, while increasing nondefense spending (relative to GDP) to the highest level in U.S. history. And it would raise taxes to historically high levels (again, relative to GDP). And all of this before addressing the impending explosion in Social Security and Medicare costs.[270]

---

266 Lillis, Mike. "Gregg: TARP is No Slush Fund," WashingtonIndependent.com. http://washingtonindependent.com/75536/gregg-tarp-is-no-slush-fund. Internet.

267 McGrane, Victoria. "White House won't use 'repaid' bank funds for jobs plan," Post-Gazette.com. http://www.post-gazette.com/pg/10037/1034087-473.stm. Internet.

268 Associated Press. "Federal deficit falls to lowest level in 4 years," MSNBC.com. http://www.msnbc.msn.com/id/16599329/ns/politics/. Internet.

269 Lagorio, Christine. "Democrats Gain Control of Congress," CBSNews.com. http://www.cbsnews.com/stories/2006/11/09/politics/main2167520.shtml; accessed 22 April 2010.

270 Boskin, Michael J. "Obama's Radicalism Is Killing the Dow," Wall Street Journal Online. http://online.wsj.com/article/SB123629969453946717.html. Internet.

Spreading the Blame Around

To be fair, Obama does not attribute all of American's problems to George W. Bush. Since taking office, he has:

- Blamed Republicans for listening to Rush Limbaugh and for fear-mongering to defeat health care reform
- Blamed talk radio and cable news shows for ginning up opposition to his health care plan
- Blamed insurers and doctors for rising health care costs
- Blamed a "stupidly" behaving white police officer for doing his job, and police in general for racial profiling
- Blamed greedy businessmen for the economic crisis
- Blamed secured creditors ("a small group of speculators") for Chrysler's bankruptcy
- Blamed the mortgage crisis on bankers and mortgage firms
- Blamed Israel for Palestinian-Israeli tensions
- Blamed America for being arrogant
- Blamed Arizona state lawmakers for passing immigration reform necessitated by the federal government's systematic failure to enforce federal immigration law

Obama held a "fiscal responsibility summit" during his first month in office, where, after his usual this-administration-inherited-a-$1.3 trillion-deficit-propaganda, he said:

> Contrary to the prevailing wisdom in Washington these past few years, we cannot simply spend as we please and defer the consequences to the next budget, the next administration or the next generation.
>
> We are paying the price for these deficits right now. In 2008 alone, we paid $250 billion in interest on our debt: One in every 10 taxpayer dollars. ...
>
> That's why today, I'm pledging to cut the deficit we inherited by half by the end of my first term in office. Now, this will not be easy. It will require us to make difficult decisions and face challenges we've long neglected. But I refuse to leave our children with a debt that they cannot repay, and that means taking responsibility right now, in this administration, for getting our spending under control.[271]

---

271 "Opening Remarks at Fiscal Responsibility Summit," New York Times. http://www.nytimes.com/2009/02/23/us/politics/23text-summit.html?pagewanted=5&_r=1. Internet.

Obama is like the trash-talking basketball player who badmouths everyone around him and everyone who came before him. He heralds himself as the team's new superstar. He gathers his fellow players in a huddle, directs the team, and calls the plays, but he cannot deliver during the game. Obama's played the game for over a year and a half, and voters are waking up to the gaping gap between rhetoric and reality.

Obama's statements sound like those of a fiscal conservative, but his fiscal policies are anything but conservative. Obama rails against the current debt and past deficits, noting that the $250 billion in interest the government paid on the federal debt in 2008 constituted "one in every ten taxpayer dollars,"[272] but the Congressional Budget Office predicts that Obama's economic policies will cause net interest on the debt to nearly triple as a percentage of GDP by 2020.

> Under the President's budget, debt held by the public would grow from $7.5 trillion (53 percent of GDP) at the end of 2009 to $20.3 trillion (90 percent of GDP) at the end of 2020. As a result, net interest would more than quadruple between 2010 and 2020 in nominal dollars (without an adjustment for inflation); it would expand from 1.4 percent of GDP in 2010 to 4.1 percent in 2020.[273]

In February 2010, Bernanke reminded the congressional Joint Economic Committee that the CBO baseline debt projection relies on several tax and spending assumptions: discretionary spending grows more slowly than nominal GDP, none of George W. Bush's expiring tax cuts are extended, and current relief from the alternative minimum tax is not extended. The assumptions are dubious. Discretionary spending continues to grow like wildfire. Obama's proposed 2011 budget extends George W. Bush's tax cuts for everyone earning less than $200,000, ($250,000 for couples), and incorporates changes to current AMT provisions; together the changes could reduce federal government revenue by $2.5 trillion or more over 10 years.[274]

---

272 Ibid.

273 "Preliminary Analysis of the President's Budget," Congressional Budget Office Director's Blog. http://cboblog.cbo.gov/?p=482. Internet.

274 Jeanne Sahadi, Jeanne. "Obama's budget: Impact on your taxes," CNN.com. http://money.cnn.com/2010/02/01/pf/taxes/obama_budget_tax_changes/index.htm. Internet. Dropping those assumptions, Bernanke warned, "the deficit at the end of 2020 would be 9 percent of GDP and the federal debt would balloon to more than 100 percent of GDP." Source: "Chairman Ben S. Bernanke: Economic Outlook,: FederalReserve.gov. http://www.federalreserve.gov/newsevents/testimony/bernanke20100414a.htm. Internet.

Obama's statements are wildly inconsistent not only with reality, but with his prior statements. In May 2009 Obama called current deficit spending "unsustainable," adding "we can't keep on just borrowing from China."[275] In December 2009, Obama said the nation must continue to "spend our way out of this recession," even while pointedly criticizing Republicans for their reckless spending.[276] Obama's promise to halve the deficit by the end of his term is pure sophistry. His 2009 stimulus package, which he used as his starting point, nearly quadrupled Bush's record 2008 deficit. Obama was actually pledging to deceptively continue unsustainable deficit spending.

After seventeen months in office, the verdict is in: Obama's blame-and-spend economic policies are failing. Following the April expiration of a tax credit, sales of new homes in the U.S. fell to the lowest level on record, sinking an astounding 33 percent month-to-month.[277] U.S. consumer confidence fell in June to 52.7, from a downwardly revised 62.7 in May. The figure, issued by the Conference Board, an industry group, was sharply lower than the average forecast from analysts polled by Reuters.[278] The Labor Department's June 2010 employment report showed a net loss of 125,000 jobs. A total of 652,000 people gave up on their job searches and exited the labor force, joining several hundred thousand others who did the same the previous month.[279] In response to the Labor Report, Obama said, "Make no mistake, we are headed in the right direction."[280]

No wonder respected pollster Scott Rasmussen concludes, "The gap between Americans who want to govern themselves and politicians who want to rule over them may be as big today as the gap between the colonies and England during the eighteenth century."[281]

---

275 Runningen, Roger and Nichols, Hans. "Obama Says U.S. Long-Term Debt Load 'Unsustainable," Bloomberg.com. http://www.bloomberg.com/apps/news?pid=2060108 7&sid=aJsSb4qtILhg&refer=home. Internet.
276 Associated Press."Obama plans to 'spend our way' out of downturn," New York Post. http://www.nypost.com/p/news/politics/obama_plans_to_spend_our_way_out_Swmgz9e2H5RuGgZuBMaWSI. Internet.
277 "Sales of U.S. New House Plunge to Lowest Level on Record," by Shobhana Chandra and Timothy R. Homan, June 23, 2010, http://www.bloomberg.com/news/2010-06-23/sales-of-u-s-new-houses-plunge-to-lowest-level-on-record.html
278 "Consumer Confidence Slumps, Home Prices Rise," by Caroline Valetkevitch, June 29, 2010 http://abcnews.go.com/Business/wireStory?id=11042110
279 "Private Sector Gains But Economy Sheds 125,000 Jobs," July 2, 2010 by Tony Marcano http://www.npr.org/templates/story/story.php?storyId=128262735
280 "Obama on jobs: 'We are headed in the right direction,'" USA Today, July 2, 2010 http://content.usatoday.com/communities/theoval/post/2010/07/obama-on-jobs-we-are-headed-in-the-right-direction/1
281 *In Search of Self-Governance*, by Scott W. Rasmussen, Rasmussen Reports, LLC, Asbury Park, New Jersey. Copyright 2009 by Scott W. Rasmussen

<u>The Four Horsemen of the Apocalypse</u>

In a 2009 interview on MSNBC's *The Rachel Maddow Show*, Senator Charles Schumer (D-NY) gleefully trumpeted the demise of limited government in America: "The hard right, which still believes when the federal government moves, chop off its hands, still believes you know, the 'traditional values' kind of arguments and strong foreign policy – all that's over."[1]

In one convoluted, but remarkably candid, sentence fragment, Schumer identified four looming horsemen of the American apocalypse. The tragedy is that he thinks they are the cavalry.

The first apocalyptic rider is government tyranny, mounted upon a federal behemoth growing ever bigger in size and power. The bureaucracy constantly invents new ways to waste taxpayer money and to control Americans' lives; Schumer even brags about it. During the February 2009 debate on the stimulus bill, Schumer boldly denounced wasteful spending critics: "Let me say this to all of the chattering class that so much focuses on those little, tiny, yes, porky amendments: the American people really don't care."[2]

Schumer's remark about "porky" amendments and his blithe dismissal of his opponents exemplifies the second horseman: arrogance. Arrogance infected all three branches of United States government a long time ago. Together, arrogance and government tyranny beget the third horseman: immorality. Schumer does not identify the "traditional values" that he disdains, but, based on his record, they surely include marriage, self-reliance, personal responsibility, integrity, honesty, the sanctity of life, and Christian faith. His worldview is indicative of a spreading secularism that denies objective truth and espouses tolerance, while demonstrating intolerance toward any idea outside the confines of political correctness.

The fourth horseman is weak foreign policy. According to Schumer, we should celebrate the demise of America's strong foreign policy. Reasonable people can disagree on what a strong foreign policy should entail, but whom, other than Schumer, advocates a weak foreign policy? Surely Americans can agree that the United States has both a right and an obligation to promulgate policies that foster and enhance its national security; two of the express purposes of the United States Constitution, are to "provide for the common defence" and to "secure the Blessings of Liberty to ourselves and our Posterity."[3]

Senator Schumer's four horsemen are not the cavalry arriving to rescue America; they are destructive forces already wreaking havoc here. If America is to survive, they must be stopped.

1 "The Rachel Maddow Show." April 8, 2009.http://www.msnbc.msn.com/id/30110064 (accessed April 19, 2010).
2 Akers, Mary Ann. "The Sleuth- Sen Schumer: Americans don't care about 'porky' amendments." February 10, 2009.http://voices.washingtonpost.com/sleuth/2009/02/sen_ schumer_americans_dont_car.html (accessed April 19, 2010).
3 "The Constitution of the United States," Preamble.

The year before Obama took office, former Comptroller General David Walker warned of the nation's grave fiscal situation. The combined burden of America's entitlement programs, federal government liabilities, commitments, and contingencies totaled $53 trillion, or "$175,000 for every man, woman, and child in the United States."[282] The stark numbers had a sobering effect on the American public. An August 2009 Rasmussen survey of likely voters showed that 71 percent of respondents believe that Obama's policies have increased the deficit.[283] By the time Obama gave his 2010 State of the Union address, Rasmussen polls showed that the public was beginning to catch on also to Obama's fiscal posturing: only 9 percent of respondents believed that Obama's promised three-year freeze on discretionary spending would reduce the federal deficit.[284] Significantly, 57 percent of likely voters supported a cut in government spending, 23 percent favored a freeze, and only 12 percent wanted an increase.[285]

The National Debt Clock

The national debt clock, viewable on the Internet at http://www.brillig.com/debt_clock/, shows a running and ever-rising tally of the government's expanding debt. You can watch the debt grow by millions between each click of the mouse.

The data is gathered from the Treasury's web site. It also contains basic information about the deficit and the debt, with simple-to-read charts, including one that shows that taking inflation into account does not diminish the scope of the problem.

Since September 28, 2007, the national debt (federal debt) has continued to increase by an average $3.78 billion per day. Moody's Investors Service, Inc. warned in 2009 and again in 2010 that the U.S. government's Aaa bond rating would come under pressure in the future if additional measures to reduce the

---

282 Levin, Mark R. Liberty and Tyranny: A Conservative Manifesto. New York: Simon & Schuster, 2009.

283 "71 percent Say Obama's Policies Have Driven Up Deficit," RasmussenReports.com. http://www.rasmussenreports.com/public_content/politics/obama_administration/august_2009/71_say_obama_s_policies_have_driven_up_deficit. Internet.

284 Another 39 percent believed the freeze would have little impact, while 42 percent believed the freeze would have no impact at all. The freeze, which would only apply to 17 percent of government spending, would not take effect until the 2011 fiscal year. "9 percent Expect Obama's Spending Freeze To Have Big Impact on Deficit," RasmussenReports.com. http://www.rasmussenreports.com/public_content/politics/obama_administration/january_2010/9_expect_obama_s_spending_freeze_to_have_big_impact_on_deficit. Internet. The freeze would not impact Medicare, Medicaid, Social Security or defense spending. Meckler, Laura and Weisman, Jonathan. "Budget Freeze Proposed," Wall Street Journal. http://online.wsj.com/article/SB10001424052748703808904575024772877067744.html. Internet.; Thomma, Steven. "Officials: Obama will propose three-year spending freeze," McClatchy. www.mcclatchydc.com/economy/story/83012.html. Internet.

285 "9 percent Expect Obama's Spending Freeze To Have Big Impact on Deficit," RasmussenReports.com. http://www.rasmussenreports.com/public_content/politics/obama_administration/january_2010/9_expect_obama_s_spending_freeze_to_have_big_impact_on_deficit . Internet.

deficit were not taken.[1] No one knows just how high the debt can rise before our economy collapses under its weight, but when the federal debt exceeds $20 trillion dollars, or 90 percent of the overall economy as the CBO projects will happen in 2020, America is engaging in a Ponzi scheme of Madoff magnitude.[2]

1   "Moody's Reiterates U.S. Spending Risks Credit Rating (Update 1), by Mary Childs, May 25, 2010 www.bloomberg.com/apps/news?pid=20670001&sid=az1YD_O3PXz4
2   Dickson, David M. "CBO report: Debt will rise to 90 percent of GDP," Washington Times. http://www.washingtontimes.com/news/2010/mar/26/cbos-2020-vision-debt-will-rise-to-90-of-gdp/print/. Internet. N.B.:Bernie Madoff, founder of Bernard L. Madoff Securities and former Nasdaq chairman, was charged on December 11, 2008 with what may prove to be the largest Ponzi scheme (excluding the Social Security Trust Fund) in American history. Madoff operated the scheme, which bilked investors of an estimated $50 billion, for many years before his house of cards folded in the wake of the economic crisis. The end came when too many of his financially stressed investors attempted to redeem their investments.

Despite the explosion of tea party protests, town hall protests, and Republican Scott Brown's election to fill Ted Kennedy's Senate seat, Congress and the White House continue their runaway spending habits, defying every measure of reason or responsibility. Democrats celebrated the first anniversary of Obama's presidency by raising the debt ceiling to approximately $14.3 trillion, an increase of $1.9 trillion over the previous debt ceiling.[286] Obama celebrated by unveiling a ten year budget proposal, with a $3.8 trillion budget for 2011 and eye-popping deficits throughout the decade. The *New York Times* noted the incongruity between Obama's rhetoric and the spiraling deficits: "President Obama declared in presenting his new 10-year budget proposal on Monday that 'our fiscal situation remains unacceptable,' but he insisted that the country pursue his ambitious domestic agenda despite facing budget deficits for the foreseeable future."[287]

The 2011 budget projected an $8.53 trillion ten-year budget deficit. The CBO reviewed the budget and found the White House's estimates to be optimistic; CBO's analysis showed that Obama's budget plans would produce $9.75 trillion in deficits over the next decade. According to the *Washington Times*:

The federal public debt, which was $6.3 trillion ($56,000 per household) when Mr. Obama entered office amid an economic

286 Alarkon, Walkter. "House raises debt limit to $14.3 trillion," The Hill. http://thehill.com/homenews/house/79861-house-raises-debt-limit-to-143-trillion. Internet.
287 Calmes, Jackie. "In $3.8 Trillion Budget, Obama Pivots to Trim Future Deficits," New York Times, 1 February 2010.

crisis, totals $8.2 trillion ($72,000 per household) today, and it's headed towards $20.3 trillion (more than $170,000 per household) in 2020, according to CBO's deficit estimates. That figure would equal 90 percent of the gross domestic product in 2020, up from 40 percent at the end of fiscal 2008.[288]

According to the 2011 budget tables released by the White House, federal government outlays as a percentage of gross domestic product (GDP) are projected to be 25.4 percent in 2010, the highest since 1945, (during World War II). That reflects a budget deficit of 10.1 percent, also the highest since 1945. Obama's planned 2010 budget deficit exceeds federal government receipts (revenue) for 1987. From 2001-2008, budget deficits totaled $2.271 trillion (constant fiscal year 2005 dollars), according to the budget tables. Even excluding the 2009 deficit of $1.28 trillion, Obama projects a three year deficit total from 2010-2012 of $3.215 trillion, dwarfing George W. Bush's *eight year* total by nearly a trillion dollars. In the last two years of his term, Obama projects spending 25.1 percent and 23.2 percent of the GDP, respectively. If he wins reelection, he intends to increase the budget each year, running deficits of 22.8 percent in 2013, 22.9 percent in 2014, and 22.9 percent in 2015.[289]

Tracing the Roots of the Deficit Crisis

Obama is not the first president to oversee an expansion of government and of the federal debt. The roots of the current debt crisis extend back over a half-century to Franklin D. Roosevelt's New Deal. Republican and Democrat presidents alike have presided over an escalating federal debt. Democrats have controlled Congress during most of this time; when the Republicans came to power with the so-called "Republican revolution" in 1994, the revolution was short-lived.

The Republican Revolution of 1994 swept into Congress with a clear reform agenda in mind. Speaker of the House Newt Gingrich led the Republican charge to create the "Contract with America" platform, which was extremely popular with the American people.

Representative Tom Coburn was a member of the freshman class of 1994 that rode into Washington on the Contract with America wave. In his book, *Breach of Trust: How Washington Turns Outsiders into Insiders,* he wrote, "We believed that we could retake our government from the career politicians in Washington who

---

288 Dickson, David M. "CBO report: Debt will rise to 90 percent of GDP," Washington Times. http://www.washingtontimes.com/news/2010/mar/26/cbos-2020-vision-debt-will-rise-to-90-of-gdp/print/. Internet.
289 Office of Management and Budget. "President's Budget, Historical Tables: Table 1.3." http://www.whitehouse.gov/omb/budget/historicals/. Internet.

had transformed a government 'for the people' into a government for themselves and for special interests."[1]

Two of the key items in the Contract with America were term limits and a balanced budget. Most of the Republican freshmen class issued term limit pledges, but the political culture of Washington is captivating and corrupting. Although many members of the Class of 1994 courageously fought for needed reform and adhered to their term limit pledges, some, having become accustomed to the perks and power of office, retracted their term limits pledges.

Under Gingrich's leadership, the Republican-controlled House passed a plan to balance the budget in seven years and cut projected spending by $1 trillion over that period; the objective was to achieve the first balanced budget since 1969. One newspaper dubbed it "the first serious attempt to reduce the role of federal spending and activities since the New Deal."[2]

The rhetoric and fear-mongering on both sides of the political aisle was intense, as was the emerging conflict between party careerists and the reform-minded freshman class. "Career Republicans were scared to death. They were terrified the public would accuse the party of not being able to govern, and we would lose our majority."[3]

Bill Clinton refused to sign appropriation bills to reduce spending, which led to continuing resolutions to keep the government functioning in accordance with the previous budget. When Bill Clinton eventually refused to sign even the continuing resolutions, the government shut down.[4]

The media had a field day. The Republicans were excoriated as extremists insensitive to the plight of senior citizens and others who relied on government assistance. Republican freshmen urged the leadership to hold firm, holding Bill Clinton to his promise to propose a plan that balanced the budget in seven years. Over 200 members of Congress stood firm on forcing the government to pare spending and balance the budget.

Gingrich, however, blinked. He urged his colleagues to vote to reopen the government. The shutdown ended. Discouraged and disheartened by his leadership's change in position, Coburn voted in favor of reopening the government, calling that decision "one of my biggest failures in Congress."[5]

Coburn marked the vote to reopen the government as the death knell for the Republican Revolution of 1994.

---

1   Coburn, Tom A. Breach of Trust: How Washington Makes Outsiders out of Insiders. Nashville: WND Books, 2003.
2   Ibid.
3   Ibid.
4   Ibid.
5   Ibid.

Obama's Czars: End-run around Congress and the Constitution

The biggest problems that we're facing right now have to do with George Bush trying to bring more and more power into the executive branch and not go through Congress at all. And that's what I intend to reverse when I'm President of the United States.[290]

Obama solemnly pledged to reverse George W. Bush's expansion of executive branch power. Instead, he installed a hemi and hit the accelerator. He has embraced most of Bush's national security policies and continued Bush's practice of issuing "signing statements" to challenge portions of federal statute, despite calling Bush's use of them an "abuse." Even liberal icons Barney Frank (D-MA) and David R. Obey (D-WI) took issue with Obama's signing statements, firing off a letter of complaint to the White House.[291]

George W. Bush's policies upset the balance of power between the executive, legislative, and judicial branches of government; Obama unfortunately picked up where George W. Bush left off by appointing an ever-expanding number of "czars" to take an increasing role in the decision-making authority of the government.

The founders understood that a president needs a small circle of trusted advisors, and indirectly provided for them in Article II, section 2, clause 1 of the Constitution, which says that the president "may require the opinion, in writing, of the principal officer in each of the executive departments, upon any subject relating to the duties of their respective offices."[292] Currently, there are fifteen executive departments. Each executive department's cabinet secretary is appointed by the president, approved by the Senate and cannot be a member of Congress or hold any other elected office.[293] The cabinet secretaries report to the president, but are accountable to Congress, which controls the secretaries' budgets and can compel testimony from any secretary.

The Russian-tinged "czar" title has been attached to many of Obama's appointees. The word "czar" is a humorous oddity on the American political scene, yet it captures the disturbing nature of the undefined authority that attends an increasing number of executive branch appointees. Some of these positions are congressionally-mandated, but many operate in new

---

290 Matthis, Nancy. "The Compleat [sic] List of Czars," American Daughter. http://frontpage. americandaughter.com/?p=2385. Internet.
291 Savage, Charlie. "Obama's Embrace of a Bush Tactic Riles Congress," New York Times. http://www.nytimes.com/2009/08/09/us/politics/09signing.html. Internet.
292 "The Constitution of the United States," Article 2, Section 2, Clause 1.
293 Longley, Robert. "More Information About the President's Cabinet," About.com. http:// usgovinfo.about.com/od/thepresidentandcabinet/a/prescababout.htm. Internet.

positions, without the confirmation of the Senate.[294] Matthew Spalding, a Heritage Foundation fellow and constitutional scholar, explained the constitutional division of powers between the executive and legislative branches in regard to presidential staff/advisors and administrative officers subject to legislative oversight:

> The President has the authority to appoint his own staff and advisors to assist in the work in his office. It is perfectly legitimate for presidential staff to advance the president's policy objectives within the administration as a matter of course, and Presidents often appoint particular advisors to advance particular, high-level policies. The executive has this authority as a separate and independent authority from officers created by the legislature to carry out the law, and Congress cannot infringe on that authority.
>
> Nevertheless, through its legislative and oversight functions, and more specifically through the Senate's participation in the appointment of officers under Article II, Congress also has significant responsibilities over the general activities of the administration in carrying out the operations of the federal government. With this legislative power in mind, a number of Senators have focused their attention on eighteen czar positions in the administration that may overstep Congress' express statutory assignment of responsibility and its oversight responsibilities.[295]

Previous presidents have appointed czars without seeking the blessing of, or receiving much resistance from, the Senate. Ronald Reagan and George H.W. Bush each appointed one. Bill Clinton appointed three, while George W. Bush appointed four.[296] Obama, in contrast, has appointed dozens of czars in less than one year.[297]

294 Spalding, Matthew. "The Threat to Self-Government: Examining the History and Legality of Executive Branch Czars," Heritage.org. http://www.heritage.org/research/thought/tst100809a.cfm. Internet.

295 Ibid.

296 Lafferty, Andrea. "How many czars does one president need?" TraditionalValues.org. http://www.traditionalvalues.org/read/3708/how-many-czars-does-one-president-need/. Internet.

297 The actual number of czars appointed by Obama is a matter of dispute, and includes some appointees who have been confirmed by the Senate. Representative Patrick McHenry (R-NC) wrote a letter to the Committee on Oversight asking that "the 44 appointed 'czars' be called before Congress to testify about their roles and responsibilities. Representative Jack Kingston (R-GA) put the number at 34. Weigal, David. "GOP Rep. Wants '44 Czars' to Testify Before Congress," The Washington Independent. http://washingtonindependent.com/58221/gop-rep-wants-44-czars-to-testify-before-congress. Internet.

It is hard to make the case that Obama's czars fit the constitutional definition of "inferior officers;" they manage critical areas of national policy, control sizable portions of the federal budget and make decisions impacting millions of Americans. In many cases they overlap, and undercut, the purpose and authority of cabinet members.

In his congressional testimony, Spalding highlighted several areas of concern associated with the proliferation of czar appointments. First, the proliferation of czars creates a confusion of responsibility and authority between various appointed positions. For example, is health care reform directed by Kathleen Sebelius, the Secretary of HHS, or by Nancy DeParle, the health care czar?

A second concern is the temptation of the White House, using a centralized command and control style of governance, to assert inappropriate political influence over normal departmental activities.

A third concern is the separation of powers. Presidential appointees who act as administrative heads rather than Article II advisors fall into the domain of Article II legislative oversight, and should be accountable to Congress.

Obama has pioneered a new path to direct the massive bureaucracy through the czar structure, thus avoiding accountability to Congress. As a possible example, Spalding cited Climate Czar Carol Browner, who circumvented the authority of the EPA administrator by leading the negotiations in establishing new automobile emission standards. Spalding warned Congress that "more and more laws – in the form of rulemaking, regulations, and policy pronouncements – are made by administrative agents not only outside of open and transparent requirements of responsible government, and without congressional approval and oversight, but generally beyond the principle that legitimate government arises out of the consent of the governed."[298]

Consequently, members of Congress have charged that Obama is evading constitutionally mandated congressional oversight by appointing dozens of czars. Susan Collins (R-ME) accused Obama of moving in "exactly the opposite direction" of his promised increase in transparency and accountability.[299] Senator Robert Byrd (D-WV) was concerned enough to send a letter to Obama, charging: "The rapid and easy accumulation

---

298 Spalding, Matthew. "The Threat to Self-Government: Examining the History and Legality of Executive Branch Czars," Heritage.org. http://www.heritage.org/research/thought/tst100809a.cfm. Internet.

299 Goler, Wendell. "Obama's Czars Draw Criticism From Both Sides of the Political Aisle," FoxNews.com. http://www.foxnews.com/politics/2009/07/15/obamas-czars-draw-criticism-sides-political-aisle/. Internet.

of power by White House staff can threaten the Constitutional system of checks and balances. At the worst, White House staff has taken direction and control of programmatic areas that are the statutory responsibility of Senate-confirmed officials."[300] Bird specifically cited three new White House offices: Health Reform, Urban Affairs Policy, and Energy and Climate Change Policy, as areas of concern.[301] Representative Jack Kingston (R-GA), criticized the abundance of czars, saying "It seems President Obama is in the midst of forming a parallel government to push his policies. Not only do [czars] duplicate existing Senate-confirmed positions, they are completely unaccountable."[302]

The American people deserve a government run by duly elected officials, not by supposed bureaucratic "experts" who are insulated from public accountability; anything less is a threat to our system of government. As the federal government's relentless expansion continues, the bureaucratic maze reaches new levels of inefficient complexity, and government moves further away from the founders' vision of a government "of the people, by the people, and for the people."[303]

So why is Barack Obama working so hard to establish critical policy-making positions and structures that avoid accountability? Obama promised to "remake America" and he is doing so by appointing extremist czars and advisors who might not survive congressional appointment hearings. Consider but a few examples:

Science Czar John Holdren: Director of the White House Office of Science and Technology Policy, Holdren is a physicist and professor whose impeccable academic credentials mask an extreme ideology and radical political agenda. In 1973, Holdren co-authored a textbook called *Human Ecology: Problems and Solutions*, which warns of dire consequences unless human population growth is halted. The book, written before the Supreme Court issued its *Roe v. Wade* decision, strongly advocates for legalized abortion, arguing that it spares "unwanted children" from

---

300 Pershing, Ben. "Byrd to Obama: Enough Already With the 'Czars,'" Washington Post. http://voices.washingtonpost.com/capitol-briefing/2009/02/byrd_enough_already_with_the_c.html. Internet.
301 Ibid.
302 "Kingston calls for transparency, accountability in presidential appointments," Kingston. House.gov. http://kingston.house.gov/News/DocumentSingle.aspx?DocumentID=137527. Internet.
303 Lincoln, Abraham. "The Gettysburg Address." http://americancivilwar.com/north/lincoln.html. Internet.

undesirable consequences, both for them and for society.[304] In a 1977 book, *Ecoscience: Population, Resources, Environment*, Holdren concluded that "compulsory population-control laws, even including laws requiring compulsory abortion, could be sustained under the existing Constitution if the population crisis became sufficiently severe to endanger the society."[305]

Green Jobs Czar Van Jones In March 2009, Obama appointed Jones to the newly-created position of Special Advisor for Green Jobs, Enterprise and Innovation at the White House Council on Environmental Quality.[306] In 1992, while still a student at Yale Law School, Jones was arrested during the riots following the Rodney King verdict. The district attorney eventually dropped the charges, but Jones later said that "the incident deepened my disaffection with the system and accelerated my political radicalization." Jones described how he was radicalized in jail at the time:

I was a rowdy nationalist on April 28th [1992] and then the verdicts came down. By August, I was a communist... I met all these young radical people of color – I mean really radical: communists and anarchists. And it was like, 'This is what I need to be a part

---

304 Jeffrey, Terence P. "Obama's Science Czar Said a Born Baby 'Will Ultimately Develop Into a Human Being," CNSNews.com. http://www.cnsnews.com/news/article/51676. Internet. Citing Swedish studies, the authors assert, "There seems little doubt that the forced bearing of unwanted children has undesirable consequences not only for the children themselves and their families but for society as well, apart from the problems of overpopulation."

305 Zahn, Drew. "Obama's science czar Holdren called for forced abortions," World Net Daily. http://www.wnd.com/index.php?fa=PAGE.view&pageId=103707. Internet. Holdren and his co-authors also imply that a newborn child is not yet a person deserving of the full protection of the law: "The fetus, given the opportunity to develop properly before birth, and given the essential early socializing experiences and sufficient nourishing food during the crucial years after birth, will ultimately develop into a human being." They accuse persons with a pro-life perspective of engaging in "unthinking actions" that help to commit the future unheard generations to misery and early death on an overcrowded planet." They even float the idea of government-mandated family size, rationalizing that "compulsory control of family size is an unpalatable idea, but the alternatives may be much more horrifying. ... If effective action is taken promptly, perhaps the need for involuntary or repressive measures can be averted." Jeffrey, Terence P. "Obama's Science Czar Said a Born Baby 'Will Ultimately Develop Into a Human Being," CNSNews.com. http://www.cnsnews.com/news/article/51676.

306 Judkis, Maura. "Obama Drafts Van Jones as Green Jobs Adviser," U.S. News & World Report. http://www.usnews.com/money/blogs/fresh-greens/2009/03/10/obama-drafts-van-jones-as-green-jobs-adviser.html.

of.' I spent the next ten years of my life working with a lot of these people I met in jail, trying to be a revolutionary.[307]

After law school, Jones became a leader in Standing Together to Organize a Revolutionary Movement (STORM), a Communist revolutionary organization with a "commitment to the fundamental ideas of Marxism-Leninism."[308] STORM and the Ella Baker Center for Human Rights, another leftist organization founded by Jones, led a vigil on September 12, 2001 to show solidarity with Arab and Muslim Americans and to mourn the civilians who died in the terrorist attacks, "as well as the victims of U.S. imperialism around the world."[309] Later, Jones signed a letter by the group 911truth.org that demanded an "immediate inquiry into evidence that suggests high-level government officials may have deliberately allowed the September 11th attacks to occur."[310]

Jones' political extremism and intense disaffection with the American capitalist system are well-documented. In recent years he has advocated using the green movement to "change the whole system."[311] In January 2008, Jones claimed that race was a factor in environmental concerns: "The white polluters and the white environmentalists are essentially steering poison into the people-of-color communities, because they don't have a racial justice frame."[312] Days before his March 2009 appointment by the Obama administration, Jones gave a lecture on energy issues in Berkeley, California in which he mocked capitalism in an exchange with an audience member who asked how the Republicans were able to "push things through" without a 60 seat majority in the Senate.

Van Jones: Well, the answer to that is: they're a**holes.

---

307 Theodosopoulos, Sam. "Fox News Notes Communist Past of the 'Green Jobs' Czar," Newsbusters.org. http://newsbusters.org/blogs/sam-theodosopoulos/2009/07/10/fox-news-notes-communist-past-green-jobs-czar#ixzz0mRS5fz2M. Internet. He explained that he subsequently changed his tactics, but not his objectives, "I'm willing to forgo the cheap satisfaction of the radical pose for the deep satisfaction of the radical ends."Kerpen, Phil. "Van Jones Returns," FOxNews.com. http://www.foxnews.com/opinion/2010/02/22/phil-kerpen-van-jones-comeback-green-jobs-obama/. Internet.
308 Klein, Aaron. "White House still listening to Van Jones 'green' advice," WorldNetDaily.com. http://www.wnd.com/index.php?fa=PAGE.view&pageId=117548. Internet; accessed 27 April 2010.
309 Klein, Aaron. "Obama 'czar' on 9/11: Blame 'U.S. imperialism'!" WorldNetDaily.com. http://www.wnd.com/index.php?pageId=108180. Internet.
310 "Van Jones' 9/11 Truther Past Raises Questions About Obama's 'Czars'," FoxNews.com. http://www.foxnews.com/story/0,2933,546602,00.html. Internet.
311 "Raw Data: Van Jones in His Own Words," FoxNews.com. http://www.foxnews.com/politics/2009/09/03/raw-data-van-jones-words/. Internet.
312 Ibid.

Questioner: I was afraid that that was the answer.

Van Jones: That's a technical, political science term. And -- Barack O -- Barack Obama's not an asshole. So -- now, I will say this: I can be an asshole. And some of us who are not Barack Hussein Obama are going to have to start getting a little bit uppity. How's that capitalism working for ya?[313]

Weeks after FOX News's Glenn Beck publicized Jones' actions, Jones resigned from his post in the Obama administration,[314] but Jones' extreme background prompted some in the media to raise questions about the vetting process of the Obama administration. Jones, however, said that his past associations were known by the White House before his appointment.[315]

Obama's view of accountability is limited to the Oval Office door. Obama has stressed the importance of the czar positions and stated that czars would report directly to him. As federal employees, the czars should not only be accountable to Obama, but to the American people. Obama's czar appointments betray his promises of accountability.

Obama asks to be held accountable, but plays the blame game. He claims to want the government to be held accountable, but implements policies that eviscerate the accountability structures already in place. No American who voted for Obama thought the "change" he promised to bring was one of less accountability, less transparency, and more divisiveness, but that is precisely what he is delivering.

---

313 Ibid.

314 Terkel, Amanda. "Van Jones to Glenn Beck: 'I see you, and I love you, brother.' ThinkProgress.org. http://thinkprogress.org/2010/02/27/jones-beck-love/. Internet.

315 Vogel, Kenneth P. "Glenn Beck won't let go of Van Jones," Politico.com. http://www. politico.com/news/stories/0310/33715.html. Internet. Senior White House Advisor Valerie Jarrett's 2009 comments about recruiting Jones to the White House support Jones's claim: "We were so delighted to be able to recruit him into the White House. We were watching him, uh, really, he's not that old, for as long as he's been active out in Oakland. "A Conversation with Valerie Jarrret – Liveblog," DailyKos. http://www.dailykos.com/storyonly/2009/8/15/767198/-A-Conversation-with-Valerie-JarrettLiveblog. Internet.

PART 2

DISTURBING TACTICS, DESTRUCTIVE ENDS

6

A Government of Laws, Not of Men

"They define a republic to be a government of laws, and not of men."
-- John Adams

We are so accustomed to living under the rule of law, and so unappreciative of its countless blessings, that we are unaware of the atrocities its creeping exile will eventually unleash. The rule of law is the very foundation, the animating principle, of our system of governance; without it, our cherished freedoms, our homes, even our lives, are at risk, subject to the whim of bureaucrats, tyrants, or dictators.

After years of suffering a "long train of abuses and usurpations" and "absolute Despotism" under the oppressive edicts of King George III, the colonists responded with the American Revolution. More than 200 years later, Americans have grown increasingly wary and weary of an ever-expanding federal government that recognizes no higher authority than its own appetite for power and control. President George Washington knew better: "The propitious smiles of Heaven can never be expected on a nation that disregards the eternal rules of order and right which Heaven itself has ordained."[316]

Red flags flap furiously in the winds of change; change that more and more Americans cannot believe in. "Take back America" has become a rallying cry for a growing number of citizens who believe if America is to endure it must return to the limited, constitutional governance, undergirded by godly morality, that the founders envisioned.

Make no mistake, a revolution is required to restore America, but it's a revolution that can be fought with the weapons of democracy. This is not a call to arms or violence – it is a call to once again

---

316 Barton, David. Original Intent: The Courts, the Constitution, and Religion. Aledo: WallBuilder Press, 2000.

tether ourselves to our core principles and values... Truth, the 'first casualty in war,' is in short supply – make it your polestar.[317]

The founders sought a government of laws, not of men; a framework grounded in God's sovereignty, which maximized individual liberties and human potential. Essential to their understanding was that every person possesses certain fundamental and unalienable rights, not because the government grants them, but because the Creator has given them. In his 1789 Thanksgiving Proclamation, Washington humbly acknowledged God's rule over all nations and people, stating, "It is the duty of all Nations to acknowledge the providence of Almighty God, to obey his will, to be grateful for his benefits, and humbly to implore his protection and favors."[318]

Washington recognized that leaders have a responsibility to insure the rights of the citizens who elect them.

> The Power under the Constitution will always be in the people. It is entrusted for certain defined purposes, and for a certain limited period, to representatives of their own choosing; and whenever it is executed contrary to their interest, or not agreeable to their wishes, their servants can, and undoubtedly will, be recalled.[319]

The founders wisely provided a framework for limited government, with checks and balances, and enumerated individual rights under the rule of law. Washington recognized that "the Constitution of the United States, and the laws made under it, must mark the line of my official conduct."[320] Fundamental to the rule of law is the principle that no one is above the law; rather, it is applied equally to each person. Every person is the beneficiary of its protections, the guardian of its liberties, and the subject of its requirements.

The founding fathers had a profound distrust of the rule of men and a profound respect for the rule of law. In order to secure the freedom

---

317 Beck, Glenn. Glenn Beck's Common Sense: The Case Against an Out-of-Control Government, Inspired by Thomas Paine. New York: Simon and Schuster, 2009.

318 Washington, George. "Thanksgiving Proclamation, 1789," The Papers of George Washington. http://gwpapers.virginia.edu/documents/thanksgiving/transcript.html. Internet.

319 Fitzpatrick, John C. The Writings of George Washington, GPO, 1931-44. Vol. 29:311. Christian obligations extend to citizens as well as leaders. Romans 13:1 instructs that "everyone must submit himself to the governing authorities." For the Christian community, this means that believers are to stand with a lawful government aligned with God's purposes. Christians are to respect governmental authority unless obedience to government would mean disobedience to God.

320 Twohig, Dorothy. "George Washington: The First Presidency," The Papers of George Washington: Articles. http://gwpapers.virginia.edu/articles/twohig_1.html. Internet.

of the new nation's citizens, "the Constitution indisputably establishes the primacy of the individual over the state."[321] Aware of the destructive potential inherent in human nature, they sought to construct the most limited system of government capable of effectively establishing a stable and ordered society. Thomas Jefferson's desire to avoid oppressive government was so great that he inferred his preference for no government over a despotic one, if forced to choose between the two:

> These societies (as the Indians) which live without government enjoy in their general mass an infinitely greater degree of happiness than those who live under the European governments. Among the former, public opinion is in the place of law, & restrains morals as powerfully as laws ever did anywhere. Among the latter, under pretence of governing they have divided their nations into two classes, wolves & sheep.[322]

A healthy suspicion of persons holding power in government is woven through our Constitution. In a speech at the 1787 Constitutional Convention, Madison noted "All men having power ought to be distrusted to a certain degree."[323]

On the continuum between the evils of anarchy and totalitarianism, the founders wisely chose a place theoretically closer to anarchy; so close that their first effort at a governing document, the Articles of Confederation, failed to provide the framework needed to facilitate commerce and mutually beneficial conduct among the states. Their second effort, the United States Constitution passed in 1787, established the greatest model for government ever devised. The founders' choice was deliberate, but not because they viewed anarchy as the lesser of evils as compared to totalitarianism; the horrific evils attributed to each are well established in human history. Rather, the founders possessed a realistic view of human nature. They understood the human appetite for the accumulation of power, and sought to constrain the governmental temptation toward despotism or totalitarianism.

> It will not be denied that power is of an encroaching nature and that it ought to be effectually restrained from passing the limits

---

321 Napolitano, Andrew P. Constitutional Chaos. Nashville: Thomas Nelson, 2004.
322 Bassani, Luigi Marco. "Life, Liberty, and...:Jefferson on Property Rights." Journal of Libertarian Studies 18, no. 1 (2004): 31-87. Ludwig von Mises Institute. [Google Docs.]
323 Advice to My Country, 1834. Brant, Irving. James Madison: Commander in Chief 1812-1836. Indianapolis: The Bobbs-Merrill Company, 1961.

assigned to it. After discriminating, therefore, in theory, the several classes of power, as they may in their nature be legislative, executive, or judiciary, the next and most difficult task is to provide some practical security for each, against the invasion of the others.[324]

Thomas Jefferson declared that the Constitution "fixed the limits" of political power in order to "bind down those whom we are obliged to trust with power." He concluded, "In questions of power, then, let no more be heard of confidence in man, but bind him down from mischief by the chains of the Constitution."[325] Today, each branch of the government has broken free of those chains, pushing outside the constitutional confines established at the country's birth. Rather than checking the power of one another, each branch has abused its own powers and acquiesced to the others' unconstitutional excesses. Congress, under the Supreme Court's absurd reading of the Commerce Clause, has found a way to regulate every facet of American life in minute detail and has ceded massive, unconstitutional powers to an un-elected Federal Reserve Board. The Supreme Court has used the concept of "the living constitution" as a license to escape constitutional boundaries and enact de facto law. The executive branch, through regulatory boards, new cabinet posts, signing statements, executive orders, czars and claims of executive privilege, has assumed more power than the founders ever dreamed of bestowing.

D.C. politicians are willfully blind to the dangers of an out-of-control, intrusive federal government. Congress and the executive branch are controlled by liberals and progressives who see government as the solution to every problem, and who criticize those who are suspicious of the growing bureaucracy. Persons of faith, independent political thinkers, home-schoolers and tea party participants have become fodder for liberals on Sunday morning news magazines as politicians legislate on everything from banking to bowl games.

> Liberalism sees no realm of human life that is beyond political significance, from what you eat to what you smoke to what you say. Sex is political. Food is political. Sports, entertainment, your inner motives and outer appearance, all have political salience for

---

324 James Madison, "Federalist #10," The Federalist Papers. http://thomas.loc.gov/home/fedpapers/fed_48.html. Internet.

325 Mayer, David N.. "By the Chains of the Constitution: Separation of Powers Theory and Jefferson's Conception of the Presidency." Perspectives on Political Science 26 (1997): 140-148.

liberal fascists. Liberals place their faith in priestly experts who know better, who plan, exhort, badger, and scold. They try to use science to discredit traditional notions of religion and faith, but they speak the language of pluralism and spirituality to defend 'nontraditional' beliefs.[326]

Historically, some government growth has benefitted the American public. The federal government occasionally proves capable of improving citizens' lives through thoughtful, constitutional legislation. Laws ending child labor, civil rights legislation and legitimate food and drug measures provide a few noteworthy examples. But power's ability to corrupt has taken a toll, and the scales long ago tipped against individual liberties. Americans are waking up to the danger of unbridled government expansion; in a June 2010 Rasmussen poll, 48 percent of Americans viewed the government as a threat to individual rights.[327]

The federal income tax has given politicians unprecedented power, and with the growth of the welfare state, much of the public has become anaesthetized to governmental misconduct. Worse, the relentless growth of government threatens to crush the private sector, America's undisputed engine of wealth creation. Between January 2008 and January 2010 the private sector lost 8.7 million jobs, while the public sector added almost 100,000 jobs.[328]

In the first quarter of 2010, a record-low 41 percent of the nation's personal income came from private wages and salaries. Government-provided benefits, such as Social Security, unemployment insurance, and food stamps accounted for a record-high 17.9 percent of personal income. Those figures do not even include the 9.8 percent of personal income paid as wages to government employees.[329] The federal budget has spiraled out of control, and so with it has the number of organizations, lobbyists, and nondisabled citizens feeding at the public trough, creating a culture of corruption, entitlement, and dependency.

---

326 Goldberg, Jonah. Liberal Fascism. New York: Doubleday, 2007.
327 "48% See Government Today As A Threat to Individual Rights," June 24, 2010 http://www.rasmussenreports.com/public_content/politics/general_politics/june_2010/48_see_government_today_as_a_threat_to_individual_rights
328 "More on My Public Sector Fat Cat Obsession," by Veronique de Rugy, http://biggovernment.com/vderugy/2010/02/23/more-on-my-public-sector-fat-cat-obsession/
329 "48% See Government Today As A Threat to Individual Rights," June 24, 2010

Rise of the Imperial Presidency

The Constitution provides for a strong chief executive and an executive branch that is co-equal in authority with the other two branches. "After much discussion, the founders created a presidential office with specific constraints as well as considerable power. They separated it from the legislative and judicial branches with a system of checks and balances designed to prevent the president from becoming a tyrant."[330]

The president is not a king; his duties and limited powers are delineated in Article 1, section 7 and Article 2 of the Constitution, and include the following: he vetoes legislation or signs it into law; he is Commander in Chief of the U.S. military; he has the power to convene one or both Houses of Congress and to receive ambassadors and other public ministers; he has the power, by and with the advice, consent and two-thirds concurrence of the Senate, to make treaties; and with the advice and consent of the Senate he appoints ambassadors, judges and officers of the United States.[331]

Article 2, section 1 of the Constitution states, "The executive Power shall be vested in a President of the United States of America." Though "the most obvious meaning of the language of this vesting clause is to confirm that the executive power is vested in a single person," Alexander Hamilton argued that this section constituted a general grant of executive power, and that the subsequent section only delineated particular cases of the preceding, more comprehensive expression.[332] "The general doctrine of our Constitution then is, that the executive power of the nation is vested in the President; subject only to the exceptions and qualifications, which are expressed in the instrument."[333] '

Madison countered that if Hamilton's view prevailed, "the most penetrating jurist would be unable to scan the extent of constructive prerogative" constitutionally granted to the President. The Supreme Court has not settled the debate that has raged ever since.[334]

Obama is not the first president to seize powers not clearly bestowed by the Constitution. Frustrated in his dealings with Congress over treaties

---

330 "Presidential Powers." Encyclopedia of American Foreign Policy, Answers.com. http://www.answers.com/topic/presidential-powers. Internet.
331 "The Constitution of the United States,", Article 1, section 7; Article 2, sections 1-3.
332 Congressional Research Service. "CRS Annotated Constitution," Law.Cornell.edu. http://www.law.cornell.edu/anncon/html/art2frag1_user.html. Internet.
333 Ibid.
334 Ibid. Myers v. United States (1926) and United States v. Curtiss-Wright Export Corp. (1936) took the more expansive view of executive power, but Youngstown Sheet & Tube Co. v. Sawyer (1952) and Medelln v. Texas (2008) appeared to retreat from that position.

with Indian tribes, Washington concluded treaties first and then asked for Senate approval, a practice followed by subsequent presidents.[335] In 1803, Jefferson dispatched James Monroe with Minister to France Robert Livingston to Paris to negotiate the purchase of New Orleans and Florida. The two accepted an offer from the French to sell all of Louisiana to the U.S. for $15 million.

Though Jefferson believed a constitutional amendment was necessary to purchase the land and drafted an amendment for that purpose, his own cabinet and party members disagreed. Setting aside his concerns, Jefferson submitted the treaty to the Senate, where it was overwhelmingly ratified.[336]

In response to a Confederate attack on South Carolina's Fort Sumter, Lincoln enlarged the Union's army and navy, blocked southern ports, arrested suspected Confederate sympathizers and spent money not appropriated by Congress. When Congress reconvened, Lincoln asked Congress to retroactively authorize his emergency actions, explaining, "These measures, whether strictly legal or not, were ventured upon under what appeared to be a popular demand and a public necessity, trusting then, as now, that Congress would readily ratify them."[337]

As the above examples illustrate, presidents during the first 100 years of the nation's existence often tested the limits of executive power, but they implicitly acknowledged that their powers were limited and struggled to justify their actions within the constitutional framework. In the last 100 years, both Republican and Democrat presidents have accelerated the expansion of executive power, abandoning constitutional checks and balances and threatening individual liberties.

Building on Hamilton's argument, presidents have employed a concept known as the "unitary executive" to exert undivided control of the executive branch and its agencies and to accept less interference from Congress. Dana D. Nelson, professor of American studies at Vanderbilt University, charges that presidents since Reagan have used the unitary executive theory to seize more and more power.[338]

---

335 "Presidential Powers." Encyclopedia of American Foreign Policy, Answers.com. http://www.answers.com/topic/presidential-powers. Internet.

336 "Louisiana Purchase." U-S-History.com. http://www.u-s-history.com/pages/h476.html. Internet.

337 Savage, Charlie. Takeover: The return of the imperial presidency and the subversion of American democracy.New York City: Little, Brown, 2007.

338 Nelson, Dana D. "The 'unitary executive' question," LA Times. http://www.latimes.com/news/opinion/la-oe-nelson11-2008oct11,0,224216.story. Internet.

Times of crisis and emergency have historically provided the most fertile soil for the growth of executive power. Responding to the country's woes during the Great Depression, Franklin Roosevelt's New Deal pushed many constitutionally suspect legislative measures through Congress. In 1935-36, the Supreme Court struck down eight of FDR's New Deal programs as unconstitutional. In 1937, FDR submitted to Congress a plan to expand the number of justices on the Court, seeking to shift the balance of power of the judiciary in his favor. FDR's court-packing power play, while not unconstitutional, was a political disaster, doomed by bi-partisan fears of the continued expansion of executive power.[339]

The "executive order," used very sparingly by presidents prior to 1900, has been a prime means of this expansion. Presidential executive orders are legal documents, generally used to direct governmental agencies or officials, which have the same effect as laws. Though generally authorized by the president's statutory or constitutional powers, many executive orders usurp legislative powers constitutionally granted only to Congress. When a president cannot advance his agenda through Congress, the executive order is a tempting alternative for circumventing Congress and the Constitution.

The legislative branch makes law; the executive branch faithfully executes, or administers, the law. The line between administration and legislation is not always a bright one, but executive orders resemble kingly edicts, a return to the "laws of men." Bruce Babbitt, Secretary of the Interior under Bill Clinton, told the Associated Press, "Here we are, having achieved 80 percent of what was sought in legislation, by administrative rule."[340] Bill Clinton advisor Paul Begala was less circumspect in his description of Clinton's use of executive orders: "Stroke of the pen, law of the land. Kinda cool."[341]

During his twelve years in office, FDR signed 3,435 executive orders.[342] For example, on April 5, 1933, FDR signed Executive Order 6102, "forbidding the Hoarding of Gold Coin, Gold Bullion, and Gold Certificates" by U.S. citizens. Order 6102 required citizens to trade in all but a small amount of their gold to the Federal Reserve, in exchange for $20.67 per troy ounce, under threat of a $10,000 fine and/or ten years

---

339 "Teaching with Documents: Constitutional Issues: Separation of Powers," Archives.gov. http://www.archives.gov/education/lessons/separation-powers/. Internet.
340 Boaz, David. "Paul Begala and the Boston Tea Party," Cato Policy Report. http://www. cato.org/pubs/policy_report/v23n1/tea-party.pdf. Internet.
341 Ibid.
342 "The Donnelly Collection of Presidential Executive Orders: Franklin D. Roosevelt," ConservativeUSA.org. http://conservativeusa.org/eo/fdroosevelt.htm. Internet.

in prison.[343] During World War II, FDR signed Executive Order 9066, which led to the relocation and interment of 120,000 Japanese Americans, Germans, and Italians.[344]

USA Today's Susan Page asserted in 2006 that George W. Bush presided over "the greatest expansion of presidential powers in a generation or more."[345] In the wake of the deadliest terrorist attacks to ever occur on U.S. soil, Bush employed a number of constitutionally-suspect security measures, including warrantless wiretapping, enhanced interrogation practices, extraordinary rendition, claims of executive privilege or state secrets, constitutionally suspect executive orders and signing statements, and denial of habeas corpus to enemy combatants.[346]

History will undoubtedly conclude that the George W. Bush administration exceeded its constitutional authority, but it will likely do so with an honest acknowledgment of Bush's fierce determination to defend the United States against a vicious enemy that had already taken 3,000 American lives. Still, civil libertarians and constitutional scholars are right to protest every measure that erodes the individual liberties the Constitution guarantees. Laws drafted to protect our freedoms, if too

343 "Executive Order 6102 - Requiring Gold Coin, Gold Bullion and Gold Certificates to Be Delivered to the Government," The American Presidency Project. http://www.presidency. ucsb.edu/ws/index.php?pid=14611. Internet.

344 "Executive Order 9066 - Authorizing the Secretary of War To Prescribe Military Areas," The American Presidency Project. http://www.presidency.ucsb.edu/ws/index. php?pid=61698. Internet.

345 Page, Susan."Congress, courts push back against Bush's assertions of presidential power," USA Today. http://www.usatoday.com/news/washington/2006-06-05-power-play_x. htm. Internet.

346 Risen, James and Lichtblau, Eric."Bush Lets U.S. Spy on Callers Without Courts," New York Times. http://www.nytimes.com/2005/12/16/politics/16program.html). Internet. DeYoung, Karen."Bush Approves New CIA Methods," Washington Post. http://www. washingtonpost.com/wp-dyn/content/article/2007/07/20/AR2007072001264.html). Internet. Mayer, Jane. "Outsourcing Torture," New Yorker. http://www.newyorker.com/ archive/2005/02/14/050214fa_fact6?currentPage=all). Internet.Page, Susan."Congress, courts push back against Bush's assertions of presidential power," USA Today. http:// www.usatoday.com/news/washington/2006-06-05-power-play_x.htm. Internet. Savage, Charlie. "Obama's War on Terror May Resemble Bush's in Some Areas," New York Times. http://www.nytimes.com/2009/02/18/us/politics/18policy.html). Internet. "Executive Order 13438: Blocking Property of Certain Persons Who Threaten Stabilization Efforts in Iraq," Slate.com. http://img.slate.com/media/94/13438-stable.pdf. Internet. "Presidential Signing Statements," Law Library of Congress. http://www.loc.gov/law/help/statements. php. Internet; accessed 27 April 2010. Napolitano, Andrew P. Constitutional Chaos. Nashville: Thomas Nelson, 2004.

broadly framed, catch not only terrorists, but also innocent citizens in their nets.[347]

The Company You Keep

If politicians are judged by the company they keep, Obama owes the public an explanation for his relationships with unrepentant terrorist Bill Ayers and convicted financier Tony Rezko. While Obama has tried to downplay his connections with criminals like Ayers and Rezko, he admits in his memoir, *Dreams from my Father*, that, even in college, he carefully selected his associates. "To avoid being mistaken for a sellout, I chose my friends carefully. The more politically active black students. The foreign students. The Chicanos. The Marxist professors and structural feminists."[1]

After transferring to Columbia University, Obama furthered his interest in leftist politics, sometimes attending the "socialist conferences" at Cooper Union.[2] Obama continued later in life to cultivate relationships with known radicals with violent histories, even launching his political career in the home of Ayers, the Weather Underground terrorist who proclaimed himself a Marxist in 2002.[3]

Based on these friends, no one with a modicum of common sense would expect Obama to be a strong defender of the rule of law. It seems radicals are not law and order types.

---

1   Obama, Barack. Dreams from my father. New York: Times Books, 1995.
2   Ibid.
3   "Barack Obama Admits: 'I Chose My Friends Carefully... Marxist Professors and Structural Feminists,'" Gateway Pundit. http://gatewaypundit.blogspot.com/2008/10/barack-obama-admits-i-chose-my-friends.html. Internet.

Whatever their views on the extent of presidential executive power, the founders spoke with one voice in seeking to prevent any president from ignoring, violating, or manipulating the law. Aware that until the English Revolution of 1688 the King of England could use his "prerogative powers" to override a law, the founders specifically guarded against a presidential usurpation of power in contravention of the law; Article 2, section 3 of the Constitution requires that the President "shall take care that the Laws be faithfully executed."

Obama's extensive history of purposeful associations with known lawbreakers and other incendiary figures was by itself enough to make his fitness for the position of chief executive suspect and to cast a shadow on the rule of law; his actions in office have only darkened the specter.

---

347 "More on Obama's first race for office in 1996," TheNewEditor.com. http://www.theneweditor.com/index.php?/archives/8076-More-On-Obamas-First-Race-for-Public-Office-in-1996.html. Internet.

Obama's dereliction of his constitutional duty to carefully and faithfully execute all of the laws of the United States is disturbing. The emerging pattern is of a president who emphasizes and follows the law when the law is useful to achieve a desired political end, and ignores, changes, or circumvents the law when it interferes with the administration's agenda. This is a far cry from the picture of America that Obama painted on his first day in office, when touting transparency and the rule of law[348] Despite his hearty assurances, the Obama administration is eviscerating the rule of law, without which the republic cannot long stand.

Excoriating Bush and Disappointing Supporters:

Obama wasted little time excoriating George W. Bush's allegedly unconstitutional actions and presenting himself as a constitutional scholar committed to faithfully upholding the laws of the land. At a campaign rally in Billings, Montana in 2008, Obama criticized George W. Bush's practice of using signing letters to circumvent the Congressional intent of certain pieces of legislation.

> What George Bush has been trying to do as part of his effort to accumulate more power in the presidency is he's been saying, 'Well I can basically change what Congress passed by attaching a letter;' That's not part of his power. But this is part of the whole theory of being Bush - that he can make laws as he's going along. I disagree with that...We're not going to use signing statements as a way of doing an end run around Congress."[349]

Instead of keeping his promise, Obama used signing statements to repudiate dozens of provisions of bills passed into law after he took office, drawing a bipartisan rebuke from Congress.[350] Obama also promised to reform use of the state secrets privilege, to thoroughly review George W. Bush's executive orders, to end the practice of extraordinary rendition, and to reject the Military Commissions Act. Seven months into his presidency, Obama had expanded the use of "state secrets" claims to block release of

---

348 Obama, Barack. "Remarks to White House Senior Staff," GPOAccess.gov. http:/www. gpoaccess.gov/presdocs/2009/DCPD200900012.htm. Internet.
349 "Obama Speaks in Billings, MT – 5/19/08," Public Radio Exchange. http://www.prx. org/pieces/26108-obama-speaks-in-billings-mt-5-19-08. Internet.
350 Eddlum, Thomas. R. "Congress Rebukes Obama on Dictatorial Claim," New American. com. http://www.thenewamerican.com/index.php/usnews/election/1402. Internet.

information, failed to comprehensively review George W. Bush's executive orders, maintained Bush's position on an extraordinary rendition lawsuit, and expressed support for the use of military commissions.[351]

The *Washington Post* and the *Huffington Post* have criticized Obama for breaking his campaign pledge to veto any telecom immunity legislation. When the *New York Times* exposed the National Security Agency's (NSA) warrantless wiretapping program in 2005, the telecom companies that had cooperated with the government were exposed to lawsuits alleging violations of the Foreign Intelligence Surveillance Act (FISA). In 2007, the George W. Bush administration asked Congress to pass legislation granting the telecom companies immunity from such lawsuits.

In October 2007, Obama spokesman Bill Burton unequivocally stated, "Barack will support a filibuster of any bill that includes retroactive immunity for telecommunications companies."[352] However, when the bill, which also expanded the government's domestic spying powers, came before the Senate, Obama didn't filibuster the bill – he voted for it.[353] The Obama administration has continued to support the warrantless wiretapping program, citing national security interests, and is even seeking dismissal of a lawsuit brought by telephone customers alleging FISA violations.[354]

Obama has abandoned his campaign promise to end constitutionally suspect policies and practices of the Bush administration in fighting terrorism. He berates his predecessor's policies even while he perpetuates them.

> When it comes to the legal framework for confronting terrorism, President Obama is acting in no meaningful sense any different than President Bush after 2006, when the Supreme Court overturned the view that the president's war time powers were effectively unlimited.
>
> ....
>
> The U.S. still reserves the right to hold suspected terrorists indefinitely without charge, try them via military tribunal, keep them imprisoned even if they are acquitted, and kill them in foreign

---

351 Tapper, Jake and de Vogue, Ariane. "Obama Maintains Bush Position on 'Extraordinary Rendition' Lawsuit," ABC News. http://blogs.abcnews.com/politicalpunch/2009/02/obama-administr.html. Internet.

352 Lane, Alexander. "Obama's wiretapping flip-flop? Yes," Politifact.com. http://www.politifact.com/truth-o-meter/article/2008/jul/14/obamas-wiretapping-flip-flop-yes/. Internet.

353 Ibid.

354 Egelko, Bob. "Obama Goes to Bat for Bush Wiretap Program," San Francisco Chronicle. http://www.commondreams.org/headline/2009/07/16-1. Internet.

countries with which America is not formally at war (including Yemen, Somalia, and Pakistan).[355]

What the White House *has* waged is a war on words designed to appease its base. John Brennan, deputy White House national security adviser for homeland security and counterterrorism, explicitly rejected use of the words "global war" and "Islamists."[356, 357] The Obama administration dropped the phrase "Global War on Terror" in favor of "Overseas Contingency Operations."[358] It rejected the concept of "enemy combatants" or the use of words such as "jihad" or "Islamic extremism."[359]

But the rhetoric masks the reality that the Obama administration has retained the core of the George W. Bush administration's constitutionally suspect policies and built upon them in ways that should shock and alarm every American.

A bit of perspective is in order before examining the terror policies and actions of the Obama administration. The Left railed against George W. Bush's national security measures (warrantless wiretapping, extraordinary rendition, alleged torture, indefinite detention without charges for persons designated by the government as unlawful enemy combatants, etc.). In his keynote address at the 2004 Democratic National Convention, Senator Obama assailed the Bush administration: "If there's an Arab American family being rounded up without benefit of an attorney or due process, that threatens my civil liberties."[360] In December 2007, reporter Charlie Savage asked Obama, "Does the Constitution permit a president to detain U.S. citizens without charges as unlawful enemy combatants?" Obama responded, "No. I reject the Bush administration's claim that the President has plenary authority under the Constitution to detain U.S. citizens without charges as unlawful enemy combatants."[361]

In the 2004 case of *Hamdi v. Rumsfield* (2004), the Supreme Court ruled that an American citizen, captured in an active combat zone and classified by

355 "The 9/14 Presidency," by Eli Lake, April 6, 2010 http://reason.com/archives/2010/04/06/the-914-presidency/

356 "The 9/14 Presidency," by Eli Lake, April 6, 2010 http://reason.com/archives/2010/04/06/the-914-presidency/

357 "Brennan Names Al-Qaeda and Affiliates as the Enemy, Silent on Hezbollah, Others," May 27, 2010 http://www.cnsnews.com/news/article/66737

358 "The 9/14 Presidency," by Eli Lake, April 6, 2010 http://reason.com/archives/2010/04/06/the-914-presidency/

359 "Don't Mention the War," by Stephen F. Hayes and Thomas Joscelyn, May 17, 2010 http://www.weeklystandard.com/articles/don%E2%80%99t-mention-war?page=4

360 "Arab Americans for Obama," http://my.barackobama.com/page/content/aahome

361 "Barack Obama's Q&A," by Charlie Savage, December 20, 2007 http://www.boston.com/news/politics/2008/specials/CandidateQA/ObamaQA/

the government as an enemy combatant, must be afforded some measure of due process in the form of a meaningful opportunity to contest the evidentiary basis for his detention before a neutral authority. The Court's decision affirmed that the wartime power of the commander-in-chief is constrained by law and the Constitution, but ruled that Hamdi's imprisonment was lawful under federal statute.[362] Justices Scalia and Stevens joined in a dissent that went further. They argued that Hamdi's indefinite detention without charges was an unconstitutional denial of due process, given that the government did not rely on the Constitution's only provision for suspending the constitutional right to a writ of habeas corpus.[363]

Hamdi and leftist histrionics notwithstanding, the Obama administration is acting upon its claim that not only does the president have authority to detain, but to destroy, U.S. citizens suspected of terrorism, with no constitutional due process at all. In an interview with *The Washington Times'* Eli Lake, Brennan said, "If an American person or citizen is in a Yemen or in a Pakistan or in a Somalia or another place, and they are trying to carry out attacks against U.S. interests, they also will face the full brunt of a U.S. response." Brennan also stated that there were "dozens of U.S. persons" who are "very concerning to us."[364]

Under Bush, the military's Joint Chiefs of Staff maintained a target list of suspected terrorists – a list that included Americans. However, unlike Obama, Bush never implemented any policy, or initiated any action, that targeted American citizens for extra-judicial assassination.

The issue is not one of killing, *on the battlefield*, American citizens who are engaging in terrorism against the U.S. The U.S. military obviously must be able to fight the enemy on the battlefield, even if the enemy is an American citizen. But the Obama administration claims authority to kill American citizens *anywhere in the world, regardless of what activity the suspect is engaged in at the time* (sleeping at home, eating dinner with the family, etc.) based on the administration's *assertion* that the citizens are actively involved in terrorism against America -- with no attempted apprehension, no arrest, no charges, no proof of evidence, no trial or opportunity to deny the charges

---

362 Hamdi v. Rumsfeld, 542 U.S. 507 (2004)

363 Hamdi v. Rumsfeld, 542 U.S. 507 (2004) A writ of habeas corpus is a judicial order providing for a court to determine whether a prisoner's incarceration is lawful and whether the prisoner should be released. Article I of the Constitution states that the right to a writ of habeas corpus can only be suspended "in cases of rebellion or invasion of the public safety." U.S. Constitution, Article 1, section 9 http://www.archives.gov/exhibits/charters/constitution_transcript.html

364 "How many Americans are targeted for assassination?" by Glenn Greenwald, June 25, 2010 http://www.salon.com/news/opinion/glenn_greenwald/2010/06/25/assassinations

– no constitutional protections whatsoever.[365] Worse, the White House has reportedly already implemented this lawless presidential assassination policy and is attempting to defend it in the court of public opinion.[366, 367, 368]

It seems inconceivable at first blush that any president could adopt such an Orwellian policy with scant political debate or media scrutiny. That the Obama administration has been able to do so reflects the Left's hypocrisy and the Right's schizophrenia. On virtually every issue except national security, conservatives easily recognize the inherent danger of a federal government unrestrained by the Constitution or the rule of law. But the Right's distrust of government too often disappears when talk turns to fighting terrorism.

All Americans, regardless of party affiliation or political perspective, should heed founder James Madison's warning: "The means of defense against foreign danger have been always the instruments of tyranny at home."[369]

---

365 "Obama authorizes assassination of U.S. citizen," by Glenn Greenwald, April 7, 2010 http://www.salon.com/news/opinion/glenn_greenwald/2010/04/07/assassinations/index.html

366 "U.S. Approves Targeted Killing of American Cleric," by Scott Shane, April 6, 2010 http://www.nytimes.com/2010/04/07/world/middleeast/07yemen.html?_r=1&hp

367 "Muslim cleric Aulaqi is 1st U.S. citizen on list of those CIA is allowed to kill," by Greg Miller, April 7, 2010http://www.washingtonpost.com/wp-dyn/content/article/2010/04/06/AR2010040604121.html?hpid=topnews

368 "The administration defends its assassination program," by Glenn Greenwald, July 1, 2010 http://www.salon.com/news/opinion/glenn_greenwald/2010/07/01/assassinations

369 Seeing American Foreign Policy Whole, by Brewster C. Denny, University of Illinois Press, 1985 For information about how fast-advancing drone technology and domestic use of drones threatens the privacy and all civil liberties of Americans, see "Drones in U.S. skies – to keep eye on us?" by Nat Hentoff, July 20, 2010 http://www.wnd.com/index.php?fa=PAGE.view&pageId=181749

BUSH POSITION	OBAMA PROMISE	OBAMA ACTION
STATE SECRETS		
Expanded use of state secrets, Including claiming power to stop a lawsuit in discovery, based on presidential assertion that continuing would expose state secrets[371]	Promised to "apply a stricter legal test" for state secrets claims, including review by Justice Dept. committee, personal approval by Atty. Gen., and annual reporting to Congress.[372]	In *OIn EFF v. Jewel*, Obama DOJ continued Bush claim that state secrets privilege bars lawsuits against administration. Added new "sovereign immunity" claim that Patriot Act bars lawsuits for illegal govt. surveillance unless there is "willful disclosure of illegally intercepted communications."[373]
EXECUTIVE ORDERS		
Issued 284 executive orders covering a wide range of subjects; took broad view of presidential authority in relation to use of executive orders.[374]	"One of my first acts as president is going to be call in my new atty. Gen. to review every single executive order … to overturn those that are undermining the Constitution, undermining our civil liberties, that are promoting this cockamamie theory of Unitary government."[375]	Issued no first-year comprehensive review of Bush executive orders; Overturned some Bush executive orders based on different policy views. Enacted 39 new executive orders on range of issues.[376]
SIGNING STATEMENTS		
Routinely used signing statements to express disagreement with, and the intention not to follow, provisions of legislation that the administration viewed as encroaching upon Executive Branch powers.	Called Bush's use of signing statements an "abuse" and vowed to use greater restraint in issuance of signing statements.[377]	Ordered review of Bush signing statements. Drew bi-partisan rebuke (429-2 vote) from Congress and ban on use of federal funds to disobey portion of bill Obama said in signing statement that he had const. authority to disregard.[378]

370 Hendler, Clint. "Parsing Obama on State Secrets," CJR.org. http://www.cjr.org/campaign_desk/parsing_obama_on_state_secrets.php.
371 Ibid.
372 Greenwald, Glen. "New and worse secrecy and immunity claims from the Obama DOJ," Salon.com. http://www.salon.com/opinion/greenwald/2009/04/06/obama/index.html
373 Archives.gov. http://www.archives.gov/federal-register/executive- orders/wbush.html
374 Pickett, Kerry. "Obama 2007 Radio Interview: My Attorney General Will Investigate Bush Executive Orders," Newsbusters.org. http://newsbusters.org/blogs/kerry-picket/2008/11/21/obama-2007-radio-interview-my-attorney-general-will-investigate-bush-e
375 Archives.gov. http://www.archives.gov/federal-register/executive-orders/obama.html
376 Savage, Charlie. "Obama's Embrace of a Bush Tactic Riles Congress," New York Times. http://www.nytimes.com/2009/08/09/us/politics/09signing.html
377 Ibid

BUSH POSITION	OBAMA PROMISE	OBAMA ACTION
MILITARY COMMISSIONS ACT		
Embraced Military Commissions Act, which provided for military trial for enemy combatants.[379]	Said "by any measure our system of trying detainees has been an enormous failure," promised to "reject the Military Commissions Act.[380]	Endorsed Military Commissions Act of 2009, which allows government to conduct military-commission trials of terror suspects held at Guantanamo detention camp.[381]
EXTRAORDINARY RENDITION		
Defended policy of extrajudicial transfer of suspect from one State to another, as vital tool to combat terrorism. Denies the U.S. tortures.[382]	Vowed to end "the practices of shipping away prisoner… to be tortured in far-off countries, of detaining thousands without charge or trial…"[383]	Continues Bush administration practice of sending suspected terrorists to third countries for detention and interrogation, but pledges more oversight to ensure no torture.[384]

378 Richey, Warren. "Obama endorses military commissions for Guantanamo detainees," Christian Science Monitor. http://www.csmonitor.com/USA/Justice/2009/1029/p02s01-usju.html

379 Ibid

380 Ibid.

381 Sourcewatch.org. http://www.sourcewatch.org/index.php?title=Extraordinary_rendition

382 Johnston, David. "U.S. Says Rendition to Continue, but With More Oversight," New York Times. http://www.nytimes.com/2009/08/25/us/politics/25rendition.html.

383 Johnston, David. "U.S. Says Rendition to Continue, but With More Oversight," New York Times. http://www.nytimes.com/2009/08/25/us/politics/25rendition.html

Civil Rights and Wrongs

Though Obama has repeatedly accused George W. Bush of violating American ideals in the treatment of suspected terrorists, some of the most alarming Obama administration actions betray a complete disregard for the basic civil rights of American citizens. On the campaign trail, Obama pledged: "When I am president we will have a civil rights division that actually is investigating crimes. We will have a civil rights division that is enforcing voting rights ... your next president will actually believe in the Constitution of the United States and will uphold that Constitution."[384]

Despite this promise, Obama failed to demand that the Department of Justice (DOJ) protect voting rights.

On Election Day 2008, Samir Shabazz and Jerry Jackson, two members of the New Black Panther Party for Self-Defense, ("New Black Panthers"), stood near the entrance to a Philadelphia polling place wearing military-style uniforms and combat boots and uttering racial slurs. Samir Shabazz was also holding a billy club.[385]

Civil rights attorney Bartle Bull, a self-described liberal who worked for Robert F. Kennedy and Jimmy Carter, witnessed some of the New Black Panther tactics in Philadelphia while visiting polling places on Election Day and filed a report with the DOJ. He later described one of the scenes, saying, "I saw two armed, uniformed, threatening men blocking the door to a polling place, screaming rudeness at voters ... one of them, for example, screamed, 'Now you will see what it is like to be ruled by the black man, cracker.'"[386] Videographer Stephen Robert Morse captured the scene on video, later viewed by more than a million people on youtube.com.[387]

Fox News reporter Rick Leventhal interviewed a Republican poll watcher on site, who alleged that poll watchers on the inside told him the New Black Panthers "told us not to come outside, because a black man is going to win this election no matter what...So, as I came back outside to

384 Nunnery, Ben. "Obama talks change in Lebanon," The Dartmouth. http://thedartmouth. com/2007/11/13/news/obama. Internet.; Obama, Barack. Speech at Lebanon High School, November 12, 2007. http://www.youtube.com/. Internet.

385 A police officer's club or baton. Billy club. Dictionary.com. Dictionary.com Unabridged. Random House, Inc. http://dictionary.reference.com/browse/billy club (accessed: April 29, 2010).

386 von Spakovsky, Hans A. "Voter Intimidation, New Black Panther Style," Newscred.com. http://www.newscred.com/article/show/title/fnc-s-o-reilly-interviews-liberal-attorney-who-witnessed-black-panther-voter-intimidation-4a2666c9e1fce/1605992. Internet.

387 Morse, Stephen Robert. "The New Black Panthers and Me," MotherJones.com. http:// motherjones.com/mojo/2009/09?page=8. Internet.

see, the nightstick turns around and says, 'You know, we're tired of white supremacy,' and starts tapping the nightstick in his hand."[388] The poll watcher called police, who escorted Shabazz away, but allowed Jackson to stay.

On January 7, 2009, the George W. Bush DOJ filed a lawsuit under the Voting Rights Act of 1965 against the New Black Panthers and members Samir Shabazz and Jackson, alleging that the group engaged in voter intimidation tactics during the 2008 general election. According to the complaint, Party Chairman Zulu Shabazz confirmed that Samir Shabazz and Jackson were placed at the Philadelphia polling place as part of a nationwide effort to deploy New Black Panthers to polling locations on Election Day. [389] The complaint also noted that Jackson was an elected member of Philadelphia's Fourteenth Ward Democratic Committee and a credentialed poll watcher for Obama and the Democratic Party.[390]

When a plaintiff, such as the DOJ, files a lawsuit against a defendant, the defendant has a set period of time during which to file an answer, either denying the claims stated in the suit or explaining the extenuating circumstances surrounding the situation. If the defendant does not respond to the suit or ask the court for more time to respond, the court treats the defendant as though he has admitted that the claims in the lawsuit are true. The plaintiff then files - and the court grants - a default judgment, which effectively means that the plaintiff wins the case. In this case, none of the defendants responded to the lawsuit.

Instead of immediately requesting a default judgment, the DOJ, now under the Obama administration, asked the court for more time to file the default judgment. The court granted the request, and on May 15, 2009, the extended default judgment filing deadline, the DOJ voluntarily dismissed the lawsuit against the New Black Panthers and Jackson, the Democratic Committee member and poll watcher. Legally, the New Black Panthers' lack of response was an admission of fault. In other words, the

---

388 "Black Panthers Cause Problems in Philadelphia (video)," DailyRadar.com. http://beltwayblips.dailyradar.com/video/black_panthers_cause_problems_in_philadelphia/. Internet.

389 "Justice Department Seeks Injunction Against New Black Panther Party," Justice.gov. http://www.justice.gov/opa/pr/2009/January/09-crt-014.html. Internet. Section 11(b) of the Voting Rights Act of 1965, prohibits intimidation, coercion or threats against "any person for voting or attempting to vote."

390 The New Black Panther Party has 28 chapters around the country and is listed by the Southern Poverty Law Center as a hate group. "Editorial: Return of the Black Panther," Washington Times. http://www.washingtontimes.com/news/2009/jul/07/return-of-the-black-panther/. Internet.

DOJ dropped its case after winning the case. The U.S. Commission on Civil Rights subsequently opened an investigation into the dismissal.

The DOJ obtained a default judgment against Samir Shabazz on May 18, 2009, but Philadelphia newspaper *The Bulletin* reported that the proposed order for the default judgment on Shabazz asked for none of the usual injunctive relief conditions the DOJ would typically seek.[391] Additionally, *The Bulletin* reported that career prosecutors wanted to proceed with the case, but Obama appointees did not.[392] Hans von Spakovsky, a former career Counsel to the Assistant Attorney General for Civil Rights, called the DOJ's decision "unprecedented:"

It is absolutely unprecedented for the Justice Department to dismiss a lawsuit after the defendants failed to answer the suit and are thus in default. And dismissing an individual who was a local Democratic party official who defaulted by not answering the complaint smacks of the worst sort of political partisanship ... It is completely contrary to all of the promises that Eric Holder made when he was confirmed to be Attorney General.[393]

Bartle Bull described the DOJ's decision as "100 percent politically motivated," adding, "The senior lawyer working on this matter, Christian Adams, said to me if this is not a case of intimidation, nothing is."[394]

Adams, a career DOJ attorney who had recently received a promotion, resigned his position in June 2010 to protest the handling of the case by Obama administration political appointees.

The New Black Panther case was the simplest and most obvious violation of federal law I saw in my Justice Department career. Because of the corrupt nature of the dismissal, statements falsely characterizing the case, and most of all, indefensible orders for the career attorneys not to comply with lawful subpoenas investigating the dismissal, this month I resigned my position ....

Threats of violence characterized elections from the end of the Civil War until the passage of the Voting Rights Act in 1965.

391 Tremoglie, Michael P. "Dept. of Justive drops New Black Panthers Case," The Bulletin. http://thebulletin.us/articles/2009/05/29/top_stories/doc4a1f42b32c161287079901. txt. Internet.
392 Ibid.
393 Ibid
394 von Spakovsky, Hans A. "Voter Intimidation, New Black Panther Style," Newscred.com. http://www.newscred.com/article/show/title/fnc-s-o-reilly-interviews-liberal-attorney-who-witnessed-black-panther-voter-intimidation-4a2666c9e1fce/1605992. Internet.

Before the Voting Rights Act, blacks seeking the right to vote, and those aiding them, were victims of violence and intimidation.
….

The assistant attorney general for civil rights, Tom Perez, has testified repeatedly that the "facts and law" did not support the case. That claim is false. If the actions in Philadelphia do not constitute voter intimidation, it is hard to imagine what would, short of an actual outbreak of violence at the polls. ….

Citizens would be shocked to learn about the open and pervasive hostility within the Justice Department to bringing civil rights cases against nonwhite defendants on behalf of white victims. Equal enforcement of justice is not a priority of this administration. Open contempt is voiced for these types of cases.[395]

In testimony before the independent, nonpartisan U.S Commission on Civil Rights, which earlier had opened an investigation into the DOJ's handling of the case, Adams described in great detail the culture of pervasive hostility within the Civil Rights Division of the DOJ toward the enforcement of civil rights protections for whites. The Commission subsequently called on the DOJ to investigate whether Adams's testimony was accurate, concluding:

Mr. Adams' (sic) testimony raises grave questions regarding whether managers and other political and career attorneys in the Civil Rights Division believe in the "color-blind" enforcement of civil rights laws, specifically, whether they should be enforced against all Americans equally and whether those protections apply with equal force to citizens of all races.[396]

Adams's sworn testimony was corroborated in affidavits subsequently filed by two other former U.S. Department of Justice attorneys.[397]

The Voting Rights Act of 1965 was designed to prevent this kind of voter intimidation.

---

395 "ADAMS: Inside the Black Panther Case," by J. Christian Adams, June 25, 2010 http://www.washingtontimes.com/news/2010/jun/25/inside-the-black-panther-case-anger-ignorance-and-/
396 Letter tp Assistant Attorney General Thomas Perez, http://www.usccr.gov/NBPH/GARtoTP_07-14-10.pdf
397 "More evidence of Justice racism," July 17, 2010   http://www.wnd.com/?pageId=180129

Without free and fair elections, a constitutional republic ceases to function. Even the slightest hint of intimidation demands a serious response by the government in order to ensure that no person is denied the opportunity to freely vote his or her conscience. Though the decision cannot be definitively attributed to Obama, it bears his imprint. "I believe President Obama owes the country an apology for this ... He appointed Eric Holder ... Martin Luther King did not die to have people in jack boots with billy clubs, block the doors of polling places," Bull told O'Reilly. "It's an absolute disgrace."[398]

Ironic Justice

It should not come as a surprise that Eric Holder's Justice Department opted against seeking justice in the New Black Panther case; conservatives panned Obama's choice for Attorney General, Eric Holder, Jr., based in part on his role in Bill Clinton's last-minute pardons of sixteen former members of a Puerto Rican terrorist group and the pardon of fugitive financier Marc Rich.

As Deputy Attorney General, Holder strongly supported severe gun control legislation, including the banning of handguns. After the D.C. Circuit Court of Appeals' 2007 decision holding that the D.C. handgun and self-defense bans were unconstitutional, Holder lamented that the decision "opens the door to more people having more access to guns and putting guns on the streets."[1]

1 "Eric Holder," Wikipedia.org. http://en.wikipedia.org/wiki/Eric_Holder.

Intimidation: The Politics of Negotiation

Under the ill-fated Articles of Confederation, the founders witnessed the injustices and economic chaos that resulted when debtor-friendly state laws unfairly benefited residents by enabling them to void or alter contracts made with residents of other states. When the founders wrote our present day Constitution, they assured the uniform enforceability of contracts across state lines.

The Contracts Clause of Article V of the Constitution prohibits states from interfering with the obligation to pay debts. The Bankruptcy Clause of Article I, Section 8, delegated to the federal government the sole authority to enact "uniform laws on the subject of bankruptcies."[399]

When the impending bankruptcy of automaker Chrysler became painfully apparent in the spring of 2009, the Obama administration

398 Ibid.
399 "The Constitution of the United States," Article 1, Section 8 and Article 5.

leveraged its power to preempt the judiciary from exercising its legal authority to administer the bankruptcy proceeding. Instead of an impartial judge applying long-standing bankruptcy laws and principles, the administration applied its own notions of fairness to achieve a quasi-bankruptcy before the fact. The government pressured lenders to surrender their contractual rights and accept payments that the government declared to be fair. The administration had a relatively easy time with the larger secured lenders, which included Goldman Sachs, Citigroup, JP Morgan and Morgan Stanley, because they all received billions of dollars of TARP funds.[400] Given the haphazard administration of the TARP program, these companies knew they were in no position to negotiate. It was a buck-the-government-and-lose-the-bucks situation; companies receiving bailout money had an incentive to cooperate with the government. By contrast, raw power was the only leverage the administration had with smaller firms that had not received bailout money.

The smaller investment firms that held out in the negotiations were first secured lenders that were entitled to be paid first under the absolute priority rule. The absolute priority rule is one of the long-standing lynchpins – the established rule of law - of such bankruptcy proceedings. It establishes a clear hierarchy of claims based on various types of security (or the lack thereof) held by a particular investor. The absolute priority rule places secured creditors at the front of the virtual payback line to receive their portions of a bankrupt company's assets. Stockholders' interests are junior to the interests of both secured and unsecured creditors. Under the rule, when similarly situated creditors do not agree with a debtor's bankruptcy plan, the court will approve the plan over the objections of the dissenting group of creditors only *if* dissenting creditors are paid in full, or if "no one with a claim or interest that is junior to the claims of the dissenting creditors will get or retain anything under the plan."[401]

During the course of the Chrysler negotiations, the Obama administration shredded the absolute priority rule and proposed that secured creditors should receive 28 cents on the dollar for the $7 billion Chrysler owed them, while the United Auto Workers Union, (UAW), a shareholder, should receive 55 percent of the reorganized Chrysler and 43

---

400 Payne, Henry. "Who drove Chrysler to bankruptcy?" National Review Online. http://corner.nationalreview.com/post//q=ZjNiZGJkNDhm)WY0MmBlW2Q5ZjM5OGJiN.html. Internet.

401 Ortiz, Nicholas. "What is the Absolute Priority Rule?" Bankruptcy Law Network. http://www.bankruptcylawnetwork.com/2007/02/19/what-is-the-absolute-priority-rule/. Internet.

cents on the dollar for its $11 billion claim.[402] It is particularly disturbing that the Obama administration structured the Chrysler deal to circumvent bankruptcy law and unfairly benefit the UAW shareholders, given that the UAW has showered over $23.7 million on Democratic campaigns since 2000.[403]

The White House did not stop at giving the UAW a sweetheart deal in contravention of longstanding bankruptcy law; White House officials also threatened secured investors that wanted to enforce their contractual rights. Tom Lauria, a bankruptcy attorney who represented a group of lenders that sought to enforce their contractual priority rights in the Chrysler bankruptcy negotiations, spoke of the administration's strong-arm tactics in the negotiations:

> One of my clients was directly threatened by the White House, and, in essence, compelled to withdraw its opposition to the deal under the threat that the full force of the White House Press Corps would destroy its reputation if it continued to fight... [Secured creditors] bought a contract that said, 'You're first in line, and in exchange for that you're gonna get a very low rate of return. I think everybody in this country should be concerned about the fact that the President of the United States, the Executive Office, is using its power to try to abrogate that contractual right. If the President will attack that contractual right, what right will it not attack?[404]

Obama made good on the White House's threats when he announced the Chrysler deal on April 30, 2009.

> While many stakeholders made sacrifices and worked constructively, I have to tell you some did not. In particular, a group of investment firms and hedge funds decided to hold out for the prospect of an unjustified taxpayer-funded bailout. They were hoping that

---

402 Will, George F. "Tincture of Lawlessness: Obama's Overreaching Economic Policies," Washington Post. http://www.washingtonpost.com/wp-dyn/content/article/2009/05/13/AR2009051303014.html. Internet.
403 Gingrich, Newt. "Once, We Would Have Called It a Scandal," Human Events. http://www.humanevents.com/article.php?id=32212. Internet.
404 "Frank talks with Tom Lauria, who represents a group of lenders that object to the Chrysler sale," NewsTalk WJR 760 AM. http://www.760wjr.com/Article.asp?id=1301727&spid=6525. Internet. Lauria was not the only person to suggest that the White House threatened creditors that resisted the Chrysler deal. Also see Carney, John. "New Allegations of White House Threats Over Chrysler," Business Insider. http://www.businessinsider.com/new-allegations-of-white-house-threats-over-chysler-2009-5. Internet.

everybody else would make sacrifices, and they would have to make none. Some demanded twice the return that other lenders were getting. I don't stand with them. I stand with Chrysler's employees and their families and communities. I stand with Chrysler's management, its dealers, and its suppliers. I stand with the millions of Americans who own and want to buy Chrysler cars. I don't stand with those who held out when everybody else is making sacrifices.[405]

Obama's claims that the firms sought to avoid any sacrifice were slanderous. Sacrifices are implicit in the nature of the bankruptcy negotiations. The creditors that protested the White House's deal were not holding out for full reimbursement of their investment, as Obama charged; instead, though they were under no legal obligation to do so, they offered to accept 50 cents on the dollar. The creditors were not looking for a taxpayer bailout; they simply opposed the government's abuse of the bankruptcy laws to coerce first lien lenders to subsidize the rehabilitation of Chrysler."[406]

George Mason law professor Todd Zywicki wrote in the *Wall Street Journal*, "The government's threats and bare-knuckle tactics set an ominous precedent for the treatment of those considered insufficiently responsive to its desires."[407] An article in *The Economist* echoed Zywicki's concerns:

America's government ... has vilified creditors and ridden roughshod over their legitimate claims over the carmaker's assets. ... Bankruptcies involve dividing a shrunken pie. But not all claims are equal: some lenders provide cheaper funds to firms in return for a more secure claim over the assets should things go wrong. They rank above other stakeholders, including shareholders and employees. This principle is now being trashed.[408]

---

405 "President Obama's remarks on Chrysler's restructuring," The Scoop: A Website for Chrysler Group Employees and their Families. http://scoop.chrysler.com/2009/04/30/president-obamas-remarks-regarding-chrysler%E2%80%99s-restructuring/. Internet.

406 "Frank talks with Tom Lauria, who represents a group of lenders that object to the Chrysler sale," NewsTalk WJR 760 AM. http://www.760wjr.com/Article.asp?id=1301727&spid=6525. Internet.

407 Zywicki, Todd. "Chrysler and the Rule of Law: The Founders put the contracts clause in the Constitution for a reason." The Wall Street Journal. http://online.wsj.com/article/SB124217356836613091.html. Internet.

408 "Mismanaging the collapse of Detroit's giants," The Economist. May 7, 2009. http://www.economist.com/opinion/displaystory.cfm?story_id=13610871

Pulitzer Prize winning commentator George Will detailed the administration's actions with this stinging rebuke:

> The Obama administration's agenda of maximizing dependency involves political favoritism cloaked in the raiment of 'economic planning' and 'social justice' ... The administration's central activity – the political allocation of wealth and opportunity – is not merely susceptible to corruption, it is corruption.[409]

Aside from the constitutional concerns, the administration's heavy hand was dangerous for an economy on the ropes. Manufacturing needs an infusion of new capital from private investors. Lenders rely on the well-established rules that govern judicial bankruptcy proceedings to protect their investments. The administration's actions place all of that into doubt.

Union Sees a Quick Return on Obama Investment

In May 2009, the Obama administration threatened to rescind California's $6.8 billion stimulus package if Governor Arnold Schwarzenegger and state lawmakers did not restore planned wage cuts to unionized home health care workers. Obama health officials charged that the wage reduction, scheduled to save financially challenged California $74 million, violated provisions of the American Recovery and Reinvestment Act, the $787 billion stimulus bill passed in 2009.[1] The administration issued the threat in response to a request from the SEIU, whose political action committee donated more than $27 million to support Obama's presidential bid in 2008.[2]

1   Halper, Evan. "U.S. threatens to rescind stimulus money over wage cuts," Los Angeles Times. http://articles.latimes.com/2009/may/08/local/me-health-cuts8. Internet.
2   Lucas, Fred. "SEIU PAC Spent $27 Million Supporting Obama's Election, FEC Filing Says," CNSNews.com.   http://www.cnsnews.com/Public/Content/article.aspx?RsrcID=40959. Internet.

---

409 Will, George F. "Tincture of Lawlessness: Obama's Overreaching Economic Policies," Washington Post. http://www.washingtonpost.com/wp-dyn/content/article/2009/05/13/AR2009051303014.html. Internet.

7

The Chicago Way:
Intimidation and Pressure

*I am sick and tired of people who say that if you debate and you disagree
with this administration, somehow you're not patriotic, and we should stand
up and say, 'We are Americans and we have a right to debate and disagree
with any Administration.'*
Hillary Clinton, April 28, 2003[410]

Obama is a protégé of Chicago's political system, considered by many
to be the most corrupt in the nation. "The political capital of the world
is now Chicago, an agreeably invigorating prospect," wrote long-time
journalist Martin Nolan shortly after the 2008 elections. Lauding the
city's self-confidence, Nolan translated its infamous reputation for hard
ball politics into a positive:

> Toughness is part of it. Rahm Emanuel does not resemble Sean
> Connery, but something about him evokes the Mephistophelean
> power of Connery's Oscar-winning performance as Jimmy Malone,
> advising Kevin Costner's Eliot Ness in *The Untouchables*: "You
> want to know how to get Capone? They pull a knife, you pull a
> gun. He sends one of yours to the hospital, you send one of his
> to the morgue. That's the Chicago way! And that's how you get
> Capone. Now do you want to do that?" [411]

---

410 "I Am Sick And Tired - Hillary Clinton (video)," Beltway Blips. http://dailyradar.com/
     beltwayblips/video/i_am_sick_and_tired_hillary_clinton/. Internet.
411 Nolan, Martin. "Obama and the 'Chicago Way'," Huffington Post. http://www.
     huffingtonpost.com/martin-nolan/obama-and-the-chicago-way_b_149128.html.
     Internet.

Obama's campaign team was so successful in fashioning his hope, change and unity message that only political junkies seemed to notice signs of the Chicago way at work during the 2008 presidential campaign. When WGN radio in Chicago scheduled an August 2008 interview with conservative writer Stanley Kurtz to talk about his research into Obama's connection to unrepentant terrorist Ayers, the Obama campaign issued a call to action via an email to supporters:

> WGN radio is giving right-wing hatchet man Stanley Kurtz a forum to air his baseless, fear-mongering terrorist smears ... He's currently scheduled to spend a solid two-hour block from 9:00 to 11:00 p.m. pushing lies, distortions, and manipulations about Barack and University of Illinois professor William Ayers... Tell WGN that by providing Kurtz with airtime, they are legitimizing baseless attacks from a smear-merchant and lowering the standards of political discourse.[412]

Zack Christenson, executive producer of "Extension 720 with

The Chicago Way

Time magazine published an article after Obama was elected president entitled "How the Chicago way helped Obama." The article acknowledged that Chicago's political history was "cartoonishly coarse and corrupt," but dismissed the characterization as an "outdated caricature."[1] Regardless of *Time's* conclusion, the sordid details surrounding disgraced Illinois Governor Rod Blagojevich's failed attempt to sell Obama's vacated senate seat following the 2008 election showed that old habits die hard.

One might expect savvy politicians to distance themselves from the Chicago way. Not so for Senior Advisor to the President David Axelrod, who proudly owns the Chicago way of doing politics, declaring "Ours is a blunt, brawling way. People are upfront about their self-interest."[2] After Obama's first year in office, Americans understand that the brawling Chicago way involves deriding citizens who express their opinions at town hall meetings. The blunt Chicago way is to categorize peaceful protestors as right-wing, anti-government extremists. Certainly this is not the change most Americans were expecting.

1 Sullivan, Amy."How the Chicago Way Helped Obama," Time. November 13, 2008.
2 Walsh, Kenneth T. "Obama's Years in Chicago Politics Shaped His Presidential Candidacy," U.S. News & World Report. http://www.usnews.com/articles/news/campaign-2008/2008/04/11/obamas-years-in-chicago-politics-shaped-his-presidential-candidacy.html. Internet.

412 McCormick, John and Schmadeke, Steve. "Obama campaign confronts WGN radio," The Swamp. http://www.swamppolitics.com/news/politics/blog/2008/08/obama_campaign_confronts_wgn_r.html. Internet.

Milt Rosenburg," said the Obama campaign declined a request to appear on the show, yet Obama supporters heeded the campaign's call to send a message, and jammed phone and email lines with howls of protest. "I definitely think that directing the phone calls and the emails of supporters was an attempt, not to shut us down, but to intimidate us."[413]

When the nonprofit "American Issues Project" (AIP) ran an ad exposing Obama's ties to Ayers, the Obama campaign's response was equally swift. It quickly produced a response ad, an entirely legitimate endeavor. It warned station managers not to run the AIP ad, pressuring advertisers, and asking the Justice Department to intervene.[414]

In September 2008, St. Louis television station KMOV Channel 4 reported that St. Louis County Circuit Attorney Bob McCulloch and St. Louis Circuit Attorney Jennifer Joyce, along with Jefferson County Sheriff Glenn Boyer, had joined the "Barack Obama Truth Squad." Both the Obama and McCain campaigns had various groups in individual states tasked with responding to information it judged to be incorrect. What was troubling about Obama's "truth squad" was the intimidation factor the campaign achieved by highlighting the inclusion of prosecutorial officials on the team. KMOV reported "The Barack Obama campaign is asking Missouri law enforcement to target anyone who lies or runs a misleading TV ad during the presidential campaign... They will be reminding voters that Barack Obama is a Christian who wants to cut taxes ... They also say they plan to respond immediately to any ads and statements that violate Missouri's ethics laws."[415]

The campaign's hardball tactics, while not illegal, offered a window into how an Obama administration would deal with adversaries. Before Obama's first year in office was complete, anyone paying attention understood who qualified as an adversary: any politician, citizen, business, or media outlet that could be demonized for the purpose of advancing the administration's agenda.

In October 2009, *Time* magazine reported on a "new White House strategy" of "issuing biting attacks on those pundits, politicians and outlets

413 Winn, Pete. "Obama Supporters Target Radio Show for Examining Ties Between Obama and Bill Ayers," CNSNews.com. http://www.cnsnews.com/news/article/34897. Internet.

414 Kuhnhenn, Jim. "Obama seeks to silence ad tying him to 60s radical," Breitbart.com. http://www.breitbart.com/article.php?id=D92PL7400&show_article=1. Internet.

415 Loesch, Dana. "Was Buffy Wicks Also Behind Missouri's Obama Truth Squad?" BigGovernment.com. http://biggovernment.com/2009/10/07/was-buffy-wicks-also-behind-missouris-obama-truth-squad/. Internet.

that make what the White House believes to be misleading or simply false claims."[416]

The Vintage Books edition back cover to Alinsky's *Rules for Radicals* quotes the *Chicago Sun Times:* "Alinsky's techniques and teachings influenced generations of community and labor organizers, including the church-based group hiring a young [Barack] Obama to work on Chicago's South Side in the 1980s …".[417] In a chapter devoted to the rules regarding the ethics of ends and means, Alinsky suggested that the perennial question, "Does the end justify the means?" becomes meaningful only when restated in all its vain ingloriousness: "Does this particular end justify this particular means?"

> ## Pragmatism: Using Any Means Necessary
>
> Pragmatism is a guiding principle for Obama, as it was for Saul Alinsky. A political organizer, according to Alinsky, "does not have a fixed truth. Truth to him is relative and changing … He is a political relativist." The organizer starts by recognizing the world as it is. He never forgets the desired end, and uses whatever tactics work.
>
> Alinsky denied the universality of any principles of truth, but made a notable exception for his own rules, which he said operated in every circumstance or time. For his disciples, this self-deception attached a sense of authority to his rules, while giving followers permission to ignore ethical considerations in the application of the rules to the extent deemed necessary for the advancement of the desired ends.

Two of Alinsky's ends/means rules suffice to demonstrate the moral vacuity of his philosophy:[418]

- Generally, success or failure is a mighty determinant of ethics. The less important the end to be desired, the more one can afford to engage in ethical evaluations of means.
- You do what you can with what you have and clothe it with moral garments.

Alinsky believed that an effective community organizer must appeal to people's base instincts in order to attack the apathy of people who have come to accept poor or unjust living conditions. To that end, he fanned hostilities, fostered resentments, agitated, and built a groundswell of anger against the established order. Alinsky espoused the effectiveness

---

416 Scherer, Michael. "Calling 'Em Out: The White House Takes on the Press," Time. http://www.time.com/time/politics/article/0,8599,1929058,00.html. Internet.
417 Rules for Radicals, a Pragmatic Primer for Realistic Radicals, Saul D. Alinsky, Copyright 1971, Vintage Books Edition, October 1989. Originally published New York: Random House
418 Alinsky, Saul. Rules for Radicals. London: Vintage Books (1989)

of agitating, and Obama is an expert agitator. The typical Alinsky method of operation is to demonize the opposition, injecting the specter of racism, greed, religious bigotry, dishonesty, or class warfare to achieve the desired end. It's a relentless, high-pressure strategy that is a go-to tactic for Obama.

The administration's unprecedented, coordinated verbal barrage against the Fox News Channel in October 2009 offered a vivid case in point. As the only conservative television news network, Fox News Channel frequently reports news the left-leaning channels avoid (i.e. Van Jones, the NPR-Obama team propaganda art campaign, Bill Ayers, ACORN scandals, the APOLLO group, the Chicago Climate Exchange scandal, etc.). Instead of taking issue with the veracity of a specific news account by Fox, the Obama team orchestrated a campaign to have other major media and the public reject Fox altogether as a news organization.

In September 2009, the White House excluded *Fox News Sunday with Chris Wallace* from a round of presidential interviews Obama gave on Sunday morning news programs. Deputy White House Communications Director Dan Pfeiffer explained, "We simply decided to stop abiding by the fiction, which is aided and abetted by the mainstream press, that Fox is a traditional news organization."[419] Anita Dunn, White House Communications Director at the time, lobbed the next salvo when she charged that Fox News was "opinion journalism masquerading as news." Asked about the comment by CNN News anchor Howard Kurtz, Dunn replied:

> The reality of it is that Fox News often operates almost as either the research arm or the communications arm of the Republican Party ... it really is not a news network at this point. ... they're widely viewed as, you know, part of the Republican Party. Take their talking points and put them on the air. Take their opposition research and put them on the air, and that's fine. But let's not pretend they're a news network the way CNN is.[420]

---

419 Rutenberg, Jim. "Behind the War Between White House and Fox," New York Times. http://www.nytimes.com/2009/10/23/us/politics/23fox.html?_r=2. Internet. N.B. President Nixon compiled a political enemies list, which included the Washington Post and New York Times, various journalists, politicians, congressmen and groups, but his administration did not use its power in an attempt to have a news organization delegitimized.

420 "Interview With White House Communications Director; Obama Wins Nobel Peace Prize," CNN RELIABLE SOURCES. http://archives.cnn.com/TRANSCRIPTS/0910/11/rs.01.html. Internet.

When asked about Dunn's comments at a White House press briefing, Gibbs said flatly, "I have watched many stories on that network that I have found not to be true."[421] Emmanuel echoed Dunn on CNN, arguing that Fox News "is not a news organization so much as it has a perspective."[422] Axelrod appeared on ABC to defend Dunn, disparage Fox News, and recruit other major media to join its anti-Fox campaign:

> The only argument Anita was making is that they're not really a news station if you watch even –it's not just their commentators – but a lot of their news programming. It's not really news; it's pushing a point of view. And the bigger thing is that other news organizations like yours ought not to treat them that way.[423]

Axelrod obviously hoped the other networks would follow the administration's cue and refuse to cover news stories originating from Fox. Obama joined in the fusillade, suggesting that Fox was not a real news channel. "I think what our advisors have simply said is that we are going to take media as it comes," Obama told NBC's Savannah Guthrie. "And if media is operating as a talk radio format then that's one thing and if it's operating as a news outlet that's another. But it's not something I'm losing sleep over."[424]

After investing a month in the "Fox-News-is-not-a-news-outlet" storyline, the administration upped the ante when the Treasury Department attempted to exclude Fox from a round of press pool interviews with the executive-pay czar Kenneth R. Feinberg.[425] The White House press pool is a well-coordinated system in which the five news networks that comprise the pool save money and time by sharing a camera and crew when recording their interviews for airing on their respective networks. Contrary to the long-standing arrangement between presidential administrations and the press pool, a Treasury representative told pool members that for the Feinberg interview, Fox would be excluded and replaced by Bloomberg.

421 Christopher, Tommy. "White House Press Secretary: Many Fox News Stories Not True," Mediaite. http://www.mediaite.com/online/robert-gibbs-many-fox-news-stories-not-true/. Internet.
422 Allen, Mike. "Fox 'not really news,' says Axelrod," Politico.com. http://www.politico.com/news/stories/1009/28417.html. Internet.
423 Ibid.
424 "Obama: Not losing sleep over Fox," MSNBC.com. http://www.msnbc.msn.com/id/3036789/vp/33429121#33427990. Internet.
425 Rutenberg, Jim. "Behind the War Between White House and Fox," New York Times. http://www.nytimes.com/2009/10/23/us/politics/23fox.html?_r=1. Internet.

The administration gambled that the other networks would go along with the snub, but the pool members stood as one, refusing to participate in the interviews unless Fox News was included. "All the networks said, that's it, you've crossed the line," said CBS News' Chip Reid. Another network bureau chief gave the rationale, "It's all for one and one for all." The White House subsequently acknowledged that a mistake was made, but denied it intentionally attempted to exclude Fox.[426]

Fox News Channel's singular success, and the other networks' continued disinterest in seriously investigating the administration's conduct, convinced the Obama team that Fox's rivals would gladly help isolate and discredit the only news network the administration did not have under its thumb. The administration's unsuccessful smear campaign against Fox News only underscored the network's effectiveness in getting under the skin of the White House.

In April 2009, Obama used the Chicago way against private citizens, publicly bullying tea party participants for their civic involvement:

> When you see, you know, those of you who are watching certain news channels on which I'm not very popular, and you see folks waving tea bags around, let me just remind them that I am happy to have a serious conversation about how we are going to cut our health care costs down over the long term, how we're going to stabilize Social Security.[427]

Obama's public derision of tea party participants was mild compared to his less publicized remarks. In an interview with Jonathan Alter, Obama employed a vulgar term with sexual connotations, charging that Republican opposition to the economic stimulus bill "helped create the tea-baggers."[428] During the health care battle, Obama reportedly told Democrat lawmakers, "Does anybody think that the teabag, anti-government people are going to

426 Shea, Danny. "Fox News Exec on Attempted Feinberg Interview Sunb: We Requested Feinberg Interview, Gibbs Acknowledged Mistake," Huffington Post. http://www.huffingtonpost.com/2009/10/24/fox-news-exec-on-attempte_n_332707.html. Internet.

427 "Obama Describes Seeing 'Folks Waving Tea Bags Around' on Channels Where 'I'm Not Very Popular,'" TVNewser. http://www.mediabistro.com/tvnewser/politics/obama_describes_seeing_folks_waving_tea_bags_around_on_channels_where_im_not_very_popular_115293.asp#. Internet.

428 "Turning 'teabagger' into a slur," by David Weigel, May 4, 1010 http://voices.washingtonpost.com/right-now/2010/05/turning_teabagger_into_a_slur.html

support them if they bring down health care? All it will do is confuse and dispirit" supporters "and it will encourage the extremists."[429]

Obama is not the only elected official in D.C. to heap scorn on citizens. When Americans began flocking to congressional town-hall-style meetings in the summer of 2009 to express frustration with Congress' health care overhaul plans, massive deficit spending, and other issues, congressional leaders issued hyperventilated denunciations of the protests.

House Speaker Nancy Pelosi (D-CA), when asked if the town hall protests represented legitimate grassroots opposition, responded, "I think they are Astroturf. You be the judge. They're carrying swastikas and symbols like that to a town meeting on health care.[430] House Majority Leader Steny Hoyer (D-MD) similarly discounted grassroots activists in an op-ed he wrote with Pelosi for *USA Today* that blasted citizens attending town halls:

> An ugly campaign is underway not merely to misrepresent the health insurance reform legislation, but to disrupt … civil dialogue. These disruptions are occurring because opponents are afraid – not just of different views – but of the facts themselves. Drowning out opposing views is simply un-American.[431]

Senate Majority Leader Harry Reid (D-NV), opted for more personal attacks, saying "evilmongers" were disrupting town halls with "lies, innuendo, and rumor."[432]

429 "Lawmakers Detail Obama's Pitch," November 7, 2009 http://prescriptions.blogs. nytimes.com/2009/11/07/lawmakers-detail-obamas-pitch/

430 "Fear or Loathing: Democrats Raise Specter of Swastikas to Cancel Town Halls," FoxNews.com. http://www.foxnews.com/politics/2009/08/06/fear-loathing-democrats-raise-specter-swastikas-cancel-town-halls/. Internet.

431 Pelosi, Nancy and Hoyer, Steny. "'Un-American' attacks can't derail health care debate," USA Today. http://blogs.usatoday.com/oped/2009/08/unamerican-attacks-cant-derail-health-care-debate-.html. Internet.

432 "Nineteen Minutes in a Car with Harry Reid," PoliticsDaily.com. http://www.politicsdaily. com/2009/08/13/nineteen-minutes-in-a-car-with-harry-reid/. Internet.

Activism v. Terrorism

An "unclassified," "law enforcement sensitive" report issued on February 20, 2009 by the Missouri Information Analysis Center (MIAC) established a profile of potential domestic terrorists entitled, "The Modern Militia Movement."[1] According to the MIAC document, "common militia symbols" include political paraphernalia such as "Libertarian material", and "Anti-Government Propaganda" such as "bumper stickers that contain anti-government rhetoric." The report even singled out supporters of third party presidential candidates, stating that militia members "are usually supporters of former Presidential Candidate (sic): Ron Paul, Chuck Baldwin, and Bob Barr." It specifically warned law enforcement personnel, that in the view of the extremists, "You are the Enemy." After the report became public and generated widespread public outcry, it was retracted.[2]

---

1   "MIAC Strategic Report: The Modern Militia Movement," Missouri Information Analysis Center. http://www.constitution.org/abus/le/miac-strategic-report.pdf. Internet.

2   Ibid.

Humana, the nation's fourth-largest health insurer and second-largest provider of Medicare benefits, learned that congressional leaders will use the Chicago way to silence opposition. On September 16, 2009, Doug Elmendorf, head of the CBO, sent a letter to Senator Max Baucus scoring Baucus' Senate Finance Committee-approved plan for health care reform, "America's Health Future Act." In the letter CBO estimated that over the 2010-2019 year period the plan would yield "savings of an estimated $123 billion" by basing Medicare Advantage program payment rates on the average of the bids submitted by plans in each market.[433]

Humana's chief medical officer, Philip Painter, M.D., subsequently sent a one-page letter, on Humana letterhead, to customers who were enrolled in its Medicare Advantage program. The letter asserted that, because of spending cuts in the health care legislation, "millions of seniors and disabled individuals could lose many of the important benefits and services that make Medicare Advantage health plans so valuable." Humana included a standard disclaimer stating that neither CMS nor the Medicare program had reviewed the information provided for accuracy or misrepresentation, and urged customers to contact their representatives.[434]

The Center for Medicare & Medicaid Services' (CMS) Teresa DeCaro fired off a cease and desist letter to Humana on September 18, 2009. The

---

433   MacDonald, Elizabeth. "Behind the Scenes in the Humana-Baucus Fight," FoxBusiness. com. http://emac.blogs.foxbusiness.com/2009/09/24/behind-the-scenes-in-the-humana-baucus-fight/. Internet.

434   "Humana letter regarding potential changes in benefits." http://big.assets.huffingtonpost. com/humanamailer.pdf.

letter alleged that Humana's Medicare recipient letter was "misleading and confusing to beneficiaries," that it "represents information to beneficiaries as official communications about the Medicare advantage program" and that it "is potentially contrary to federal regulations and guidance." CMS instructed Humana to immediately end all such mailings and to remove all related materials from its website. The letter concluded: "Please be advised that we take this matter very seriously and, based upon the findings of our investigation, will pursue compliance and enforcement actions." On September 21, CMS also issued a cease and desist memo to all Medicare Advantage Plan providers that essentially mirrored the letter to Humana. The memo included the threat of compliance/enforcement actions.[435]

Senator Baucus, Chair of the Senate Finance Committee, followed with a press release headlined, "AT BAUCUS' URGING, CMS CRACKS DOWN ON INSURANCE COMPANY SCARE TACTICS." In the release, Baucus stated that his health care reform bill strengthened Medicare and did not cut benefits covered under the Medicare program. He alleged that Humana's letter was misleading and "wholly unacceptable."[436]

Republican Senate Minority leader Mitch McConnell called the CMS action an outrageous federal gag order instructing companies that communicate with clients on the health care issue to, "shut up – or else." House Republican leader John Boehner alleged that the Obama administration requested the gag order.[437] As a health insurer, Humana is subject to a litany of federal regulations and guidelines that detail its obligations under federal law. CMS has authority to ensure that Humana meets its legal requirements in its communications with customers, which include clearly distinguishing between official Medicare program information and advocacy communication. Media Matters, a liberal media watchdog, alleged that the letter was included in an envelope with "important information about your Medicare Advantage plan – open today!" printed on it.[438]

435 Wolfe, Byron. "Shut Up! The Government Says" - McConnell on Humana Letter," ABCNews.com. http://blogs.abcnews.com/thenote/2009/09/shut-up-the-government-says-mcconnell-on-humana-letter.html. Internet.
436 MacDonald, Elizabeth. "Behind the Scenes in the Humana-Baucus Fight," FoxBusiness.com. http://emac.blogs.foxbusiness.com/2009/09/24/behind-the-scenes-in-the-humana-baucus-fight/. Internet.
437 Wolfe, Byron. "Shut Up! The Government Says" - McConnell on Humana Letter," ABCNews.com. http://blogs.abcnews.com/thenote/2009/09/shut-up-the-government-says-mcconnell-on-humana-letter.html. Internet.
438 "Beck, Fox News lead conservative media in uniformly decrying 'McCarthy' – like violation of Humana's 'free speech' rights," MediaMatters.com. http://mediamatters.org/mobile/research/200909230028. Internet.

A combination of factors evinces a political motive behind the CMS cease and desist letter. Most telling is that the issuance of the letter came at the request of Senator Baucus, chief proponent of the legislation. Also, CMS claimed the Humana letter was "potentially contrary to federal regulations and guidance for the MA and Part D programs and other federal law, including HIPAA," yet it did not cite any specific legislative or regulatory language.[439] In fact, CMS noted it would "continue our research into this issue."[440] Finally, CMS issued a system-wide gag order without providing any evidence of a system-wide problem.

In short, CMS overreached with its aggressive and intimidating response that leapfrogged over more a number of more restrained alternatives. CMS could have continued its research before taking any action, or instructed insurers on how best to assert its constitutional free speech rights without offending federal laws or regulations. It could have limited its response to only Humana. It could have omitted the threatening language. But it did none of these – it simply said, in effect, "shut up."

Humana was only stating the facts in alerting customers to the potential loss in benefits and coverage that could attend the $123 billion in "savings" outlined by the CBO; in fact, the day after CMS issued its cease and desist memo, the CBO sent a letter to Senator Baucus that described how under "America's Healthy Future Act," families would pay more money for less coverage than they would under current law. [441]

The $871 billion health care reform bill that eventually became law contained roughly $500 billion in Medicare cuts over a ten year period.[442]

The Obama administration does not hesitate to use the Alinskyite tactic of pressure and intimidation against any group, business or entity that stands in the way of its agenda.

In his 2010 State of the Union speech, Obama assailed the Supreme Court, sitting together in the front rows: "With all due deference to separation of powers, last week the Supreme Court reversed a century of law that, I believe, will open the floodgates for special interests, including

---

439 Ibid.
440 Silva, Chris. "CMS probes Humana's lobbying tactics on reform," AMedNews.com. http://www.ama-assn.org/amednews/2009/10/05/gvsa1005.htm. Internet.
441 "CBO Letter to Max Baucus: October 7, 2009." http://www.cbo.gov/ftpdocs/106xx/doc10642/10-7-Baucus_letter.pdf
442 Silverlieb, Alan. "Senate approves health care reform bill," CNN.com. http://www.cnn.com/2009/POLITICS/12/24/health.care/index.html. Internet.

foreign corporations, to spend without limit in our elections." Obama urged Congress to help "correct some of these problems."[443]

Obama's swipe at the Court mischaracterized its ruling in *Citizens United v. Federal Election Commission*, decided a few weeks before his speech. *Citizens United* upheld the plain language of the First Amendment that "Congress shall make no law … abridging the freedom of speech." Federal statute 2 U.S.C. Section 441b, which the Court held violated the First Amendment, constituted an outright ban on corporate speech, with criminal sanctions. The Court has long recognized that free speech rights extend to corporations, and its application of a strict scrutiny standard was consistent with case precedent involving political speech (notwithstanding *Austin*, which the Court held to be an aberration).[444]

Even ABC News took exception to Obama's claim that the *Citizens United* ruling would "open the floodgates" to special interests and interference from foreign corporations in American elections. ABC quoted current federal law that forbids foreign corporations from interfering in U.S. elections.[445]

The Obama administration's response to what the president called the worst environmental disaster in U.S. history continued a pattern of demagoguery wedded to political exploitation of a crisis. On April 20, 2010 an explosion aboard the offshore oil rig Deepwater Horizon killed eleven workers and caused a massive deep sea oil gusher of a well owned by BP. During the second week of June, U.S. government scientists estimated that the ruptured well was continuing to spew up to 40,000 barrels of oil per day into the Gulf of Mexico. By day 53 an estimated two million barrels of oil had poured into the ocean, eight times the amount spilled in the 1989 Exxon Valdez disaster.[446]

As days turned to weeks turned to months, public concern mounted along with demands to know how and when the leak would be plugged. Concerned citizens sought assurance that both BP and the government were doing everything possible to cap the hole, mitigate the damage, and clean up the spill.

---

443 "Fact Check: President Obam's State of the Union 2010," by Huma Khan, January 27, 2010 http://www.abcnews.go.com/print?id=9680549
444 http://www.scotusblog.com/wp-content/uploads/2010/01/citizens-opinion.pdf
445 "Fact Check: President Obam's State of the Union 2010," by Huma Khan, January 27, 2010 http://www.abcnews.go.com/print?id=9680549
446 "Factbox: The Gulf BP spill: How much Oil is it anyway?" by Chris Baltimore and Elieen O'Grady, June 11, 2010 http://www.reuters.com/article/idUSTRE65A5IA20100611

In response, Interior Secretary Ken Salazar said administration officials would keep their "boot on the throat" of BP. During a press briefing, White House Press Secretary Robert Gibbs used the same violent imagery.[447] Obama reacted to charges that the administration was bogged down in academic musings instead of stopping the uncontrolled gusher and holding BP responsible by explaining, "I don't sit around just talking to experts because this is a college seminar. We talk to these folks because they potentially have the best answers, so I know whose ass to kick."[448]

The unprecedented environmental catastrophe merited Obama's first Oval Office speech, on June 15, 2010, nearly seventeen months into his presidency. Obama devoted a total of three sentences, or two percent of his speech, to explaining what tangible actions the government was taking to stop the leak.[449]

As Obama spoke, oil continued to flow into the Gulf, even as the U.S. rejected offers of help from around the world. Finally, on day 70 after the spill, the State Department announced that the U.S. was working out the details for accepting help from 12 countries and international organizations, of the more than 30 international offers of assistance it had received.[450]

Obama spent 32 percent of his speech on the need for alternatives to oil and for cap-and-trade legislation, which, according to Obama in 2008, would cause electricity rates to "necessarily skyrocket."[451] On June 25, 2010 Politico reported, "His [Obama's] hoped-for third act – a wide-ranging climate change and energy bill – is next on Obama's docket .... Obama plans to press his advantage – to try and salvage one more legislative win out of the depths of the BP oil spill tragedy."[452]

447 "BP Will Feel Either 'Boot on the Throat' Or 'Feet to Fire'," by Frank James, May 3, 2010 http://www.npr.org/blogs/thetwo-way/2010/05/bp_will_feel_either_boot_on_th.html
448 "Obama looking for 'whose ass to kick," June 8, 2010 http://www.cnn.com/2010/POLITICS/06/07/gulf.oil.obama/index.html
449 "Transcript of Obama's First Oval Office Speech," June 15, 2010 http://www.foxnews.com/politics/2010/06/15/transcript-obamas-oval-office-speech/
450 "US accepts international assistance for Gulf spill," Associated Press, June 29, 2010 http://finance.yahoo.com/news/US-accepts-international-apf-4104246595.html?x=0&.v=2
451 "Pence claims that Obama said energy costs will skyrocket with a cap-and-trade plan." Politifact.com. http://www.politifact.com/truth-o-meter/statements/2009/jun/11/mike-pence-claims-Obama-said-energy-costs-will-skyrocke/. Internet.
452 "Obama: 'On the brink' of Wall St. bill," by Carrie Budoff Brown and Meridith Shiner, June 24, updated June 25 http://www.politico.com/news/stories/0610/38976.html

8

Crisis and Emergency:
Act Now or Die

"The sky is falling! The sky is falling!"
-Chicken Little

Never Waste a Crisis

In the midst of the multitude of crises the U.S. economy endured in 2008 and 2009, some seized opportunity. Multi-billionaire and behind-the-scenes political puppeteer George Soros said, "I'm having a very good crisis."

Chief of Staff Rahm Emmanuel, apparently giddy more than guarded in the wake of his man's November triumph, remarked, "You never want a serious crisis to go to waste. ... It's an opportunity to do things you think you could not do before." Secretary of State Hillary Clinton, echoed Emmanuel: "Never waste a good crisis," she said, seeing the supposed global warming crisis as an opportunity to develop greener energies. Just a few days later, in his Saturday radio address, Obama urged Americans to "discover great opportunity in the midst of great crisis."

Like radical environmentalists, the administration knows the public will never adopt its agenda unless it fears looming disaster. So the crisis represents opportunity. To maximize the opportunity the administration must maximize the crisis. Exploit fear and uncertainty? Yes they can![1]

---

1   "Editorial: Obamanomics," Washington Times. http://www.washingtontimes.com/news/2009/mar/16/obamanomics/. Internet.

Pressing issues call for timely legislative action. The appropriate legislative process in a democratic republic includes adequate time for debate and amendment of any proposed bill; otherwise, demagogues gain the upper hand and exploit a crisis. A strong, democratic leader cultivates a climate of calm, courageous resolve in the midst of crisis. In the Obama administration, cultivating a climate of crisis is a political strategy. Though previous administrations have been guilty of capitalizing on crises for political purposes, the Obama administration appears to be the first to publicly extol the practice.

> Crisis is routinely identified as a core mechanism of fascism because it short-circuits debate and democratic deliberation. Hence all fascistic movements commit considerable energy to prolonging a heightened sense of emergency. Across the West, this was the most glorious boon of World War I.[453]

A Promise Kept – for Nine Days

Acknowledging the public's concern for open, deliberative government, Obama pledged on the campaign trail that he would give the American public five days to review and comment on any non-emergency bills before he signed them into law. He called it "sunlight before signing."[1]

Obama broke that promise on his ninth day in office when he signed the Lily Ledbetter Fair Pay Act of 2009, named for an Alabama woman who filed a charge of equal-pay discrimination suit with the Equal Employment Opportunity Commission (EEOC) after taking early retirement from her job at Goodyear Tire and Rubber Company. Ledbetter won a $3 million dollar jury verdict, reduced to $300,000 in accordance with Title VII's damages cap, but nine years later the Supreme Court overturned the verdict. The Court held that Ledbetter's claims were time barred because the discriminatory pay decision had been made more than 180 days (the statute of limitations under Title VII) prior to the date charges were filed with the EEOC. The Ledbetter Act adds a provision to Title VII that effectively restarts the statute of limitations clock each time an individual receives wages or other compensation resulting in whole or in part from a discriminatory pay decision.[2]

Regardless of the legislation's merits, passage of the legislation clearly did not constitute an emergency. The Lily Ledbetter Fair Pay Act of 2009 was introduced in the Senate on January 8, 2009. The Senate approved the bill on January 22, 2009, followed by House approval on January 27. Two days later, Obama signed the bill into law.[3]

Since the Ledbetter Act, Obama has repeatedly signed non-emergency legislation prior to the expiration of the promised five-day window. On February 4, 2009, Obama signed a bill expanding the State Children's Health Insurance Program just hours after the bill passed through Congress. Since the bill did not become effective until April 2009, the legislation could hardly be termed an

1 "Allow five days of public comment before signing bills," Politifact.com. http://politifact.com/truth-o-meter/promises/promise/234/allow-five-days-of-public-comment-before-signing-b/. Internet.
2 "S.181 - Lilly Ledbetter Fair Pay Act of 2009," OpenCongress.org. http://www.opencongress.org/bill/111-s181/show. Internet.
3 Grossman, Joanna L. "The Lily Ledbetter Fair Pay Act of 2009," Findlaw.com. http://writ.news.findlaw.com/grossman/20090213.html. Internet.

453 Goldberg, Jonah. Liberal Fascism. New York: Doubleday, 2007.

emergency. In May 2009, the president signed a credit card disclosure reform bill just two days after the bill was finalized in Congress.[4]

The president's end-run around this promise is simple: everything is an emergency.

4   "Allow five days of public comment before signing bills," Politifact.com. http://politifact.com/truth-o-meter/promises/promise/234/allow-five-days-of-public-comment-before-signing-b/. Internet.

The crisis tactic is essential to radicals who want to destroy the deliberative process the founders built into the system of checks and balances. American governance is utterly dependent upon a free flow of information, adequate time for reflection and a full opportunity for vigorous debate.

Some crises are real, but many are manufactured by politicians eager to short-circuit the legislative process or to maneuver past constitutional safeguards. The cry goes out to the public that quick action is imperative, and that the one unacceptable option is to do nothing. But the wrong action in the midst of a crisis will often make a bad situation much worse. The law of unintended consequences never sleeps, and when government acts to "solve" a manufactured crisis it often plants the seeds for a real future crisis.

Nonetheless, Obama often uses the false argument that *any action* is better than inaction. He argues that special interests, through their longstanding malfeasance or inertia, have created a crisis that demands an immediate remedial response. Obama used this tactic ad nauseum in the health care debate. He used it to push through the massive 2009 stimulus bill. Regarding the automobile industry bailout, Obama said, "(W)e decided that while providing additional assistance was a risk, the far greater risk ... was to do nothing."[454]

Obama's push for financial reform fit the usual template:

Special interests have waged a relentless campaign ... the financial industry and its powerful lobby have opposed modest safeguards against the kinds of reckless risks and bad practices that led to this very crisis. .... But this is certain: one way or another, we will move

454 "Obama calls for passage of financial reform bill," April 24, 2010   http://politicalticker.blogs.cnn.com/2010/04/24/obama-calls-for-passage-of-financial-reform-bill/?fbid=GmyQE4H4nkx

forward. This issue is too important. The costs of inaction are too great. We will hold Wall Street accountable."[455]

Not surprisingly, the financial reform bill supported by Obama fails to reign in Fannie Mae and Freddie Mac. Through these mortgage behemoths, pursuant to the Community Reinvestment Act, millions of bad loans were made to home buyers who could not afford houses, helping to precipitate a mortgage crisis that led to the 2008 economic crisis. In fact, the two congressmen at the forefront of shaping the financial reform legislation, Senator Chris Dodd (D-Conn.) and Representative Barney Frank (D-Mass.) were key players over a period of years in helping lay the seeds for the Fannie and Freddie fiasco.

Scare Tactics: The Evolution of a Crisis

Obama pushed the $787 billion stimulus package through Congress at a neck-breaking speed by feeding on the fear of the unknown. In less than a month, U.S. economic troubles devolved from a bad situation into a catastrophe in the untempered universe of Obama's rhetoric:

- In short, a bad situation could become dramatically worse if Washington doesn't go far enough to address the spreading crisis… I don't believe it's too late to change course, but it will be if we don't take dramatic action as soon as possible.[456]
- The unemployment rate is now over 7 percent. Clearly, the situation is dire, it is deteriorating, and it demands urgent and dramatic action … For the sake of our economy and our people, this is the moment to act, and to act without delay.[457]
- We are experiencing an unprecedented economic crisis that has to be dealt with and dealt with rapidly.[458]

455 The White House "Weekly Address: President Obama Says We Must Move Forward on Wall Street Reform," April 17, 2010 http://www.whitehouse.gov/the-press-office/weekly-address-president-obama-says-we-must-move-forward-wall-street-reform

456 Loven, Jennifer."Obama warns of dire consequences without stimulus," Breitbart.com. http://www.breitbart.com/article.php?id=D95J4DV00. Internet.

457 Tozzi, Lisa. "Obama Calls Job Report 'Stark Reminder' of Need for Urgent Action," New York Times. http://thecaucus.blogs.nytimes.com/2009/01/09/obama-calls-jobs-report-stark-reminder-of-need-for-urgent-action/. Internet.

458 "Obama sees stimulus package by mid-February," MSNBC.com. http://www.msnbc.msn.com/id/28811470/. Internet.

- We've inherited an economic crisis as deep and dire as any since the Great Depression.[459]
- If we do not move swiftly to sign the American Recovery and Reinvestment Act [ARRA] into law, an economy that is already in crisis will be faced with catastrophe.[460]

The U.S. economy was in recession at the time of Obama's remarks, but the immediate crisis had abated several months before he made the foregoing comments. Perhaps the public is lucky that Obama signed the stimulus package before his speeches escalated our economic woes to the level of a global meltdown. Then again, the wildly expensive, pork-laden legislation moved the government one step closer to an approaching fiscal day of reckoning.

In a January 2009 white paper study, "The Job Impact of the American Recovery and Reinvestment Plan," the Obama administration projected that unemployment would peak at just over 8 percent without the stimulus, but would be contained under 8 percent with the stimulus.[461] Seven percent employment was "dire" and "deteriorating" in January 2009, according to Obama, but in June 2009 he said the prospect of 10 percent unemployment was just "a lagging indicator." "I think that what you've seen is that the pace of job loss has slowed ... we will end up seeing recovery shortly."[462]

In 2004, Obama sang a completely different tune in decrying George W. Bush's legislative strategy, complaining that Bush used urgency and intimidation to hurry bills through Congress without allowing time for members to read or debate the bills.

Obama: When you rush these budgets that are a foot high and nobody has any idea what's in them and nobody has read them.

Randi Rhodes: 14 pounds it was!

Obama: Yeah. And [when] it gets rushed through without any clear deliberation or debate, then these kinds of

---

459 Obama, Barack. "The Action Americans Need," Washington Post. http://www. washingtonpost.com/wp-dyn/content/article/2009/02/04/AR2009020403174.html. Internet.

460 Cover, Matt. "Unemployment Worse with Stimulus than Without," CNSNews.com. http://www.cnsnews.com/Public/Content/Article.aspx?rsrcid=50521. Internet.

461 "The Job Impact of the American Recovery and Reinvestment Plan." http://otrans.3cdn. net/45593e8ecbd339d074_l3m6bt1re.pdf. Internet.

462 Tapper, Jake. "President Obama Predicts Unemployment Will Hit 10% This Year," ABCNews.com. http://blogs.abcnews.com/politicalpunch/2009/06/president-obama-predicts-unemployment-will-hit-10-this-year.html. Internet.

things happen. And I think that this is in some ways
what happened to the Patriot Act... It was so quick
after 9/11 that it was introduced that people felt very
intimidated by the administration."[463]

Obama's criticism of Bush was on point, but it was no more than
political posturing. Instead of developing a plan to change the way bills
were rushed through Congress during the George W. Bush years, Obama
was studying how to perfect the process.

Few politicians can match the Obama administration when it comes to
cultivating an urgent sense of crisis. As president-elect in December 2009,
Obama was sounding the warning on climate change: "The time for delay
is over; the time for denial is over ... We all believe what the scientists have
been telling us for years now, that this is a matter of urgency and national
security."[464] In June 2009, in an attempt to influence Congress' climate
bill vote, the Obama administration released a climate change report that
a former chair of the American Meteorological Society described as "not a
work of science but an embarrassing episode for the authors."[465] Two months
before the global warming research scandal dubbed "Climategate" erupted,
Obama channeled Al Gore in his first address to the United Nations:

The danger posed by climate change cannot be denied. Our
responsibility to meet it must not be deferred. If we continue
down our current course, every member of this Assembly will
see irreversible changes within their borders. Our efforts to end
conflicts will be eclipsed by wars over refugees and resources.
Development will be devastated by drought and famine. Land that
human beings have lived on for millennia will disappear. Future
generations will look back and wonder why we refused to act.[466]

463 "Obama 2004: Bush Rushed Legislation Without Allowing Time to Read, Debate," Real
Clear Politics. http://www.realclearpolitics.com/video/2009/07/27/obama_2004_bush_
rushed_legislation_without_allowing_time_to_read_debate.html. Internet.

464 Borentstein, Seth."As warming crisis looms, Obama pushes change," Anchorage Daily
News. http://www.adn.com/2008/12/14/623339/as-warming-crisis-looms-obama.html.
Internet.

465 Morano, Marck. "'Scaremongering': Scientists Pan Obama Climate Report," Canada
Free Press. http://www.canadafreepress.com/index.php/article/12050. Internet.

466 "President Obama's Address to U.N. General Assembly: September 23, 2009," America.
gov. Avaialable from http://www.america.gov/st/texttrans-english/2009/September/2009
0923110705eaifas0.3711664.html. Internet.

Global warming, now politically positioned as "climate change," is a contentious issue boiling in a stew of transparent political agendas and controversial, pseudo-scientific theories. Gore's hypocritical hyperbolism alone should be enough to sound the scam alert.[467] There are intelligent, sincere voices on each side of the debate, but the science of climate change is still in its infancy. Meteorologists have difficulty predicting weather patterns five days in advance, yet Obama has no problem predicting a global, meteorological meltdown if America does not immediately respond to the impending danger. This is not leadership, but hysteria and fear-mongering.

To be fair, screaming "emergency" and fear-mongering are not tactics exclusive to the Left. Republicans have cried "emergency" to rush major initiatives to enactment, including the Patriot Act. The bill, which expanded the federal government's ability to gather intelligence, engage in domestic surveillance and secret searches, and detain suspected terrorists, was considered on the floor of the House of Representatives the same day it was introduced. Few, if any, members had an opportunity to read the bill before debating it. The House overwhelmingly passed the bill on October 24, 2001. The Senate passed the bill the following day and Bush signed it into law on October 26, 2001.[468] The justification, at least in this example, was that

---

467 Former vice-president Al Gore's 2006 film on global warming, "An Inconvenient Truth" catapulted him to hero status among climate change believers as the leading prophet of doom. In 2007, British High Court Justice Michael Burton, identifying nine factual inaccuracies in the film, characterized it as "alarmism and exaggeration." Gore has warned of an impending rise in sea levels of up to 20 feet, though the Intergovernmental Panel on Climate Change has projected a possible rise of just 7 to 23 inches by 2100. Among the other dire but dubious "facts" Gore has attributed to global warming: climate change is settled science, polar bears are drowning, populations are being forced to evacuate low-lying areas, and an alleged correlation between rising temperature and C02 levels is "an exact fit." Gore testified before Congress in support of cap and trade legislation, equating critics of global warming with those who believe the Apollo moon landing was staged. Glover, Daniel K. "The Nine Lies of Al Gore." http://www.noteviljustwrong.com/blog/general/218-the-nine-lies-of-al-gore. Internet. Though Gore denies profiting from his global warming work, he has enlarged his net worth from less than $2 million when he left government in 2001 to estimates in the hundreds of millions of dollars through his dual role as investor and climate change advocate. Broder, John M. "Gore's Dual Role: Advocate and Investor," New York Times. http://www.nytimes.com/2009/11/03/business/energy-environment/03gore.html. Internet. Gore has admitted to being a meat eater, while acknowledging the major contribution of meat production in the world's total greenhouse gas emissions. Whitlock, Scott. "Surprise: ABC's Sawyer Hits Gore on Profits From Global Warming, Plays Glenn Beck Attack," Newsbusters.org. http://newsbusters.org/blogs/scott-whitlock/2009/11/03/surprise-abc-s-sawyer-hits-gore-profits-global-warming-plays-glenn-b. Internet.

468 Blumenthal, Paul. "Congress Had No Time to Read the USA PATRIOT Act," Sunlight Foundation. http://blog.sunlightfoundation.com/2009/03/02/congress-had-no-time-to-read-the-usa-patriot-act/. Internet.

improving security after radical Islamic terrorists murdered 3000 Americans civilians *was* an emergency; even so, the process left much to be desired.

When politicians forego careful consideration of legislation in the name of emergencies, they disserve the citizenry. Citizens should worry when any party or politician warns that dire consequences will ensue if immediate action is not taken to avert disaster or resolve a crisis. Even in a crisis, the quickest way to exacerbate a situation is to take the wrong action.

Extenuating Circumstances

Politicians use many ploys when rushing radical, often unconstitutional, bills into law. Here are just a few of the most popular frenzy-inducing tactics as applied to the 2009 health care debate.

- <u>The issue has already been debated for years</u>
  In his September 9, 2009 address to the joint session of Congress, Obama noted: "I am not the first President to take up this cause, but I am determined to be the last. It has now been nearly a century since Theodore Roosevelt first called for health care reform … The time for games has passed. Now is the season for action."[1] Just because an issue has been around for years does not mean enough time has been given to debate a *specific bill*. The details of the proposed bill are what must be fully exposed and fully debated.

- <u>The opposition would have us do nothing</u>
  President Obama reverted to this siren song when speaking before the AFL-CIO in September 2009. Referring to those who criticize his approach to health care, he said, "Their answer is to do nothing."[2] His claim is categorically untrue, but the congressional majority and the administration clanged this bogus bell loudly enough to drown out the voice of anyone offering an alternative to their proposals. In the health insurance debate alone, Republicans drafted multiple bills with a host of alternatives to reform health care, including tort reform, portability of policies, interstate health policies, extending tax breaks currently reserved for businesses to individuals, improved health savings accounts, and health insurance comparison-shop services.

- <u>Opponents of the bill are greedy liars</u>
  In logical construction, attacking an opponent personally instead of the opponent's argument is a fallacy called *ad hominem abusive*. In politics, the same tactic is called standard operating procedure. Smearing the opposition was the current administration's real workhorse tactic in the health

---

1 "Remarks by the President to a join session of Congress on health care," WhiteHouse.gov. http://www.whitehouse.gov/the_press_office/remarks-by-the-president-to-a-joint-session-of-congress-on-health-care/. Internet

2 "The White House: Remarks by the President at AFL-CIO Labor Day Picnic," WhiteHouse. gov http://www.whitehouse.gov/the_press_office/Remarks-by-the-President-at-AFL-CIO-Labor-Day-Picnic/. Internet.

care debate. Everyone was fair game – members of Congress, insurance companies, doctors and citizens

- Dismiss the public's objections

This tactic involves responding to specific criticism with vague or illusory promises. For example, in claiming that the health care reform would be deficit-neutral, the Obama administration indicated that about two-thirds of the trillion dollar health care legislation would be financed by eliminating waste, fraud, and abuse in the health care system. Senator Baucus's reform bill projected that about half of the revenue needed to offset its cost would come from anti-fraud and waste efforts in Medicare and Medicaid. The inefficiency of the government's current involvement in health care would lead any rational individual to question the logic of turning the entire system over to a bungling bureaucracy. Administrations dating back to President Jimmy Carter's have attempted, without success, to streamline Medicare and Medicaid. Obama announced the creation of a task force to look for ways to achieve health care system savings, but no realistic plan for doing so has been offered.[3]

- When in doubt, exaggerate

Most politicians are too practiced in the art of deception to offer up obvious lies, so when a politician makes a demonstrably false statement, it is a sign of desperation. Consider Obama's assertion that a surgeon might choose to amputate a patient's foot because he makes between thirty and fifty thousand dollars for an amputation, but just a pittance for more appropriate, less drastic treatments.[4] One can only speculate where Obama obtained that figure, if not out of thin air. The American College of Surgeons gave this scathing response to Obama's assertion:

> Yesterday during a town hall meeting, President Obama got his facts completely wrong. He stated that a surgeon gets paid $50,000 for a leg amputation when, in fact, Medicare pays a surgeon between $740 and $1,140 for a leg amputation. This payment also includes the evaluation of the patient on the day of the operation plus patient follow-up care that is provided for 90 days after the operation.
>
> Three weeks ago, the President suggested that a surgeon's decision to remove a child's tonsils is based on the desire to make a lot of money. That remark was ill-informed and dangerous, and we were dismayed by this characterization of the work surgeons do. Surgeons make decisions about recommending operations based on what's right for the patient...

---

3   Brady, Demian. "Tacking Waste, Fraud, and Abuse in Medicare and Medicaid," Government Bytes. http://blog.ntu.org/main/post.php?post_id=4863. Internet.
4   "Obama: Doctors May Choose Amputation Because of Reimbursement," RealClearPolitics. com. http://www.realclearpolitics.com/video/2009/08/11/obama_doctors_may_choose_amputation_because_of_reimbursement.html. Internet.

9

The Permanent Campaign:
Propaganda and Indoctrination

"This is a new innovation from Obama and I think it's a great thing for the Democratic Party. ... Now we don't just have a permanent campaign for electing Democrats; we have a permanent campaign for influencing policy. It brings us a little closer to the European model."
– Howard Dean, former Chair of the Democratic National Committee[469]

Welcome to the age of the permanent campaign. Even Americans who avoid politics recognize the distinctive characteristics of a politician in campaign-mode: lots of vague promises, empty rhetoric, half-truths, flip-flopping, positioning, and a win-at-all-costs mentality. In a November 2009 Rasmussen poll, only four percent of voters say most politicians keep their campaign promises.[470]

According to the poll, 68 percent of Republicans and 52 percent of Independents think that when candidates break campaign promises, it is because they deliberately lied. By contrast, 74 percent of Democrats attribute broken promises to the occurrence of unforeseen events post-election.

Dean's permanent campaign mode is not exactly a new development; what *is* new is the brazen manner in which Dean extolled its virtues. The permanent campaign mentality infects not only both political parties but schools and colleges, scientific and arts communities, media establishments, community organizer coalitions, television and movie studios, corporate

---

469 http://www.breitbart.tv/howard-dean-declares-debate-between-capitalism-and-socialism-to-be-over/
470 "Just 4% Say Most Politicians Keep Their Campaign Promises," November 9, 2009 http://www.rasmussenreports.com/public_content/politics/general_politics/november_2009/just_4_say_most_politicians_keep_their_campaign_promises

boardrooms, and even military bases, the U.S. Justice Department ... and the current presidential administration.

Americans expect presidents to cease campaigning after the election and to begin governing; to do otherwise is to politicize every policy decision. Dean not only acknowledged this, he praised it: "Now we don't just have a permanent campaign for electing democrats; we have a permanent campaign for influencing policy."

President Obama's decision to implement a campaign mentality for accomplishing policy objectives is much more than symbolic. Its roots go deep into the structural specifics of *how* his administration seeks to bring about the fundamental change to America that he promised.

The signature temptation for campaigns is to "win at all costs" – to do whatever it takes to get elected. According to Saul Alinsky, a true leader must be willing to sacrifice his personal conscience for the good of the masses, to be "corrupted" for them.[471]

President Obama has often noted that politics is about the "art of the possible," with a practical focus on whatever works.[472] His views echo those of Alinsky, the father of political organizers and a strong influence on President Obama. In *Rules for Radicals*, Alinsky wrote:

> The man of action views the issue of means and ends in pragmatic and strategic terms. ... He asks of ends only whether they are achievable and worth the cost; of means, only whether they will work. To say that corrupt means corrupt the ends is to believe in the immaculate conception of ends and principles. The real arena is corrupt and bloody. Life is a corrupting process ... he who fears corruption fears life.[473]

According to Obama, everything is relative. He talks of universal values but rejects the concept of objective, universal truth; truth itself becomes but another means, a servant to the desired end. By Obama's measure, a means is true if it works. This is no garden variety, commonsense practicality, but an ideologically driven, progressive pragmatism, as dangerous as it is deceptive.

The effectiveness of a particular means can never be the only standard; morally wrong means are still wrong no matter how well they work. Brainwashing, propagandizing, lying, deceiving, extorting, bribing, indoctrinating, and demonizing are all tactics that may work to achieve

---

471 Alinsky, Saul. Rules for Radicals. London: Vintage Books (1989) p. 25
472 Obama, Barack. The Audacity of Hope. New York: Crown, 2006. p. 219
473 Alinsky, Saul. Rules for Radicals. London: Vintage Books (1989) pp 24-25.

an end. Wise citizens rightly reject them as unethical actions destructive to civil society.

The current administration and its allies are using many of these illicit means to advance a fundamental transformation of America, characterized by the continued centralization of government power and control, including an emphasis on allegiance to the state quickened by the purposeful weakening of traditional values such as faith, family, and morality. The path toward these ends was well-trodden long before President Obama came into power – he is just accelerating the pace.

The Permanent Campaign in Public Schools

Shortly after President Obama announced that he would make a speech to all public school students on September 8, 2009 – the first day back to school for many students – a firestorm of protest erupted. Opponents called Obama's plans socialist indoctrination, a violation of church and state, and an affront to parents. Some schools opted not to show the speech live, and many schools and districts made arrangements to accommodate students whose parents wanted their child not to listen to the speech.

In Valdosta, Georgia, hundreds of people showed up at the city's Board of Education meeting to demand the resignation of Valdosta City School Superintendent Dr. Bill Cason, who made the decision not to show the speech during school hours across the predominantly black school system. Floyd Rose, president of the Valdosta/Lowndes chapter of the Southern Leadership Conference, played the race card:

> If Dr. Cason were black and eighty percent of the school children in his district were white, and he arbitrarily decided not to allow white children to watch a white president's 'back to school' speech, and whites came here tonight in the numbers that blacks have come to protest, he would resign, or be fired. And we are here to demand no less.[474]

The controversy highlighted just how polarizing a figure the man supporters touted as "post-partisan" had become, less than eight months into his presidency. At first glance, the opposition to the speech seemed

---

474 Controversy leads to resignation request," by Johnna Pinholster, September 15, 2009. http://www.valdostadailytimes.com/homepage/local_story_258000146.html

overblown. White House spokesman Robert Gibbs called it "silly season."[475] According to the Department of Education website, President George H.W. Bush addressed students in 1991 on live television from an American history classroom at Deal Junior High in Washington, D.C.[476] The announced purpose of President Obama's speech, "to challenge students to work hard in school, to not drop out, and to meet short-term goals like behaving in class...," seemed innocuous. Why the fuss?[477]

The short answer is simply that many Americans do not trust the President, even with something as seemingly harmless as an address to encourage students. They don't trust his motivations and his intentions. They are aware of his call to create a civilian volunteer force just as strong and well-funded as the military. They are aware of his ties to unrepentant terrorist William Ayers and the radical political agenda embedded in his Chicago Annenberg Challenge program for Chicago schools.[478] They respect the office of the President, but reject the idea of Obama personally "assisting" in the education of their children, especially with them not present.

It didn't take long for parents' suspicions to be at least somewhat borne out. The original top-down lesson plans promulgated by the Department of Education (and written by the White House Teaching Fellows, which includes several activist educators) included just the type of politicization that critics had feared.[479]

The detailed plans offered questions and guided activities for before, during, and after the speech. For grades pre-k through sixth grade, the original lesson plans (later reworded amid the criticism) recommended that teachers have students "write letters to themselves about what they can do to help the President. These would be collected and redistributed

475 "Gibbs: Resistance to Obama school speech just plain 'silly'" by Matthew Shaer, September 4, 2009. http://features.csmonitor.com/politics/2009/09/04/gibbs-resistance-to-obama-school-speech-just-plain-silly/

476 "President Barack Obama Makes Historic Speech to America's Students," http://www.ed.gov/admins/lead/academic/bts.html

477 "President Barack Obama Makes Historic Speech to America's Students," http://www.ed.gov/admins/lead/academic/bts.html

478 "Obama and Ayers Pushed Radicalism on Schools," September 23, 2008, by Stanley Kurtz. http://online.wsj.com/article/SB122212856075765367.html

479 "Obama's classroom campaign: No junior lobbyist left behind," by Michelle Malkin, September 2, 2009. http://michellemalkin.com/2009/09/02/obama%E2%80%99s-classroom-campaign-no-junior-lobbyist-left-behind/

at an appropriate later date by the teacher to make students accountable to their goals."[480]

The plans included suggested questions for teachers to have the children think about during the speech, as they took notes, including, "What is the president asking me to do?" and "What specific job is he asking me to do?" Post-speech questions were of a similar vein. Teachers could extend learning by having students create posters in which they named three steps for achieving goals in each of the following areas: "personal, academic, community, and country."[481]

The lesson plans for students in grades 7-12 were less politicized, but included pre-speech questions such as "How will he inspire us?" and post-speech questions such as "Is President Obama inspiring you to do anything?"[482] Lost in the minutia about the specifics of the lesson plans was the impropriety of the White House or the Department of Education directing the specifics of classroom discussions and activities across the nation.

The speech itself was largely uncontroversial. President Obama's admonition that students take responsibility for their own education, work hard and persevere was on target. Duty to country was a central focus. The teaching of civic responsibility is commendable; the problem is one of context. The speech was delivered to a captive audience of children as young as four or five years old, in a setting where "duty to God" has been banished, and accompanied by politically calculated examples of what that service might entail. President Obama told students they would need math and science skills to "develop new energy technologies and to protect our environment," and that they would need skills gained in history and social studies to "fight poverty and homelessness, crime and discrimination, and make our nation more fair and more free."[483] Laudable goals all, except that most of these issues are politically charged agenda items of the Obama administration.

Adding to the rising discontent of conservatives during this same time period was the re-emergence just days before Obama's school speech of a public service video titled "I serve," made by a number of Hollywood celebrities, originally released in January 2009. The beginning and the end

480 "Critic Decry Obama's 'Indoctrination' Plan for Students," by Joshua Rhett Miller, September 2, 2009. http://www.foxnews.com/politics/2009/09/02/critics-decry-obamas-indoctrination-plan-students/?utm_source=feedburner&utm_medium=feed&utm_campaign=Feed%25253A+foxnews%25252Fpolitics+(FOXNews.com+-+Politics)
481 http://www.ed.gov/teachers/how/lessons/prek-6.pdf
482 http://www.ed.gov/teachers/how/lessons/7-12.pdf
483 http://www.whitehouse.gov/MediaResources/PreparedSchoolRemarks/

of the video featured a full screen image of Barack Obama. When shown to students at a public school in Utah, the video prompted an outcry from parents due to some of the leftist political content, including pledges to support stem cell research, to drive a hybrid vehicle, to drink less bottled water, to "flush only after a deuce," to be of service to Barack Obama, and to go to an administration website. The last pledge on the video: "I pledge to be a servant to our president…"[484]

The video is pure political propaganda. It has no place in public schools. It illustrates the totalitarian nature of progressive thinking. Children at a public school are fed propaganda so they can advise their family about what kind of water containers to drink from, what kind of cars to drive, and even about when to flush the toilet. From the progressive perspective, the government has a right to exercise control of citizens' bathroom activities for the common good and the federal pocketbook. Thankfully, a "pay-per-flush" toilet tax such has been proposed in Canada seems not to be on D.C.'s radar as of yet.[485]

Another controversial school video, "The story of stuff," is a twenty minute film harshly critical of U.S. consumerism, produced in 2007 by Free Range Studios and funded by the left-wing Tides Foundation. According to the *New York Times*, the web video has been viewed by millions on the Internet and has been seen by public school students across the country.[486]

The video has won praise for facilitating needed discussion and has been loudly condemned for its factual inaccuracies, negative depiction of corporations, and anti-capitalist stance. The wasteful effect of rampant consumerism is an issue that should be discussed in America, including in its schools. But the video is little more than leftist propaganda; such indoctrination has no place in schools, especially if shown to students younger than high school age.

Perhaps the most offensive videos were not those produced in a studio, but in schools from New York to Georgia, depicting mostly young American public schoolchildren singing President Obama's praises at the direction of their teacher. The first video leaked to the public showed second grade

---

484   http://www.youtube.com/watch?v=51kAw4OTlA0

485   "Householders to be charged for each flush of toilet," February 17, 2009, by Karen Hawthorne.
      http://network.nationalpost.com/np/blogs/posted/archive/2009/02/17/householders-to-be-charged-for-each-flush-of-toilet.aspx

486   "A Cautionary VideoAbout America's Stuff," by Leslie Kaufman, May 10, 2009. http://www.nytimes.com/2009/05/11/education/11stuff.html?pagewanted=1&_r=1

students at B. Bernice Elementary School in Burlington Township, New Jersey singing a rap song:

> Mmm, mmm, mmm! Barack Hussein Obama.
> He said red, yellow, black or white
> All are equal in his sight.
> Mmm, mmm, mmm! Barack Hussein Obama.[487]

Churchgoers would recognize the borrowed lines:

> Jesus loves the little children,
> All the children of the world,
> Red and yellow, black or white,
> All are precious in his sight ...

The lyrics to the second song sung by the young students were in the same adulatory vein. [488]

According to school officials, the video was made in February 2009 and was part of the school's celebration of Black History Month. In a released statement, District Superintendent Christopher Manno said, "There was no intention to indoctrinate children," and "there was no political agenda underlying the activity."[489]

Eleven similar videos were made public after being anonymously emailed to Big Hollywood, a website of breitbart.com.[490, 491] The point is not that the Obama administration had anything to do with the staging of these events; there is no evidence it did. But parents should be aware that while kindergarteners may not be free to pray at school, they may be pressured to praise the president in song.

487 "Mmm mmm mmm: New details about the Dear Leader song video," September 24, 2009, by Michelle Malkin. http://michellemalkin.com/2009/09/24/mmm-mmm-mmm-new-details-about-the-dear-leader-song-video/

488 "Mmm mmm mmm: New details about the Dear Leader song video," September 24, 2009, by Michelle Malkin. http://michellemalkin.com/2009/09/24/mmm-mmm-mmm-new-details-about-the-dear-leader-song-video/

489 GOP claims video shows public B. Bernice Elementary School students made to sing about Obama," http://www.politifact.com/truth-o-meter/statements/2009/sep/25/michael-steele/gop-claims-video-shows-b-bernice-young-elementary-/

490 "Feeling the Obama Love," by Bethany Stotts, November 6, 2009. http://www.academia.org/feeling-the-obama-love/print/

491 "ELEMENTARY EPIDEMIC: 11 Uncovered Videos Show Schoolchildren Singing Praises to Obama," November 4, 2009, by John Nolte http://bighollywood.breitbart.com/jjmnolte/2009/11/04/elementary-epidemic-11-uncovered-videos-show-school-children-performing-praises-to-obama/

Public School Indoctrination by Design

In the first pages of *On Being a Teacher,* written by today's most influential writer of K-12 public education in America after he visited Cuba in the 1970's, Jonathan Kozol writes, "We have not yet evolved a system of education that is not a system of indoctrination." Bernard Goldberg, in *100 People who are Screwing Up America*, writes, "Kozol is the patron saint of today's liberal educational establishment. ... He believes that education cannot and should not be politically neutral. Indeed, the once-outrageous idea that teachers should use their classrooms to espouse liberal/radical political views – i.e. to propagandize – can be traced directly to Jonathan Kozol."[1]

Today, in many public schools, traditional moral principles and perspectives are avoided as an unconstitutional establishment of religion while anti--Christian viewpoints are routinely labeled as secular and thus approved. Darwin is in, intelligent design is out; "Earth Day" is in, prayer is out; *Queer 13* is in, the Bible is out; political correctness is in, the Ten Commandments are out.

1 Goldberg, Bernard. 100 People who are screwing up America, Harper Collins. New York. 2005. p. 170

Conservatives have long lamented the secularization of public schools, but have often focused more on wedge issues - such as school prayer, on which even conservatives have varying views - than on the main issue of curriculum content, where the ideological battles rage.

A central figure in the battle today is Kevin Jennings, who was appointed to head the Office of Safe and Drug-free Schools by Obama Education Secretary Arne Duncan. Jennings is the founder of the Gay, Lesbian and Straight Education Network (GLSEN), the leading organization in the advancement of the homosexual agenda in schools. GLSEN uses the concept of "safe schools" as a political device to implement its homosexual education agenda. The irony of a homosexual activist administrating the government's safe schools program has not been lost on outraged critics, who have called for Jennings' removal. A group of 53 House Republicans wrote President Obama in October 2009, stating that Jennings was unfit for the position due to his homosexual advocacy.[492]

In his book *Always My Child,* Jennings urges an educational "diversity policy that mandates including LGBT [lesbian, gay, bisexual, transgender] themes in the curriculum." He wrote the forward for a book titled, *Queering Elementary Education.*[493] At a GLSEN conference held October 25, 1997 at

492 53 Republicans demand firing of 'safe schools' czar Kevin Jennings," October 15, 2009, by Michael O'brien. http://thehill.com/blogs/blog-briefing-room/news/63249-53-republicans-demand-firing-of-safe-schools-czar
493 Kevin Jennings – Unsafe for America's Schools," June 29, 2009. http://www.humanevents.com/article.php?id=32472

Grace Church School in New York City, Jennings said, "Sane people keep the world the same [sh*tty] old way it is now. It's the people who think, no, I can envision a day when straight people say, 'So what if you're promoting homosexuality?' ... That is our mission from this day forward."[494]

During the same conference another GLSEN activist and New York City teacher Jaki Williams led a workshop titled, "Inclusive Kindergartens," in which she taught how to indoctrinate little schoolchildren. At that age, children are "developing their superego," so "that's when the *saturation process* needs to begin (emphasis added)." To initiate conversation with the children toward that end, she recommended having students read from an assortment of pro-homosexual books, such as *Heather Has Two Mommies.*

In a speech to Marble Collegiate Church on March 20, 2000, Jennings reportedly said, "We have to quit being afraid of the religious right. We also have to quit — ... I'm trying to find a way to say this. I'm trying not to say, '[F---] 'em!' which is what I want to say, because I don't care what they think! Drop dead!"[495] After the statement surfaced again in 2009, Jennings said he had no recollection of having made the statement.

At the aforementioned 1997 GLSEN conference, Jennings offered praise for a gay rights pioneer who had supported the pro-pedophilia North American Man-Boy Love Association (NAMBLA): "One of the people that's always inspired me is Harry Hay, who started the first ongoing gay rights group in America."[496] According to NAMBLA's website, Hay made the following statement in 1983 at New York University:

In the gay community the people who should be running interference for NAMBLA are the parents and friends of gays. Because if the parents and friends of gays are truly friends of gays, they would know from their gay kids that the relationship with an older man is precisely what thirteen-, fourteen-, and fifteen-year-old kids need more than anything else in the world.[497]

494 Kevin Jennings 1997 Transcript..." http://americansfortruth.com/news/kevin-jennings-1997-transcript-promoting-homosexuality-in-schools-glsen-good-for-kids.html#more-2863

495 When Silence Would Have Been Golden," April 10, 2002, by Peter J. Labarbera. http://www.cwfa.org/articledisplay.asp?id=2580&department=CFI&categoryid=papers

496 This is Not Your Father's School Safety," by Rachel Abrams, October 3, 2009 http://www.weeklystandard.com/weblogs/TWSFP/2009/10/this_is_not_your_fathers_schoo.asp

497 A Quest for Knowledge: Harry Hay, at Tufts University, 1983. http://www.nambla.org/nyu1983.htm

GLSEN and other homosexual activist organizations are implementing their vision in an increasing number of public school systems in America, including schools in California, Minnesota, and Illinois. For example, in Deerfield, Illinois, Deerfield High School required fourteen year old freshmen to attend a Straight Gay Alliance Network panel discussion led by gay and lesbian students. The "freshman advisory class" included sexually explicit discussions of homosexual behaviors. Not only were parents not informed about the panel discussion, students were required to sign a confidentiality agreement in which they promised not to tell anyone – including their parents – about the discussion. Although the district school superintendent subsequently admitted the district made a mistake by requiring children to sign the agreement, parents continued to be banned from sitting in on the freshman advisory class and were not permitted access to materials used in formulating the class curriculum.[498]

In May 2009 the Alameda (California) County Board of Education approved a mandatory diversity sensitivity training program for students from kindergarten through fifth grade. The program, officially titled "LGBT Lesson #9," includes the pro-homosexual book, *Tango Makes Three*, as required reading for second grade students. In the book, two gay penguins raise a happy baby penguin. Third grade students' instruction includes the film "That's a Family," which features both homosexual couples and traditional families. Fifth grade students learn to "identify stereotypes about lesbian, gay, bisexual and transgender people" and are informed that "LGBT people have made important contributions within the United States and beyond." The school refused to allow parents to opt their children out of lessons, prompting a lawsuit filed by Pacific Justice Institute that seeks enforcement of the opt-out requirements of the California Education Code.[499]

Jennings' appointment as the nation's safe-schools czar exemplifies the influence and success activists continue to have in embedding indoctrination into the public school curriculum. The National Education Association is also advancing a homosexual agenda under the guise of diversity.[500]

---

498 School Official in Basketball Flap is No Stranger to Controversy," by Jana Winter, May 13, 2010 http://www.foxnews.com/us/2010/05/13/school-official-suzan-hebson-no-stranger-controversy/

499 "Mandatory 'gay' lessons spark lawsuit," August 14, 2009 http://www.wnd.com/?pageId=106819

500 Eagle Forum, "The NEA Spells Out its Policies," August 2008, Vol. 42, No. 1 http://www.eagleforum.org/psr/2008/aug08/psraug08.html

The ten billion dollar textbook business, dominated by only three publishers, is ground zero in the ideological education war. In twenty states, the state board of education chooses textbooks for the entire state, based on the recommendations of "textbook adoption committees." Various interest groups pressure the committees to choose textbooks that reflect their particular perspective. The committees wield enormous influence with textbook publishers, especially in Texas, because it is the largest state that adopts books on a statewide basis.[501]

Textbook publishers also have multicultural advisory committees typically consisting of representatives from the various interest groups. Diane Ravitch was appointed by President Bill Clinton to work on a national test and later authored *The Language Police.* In an interview with Fox News correspondent Tucker Carlson, Ravitch explained how the advisory committees function:

Ravitch: And so you have people who are trained to find bias where no one else would see it. Someone might find "mice" offensive.

Carlson: Who would that be insensitive to?

Ravitch: People who are afraid of mice, just to show you how silly it gets. Most of the publishers have a list of images you can't use. You can't show women with big hair ... You can't have a picture of a woman cooking. That's considered a biased image because women are not supposed to cook. ... "Waiter" or "waitress," these are biased words. A couple of dictionaries have introduced the word "waitron."[502]

The "silent censorship" by publishers has become so ingrained that it is now done as a matter of course. U.S. and world history textbooks that emerge from this process are short on historical fact and long on politically correct doctrine.

---

501 The Trouble with Textbooks," by Tucker Carlson, Foxnews.com, September 3, 2009
http://www.foxnews.com/opinion/2009/09/03/tucker-carlson-textbooks/
502 The Trouble with Textbooks," by Tucker Carlson, Foxnews.com, September 3, 2009
http://www.foxnews.com/opinion/2009/09/03/tucker-carlson-textbooks/

Islam in the Classroom

The American Textbook Council, an independent New York based educational research organization founded in 1989, issued a 41 page 2008 report, "Islam in the Classroom," after sampling ten widely adopted junior and senior high textbooks. Among the findings of Gilbert Sewell, author of the report:

- *History Alive! The Medieval World and Beyond*, published by the privately held Teachers Curriculum Institute for seventh-graders and reportedly used by over 300 California school districts, is full of factual inaccuracies and historical distortions.[1]
- "Among the textbooks examined, the editorial caution that marks coverage of Christian and Jewish beliefs vanishes in presenting Islam's foundations. ... (T)he seventh-grade textbooks cross the line into ... scripture, or myth," and also include "lavish textbook praise of Islam" and "glowing declarations of Muslim social conscience."[2]
- "While seventh-grade textbooks describe Islam in glowing language, they portray Christianity in harsh light. Students encounter a startling contrast. Islam is featured as a model of interfaith tolerance; Christians wage wars of aggression and kill Jews. Islam provides models of harmony and civilization. Anti-Semitism, the Inquisition, and wars of religion bespot the Christian record. ... When the Seljuks or other Muslim groups attack Christian peoples, kill them and take their lands, the process is referred to as 'building' and empire. Christian attempts to restore those lands are labeled as violent attacks or 'massacres.'" Similarly, crusading Christians are "invaders," while the Seljuks are depicted as "migrating" into Christian territories.[3]

---

1 http://www.historytextbooks.org/islamreport.pdf p. 7
2 IBID, page 12
3 IBID, Page 19

As disturbing as the biased textbook approach to religion and sexuality is the uniquely critical coverage of American history. In a time when American high school students' mastery of history is abysmal, publishers sacrifice coverage of U.S. achievements and foundational instruction in American history in order to excoriate the United States for its past slavery and racism, its treatment of American Indians, its internment of Japanese during World War II, and other lowlights of American history.

The same textbooks often heap praise on, or at least fail to critically evaluate, non-American cultures. As a result, students receive a distorted, negative perspective of America. Concludes Fox News commentator Tucker Carlson: "A thorough cover-to-cover reading of almost any high school history text leaves you with the impression that the United States is at best embarrassing, and at worst a menace to world peace."[503]

All of these textbook distortions predate the election of Barack Obama as President. Unfortunately, they seem to line up seamlessly with his views and those of his administration. The difference is that textbook publishers' revisionism can be largely attributed to pressure from fringe special interests on the outside; the same fringe groups are in many cases on the inside of the Obama administration directing its permanent propaganda campaign.

Taxpayer-funded Art as a Political Tool

The power of art lies in its capacity for communicating to the human spirit at a deeper level than mere words. It uses symbolism and aesthetics to connect with the emotions and feelings of the viewer. As a presidential candidate, Barack Obama benefitted from the now-famous "HOPE" poster portrait of him created by street artist Shepherd Fairey, which became a familiar emblem in his campaign. Hundreds of thousands of copies of the poster were sold.[504] Similarly, musician will.i.am's "Yes We Can" song and music video helped sustain a positive momentum for the Obama campaign.

Like most successful campaign teams, Obama's campaign strategists effectively used art, symbolism, and imagery to political advantage. Symbolism was a potent weapon in Obama's presidential campaign. For many voters, he symbolized the advent of a new, post-racial America. He used his youthful appearance and cult-of-entertainment persona to connect to the younger generation. His campaign wasted no opportunity and no image in cultivating a presidential aura for their politically inexperienced candidate. In Berlin, Obama used the Victory Column as a backdrop for his speech. The campaign converted the presidential seal into an "OBAMA for AMERICA" logo and website advertisement, but abandoned that effort after it was criticized.[505] When Obama spoke at the Democratic National

---

503 The Trouble with Textbooks," by Tucker Carlson, Foxnews.com, September 3, 2009 http://www.foxnews.com/opinion/2009/09/03/tucker-carlson-textbooks/

504 AP Accuses Obama Artist Shepard Fairey of Copyright Infringement," February 4, 2009, by Hillel Italie. http://www.huffingtonpost.com/2009/02/04/ap-accuses-shepard-fairey_n_164045.html

505 Obama's presidential seal gone after one use," June 23, 2008, http://politicalticker.blogs.cnn.com/2008/06/23/obama%E2%80%99s-presidential-seal-gone-after-one-use/

Convention, a Reuters story described the backdrop as "an elaborate columned stage resembling a miniature Greek temple... reminiscent of Washington's Capitol building or even the White House."[506]

In an example of permanent campaign mode, the Obama administration attempted to mobilize the arts community, through the taxpayer funded National Endowment for the Arts (NEA). But a film producer cried foul when the NEA and the White House together asked a group of influential artists to help support President Obama's political agenda.

The conference call, hosted by the NEA, the White House Office of Public Engagement and United We Serve (a nationwide initiative by the White House allegedly focused on increasing volunteerism) took place on August 10, 2009 with 75 artists, musicians, writers, poets, film producers and others. Los Angeles film producer Patrick Courrielche accused officials on the call of encouraging the artists to apply their talents to further the president's political agenda.

White House spokesman Shin Inouye, responding by email, said the teleconference "was not meant to promote any legislative agenda … it was a discussion of the United We Serve effort and how all Americans can participate."[507] The NEA denied that it issued the invitations to the teleconference, but a subsequently leaked NEA email sent prior to the conference call reminded artists of the call and asked for their participation.[508]

The denials likely would have quelled further criticism if Courrielche had not secretly recorded the hour long phone conversation. The transcript left no doubt as to the political nature of the call. Michael Skolnik, a film-maker and the political director for hip-hop mogul Russell Simmons, told the callers that "the goal of all this and the goal of this phone call" included

506 Obama's columned backdrop draws GOP sneers," August 27, 2008, by Muriel Kane. http://www.rawstory.com/news/2008/Obamas_columned_backdrop_draws_GOP_sneers_0827.htm

507 NEA Reassigns Communications Director Following Uproar Over Obama Initiative," September 11, 2009. http://www.foxnews.com/politics/2009/09/11/nea-reassigns-communications-director-following-uproar-obama-initiative/

508 Art for Obama's Sake – the NEA pushes the White House agenda," August 27, 2009, by Kerry Picket. http://www.washingtontimes.com/weblogs/watercooler/2009/aug/27/art-obamas-sake-nea-pushes-white-house-agenda/ "The Rest of the Story," September 21, 2009. http://www.powerlineblog.com/archives/2009/09/024559.php

the effort "to support some of the president's initiatives" and "to push the president and push his administration."[509, 510]

According to Skolnik, the White House initiated plans for the call for the purpose of advancing the president's political agenda. Skolnik referenced Fairey's "HOPE" political poster as a "great example" of the "role that we played during the campaign for the president..."[511] He said "the president has a clear arts agenda and has been very supportive of using art and supporting art in creative ways to talk about issues that we face here in our country and also to engage people."[512]

NEA Director of Communications Yosi Sergant, explained how the artists, using the platform of the United We Serve campaign, could advance the president's agenda:

> This is an amazing opportunity for each of us not only to do what we do daily but to do it within an infrastructure and framing of a national program.... Nobody knows better how to make a stink about it ... What does that mean? How does it fit within this initiative? What the hell is national service? ... It means whatever we want it to mean. I would invite you to pick something whether it's health care, education, the environment, you know, there's four key areas the corporation has identified as the areas of service. My ask would be to apply ... your artistic creative communities' utilities and bring them to the table. ....[513]

Making a stink is not the way to encourage volunteerism, but it is the way to exert public pressure towards helping the President to pass health care reform, education reform, and cap and trade legislation. Sergant repeated the "make a stink" comment three times during the conference call.

The Hatch Act restricts the political activity of federal executive branch employees, and various laws prohibit the use of federal funds for lobbying efforts. White House lawyers reportedly denied that the NEA call violated the law, though some critics disagreed.[514] Everyone agreed that at the very least, the conference call crossed the line of propriety. The White House

---

509 Full NEA Conference Call Transcript and Audio," by Patrick Courrielche. http://bighollywood.breitbart.com/pcourrielche/2009/09/21/full-nea-conference-call-transcript-and-audio/
510 IBID, page 9
511 IBID, page 8
512 IBID, page 8
513 Ibid, pp 25, 30
514 George Will: NEA Call for 'Recovery Agenda' Art Likely Broke Some Laws," http://www.breitbart.tv/george-will-nea-call-for-recovery-agenda-art-likely-broke-some-laws/

vowed to issue new guidelines to prevent such a call from happening again and to correct any "misunderstanding" about the NEA's role in supporting the national service initiative.[515] It also reassigned Sergant.

The National Endowment for the Arts was created in 1965 as an independent public agency of the federal government. According to its website, it is "dedicated to supporting excellence in the arts, both new and established; bringing the arts to all Americans; and providing leadership in arts education."[516] But the Obama administration appears to view the NEA as a resource for propaganda. Despite the White House's reiteration of its policy that "grant decisions should be on the merits," no objective reader of the teleconference transcript would anticipate that in the Obama administration the NEA will be non-partisan in its funding of art projects; it sees itself as a servant of the president's agenda.[517]

Climate Change, the EPA, and "Climategate"

Carbon dioxide (CO_2) is among earth's most basic natural atmospheric gases. Botanists have known for over two hundred years that green plants consume carbon dioxide during photosynthesis and release oxygen. Humans and all animals breathe in oxygen and breathe out CO_2, completing nature's cycle of life. Several decades ago scientists began studying how weather processes and certain gases create a natural greenhouse effect that keeps the surface of the earth warm. Naturally occurring greenhouse gases include water vapor, carbon dioxide, methane, nitrous oxide, and ozone.[518] In recent years, scientists have focused on the effect of CO_2 as a greenhouse gas and hypothesized that an increase in the level of atmospheric CO_2 will cause an increase in the earth's greenhouse effect, causing a rise in the earth's temperature.

Based on studies using complex computer models, leading global warming theorists for years have portended planetary calamity within a few short decades if action is not taken to reduce the amount of CO_2 being produced by human activities such as the mining of coal and oil,

515 Political Punch," September 22, 2009 by Jake Tapper. http://blogs.abcnews.com/politicalpunch/2009/09/after-inappropriate-nea-conference-call-white-house-pushes-new-guidelines.html
516 http://www.arts.gov/about/index.html
517 Political Punch," September 22, 2009 by Jake Tapper. http://blogs.abcnews.com/politicalpunch/2009/09/after-inappropriate-nea-conference-call-white-house-pushes-new-guidelines.html
518 What are Greenhouse Gases?" by Larry West http://environment.about.com/od/faqglobalwarming/f/greengases.htm

the burning of fossil fuels, the breeding of cattle for meat consumption ... and breathing. Their prognosticative track record is less than exemplary, to be kind.[519]

The complexity of earth's weather system has to-date prevented scientists from creating reliable computer models able to adequately account for either the causes or the consequences of increased atmospheric levels of CO_2. A host of factors, known and yet unknown, impact earth's climate, including natural centuries-long climate cycles, sunspot activity, precipitation systems, and ocean warming/cooling cycles. The multiplicity of factors makes proving cause-effect relationships particularly difficult. Some scientists, for example, have suggested that rather than CO_2 producing warmer oceans, ocean warming causes increased CO_2 levels.[520] Scientists who are skeptical about manmade global warming theories argue that current climate models are too primitive and unstable to have predictive value; in other words, they fail to mimic the real world weather system, which shows a stability not reproduced by the computer models. A December 2007 Senate Report detailed the findings of over 400 prominent scientists from over two dozen countries who disputed the so-called consensus regarding man-made global warming.[521]

More than 30,000 scientists have signed a petition which states:

> There is no convincing scientific evidence that human release of carbon dioxide, methane, or other greenhouse gases is causing or will, in the foreseeable future, cause catastrophic heating of the Earth's atmosphere and disruption of the Earth's climate. ... Moreover, there is substantial scientific evidence that increases in atmospheric carbon dioxide produce many beneficial effects upon the natural plant and animal environments of the Earth. ... The proposed limits on greenhouse gases would harm the environment, hinder the advance of science and technology, and damage the health and welfare of mankind.[522]

---

519 See "Is the Sky Really Falling? A Review of Recent Global Warming Scare Stories," August 23, 2006 by Patrick J. Michaels http://www.cato.org/pubs/pas/pa576.pdf

520 CO2, Pollution and Global Warming," by Roberta C. Barbalace, http://environmentalchemistry.com/yogi/environmental/200611CO2globalwarming

521 U.S. Senate Report: Over 400 Prominent Scientists Disputed Man-made Global Warming Claims in 2007," http://www.scribd.com/doc/2603317/Global-Warming-US-Senate-Report

522 When is a Consensus on Climate Not a Consensus?" May 19, 2008, by Janet Raloff http://www.sciencenews.org/view/generic/id/32328/title/Science_%2B_the_Public__When_Is_a_Consensus_on_Climate_Not_a_Consensus%3F

Nevertheless, on December 7, 2009 the Environmental Protection Agency (EPA) issued a final ruling that the atmospheric combination of six greenhouse gases, including carbon dioxide, threatens public health and safety and that the combined emission of these gases from new motor vehicles constitutes air pollution. The move cleared the way for the EPA to regulate, without any action from Congress, a whole host of CO2-emitting industries.[523]

The science of climate change is still in its infancy. Science, by its very nature, depends on cold, unbiased objectivity. Its quest for knowledge is wholly dependent upon the integrity of the scientists and their commitment to the scientific method as they seek new understandings of the earth's physical realities. *If* reputable scientists had persuasive empirical evidence that global warming is occurring, that human activity is a substantial cause, and that the earth's warming poses a substantial threat to the planet, *then* collaborative worldwide efforts to find a solution would be imperative.

Global warming is a legitimate area of scientific study. It is possible that man-made global warming is a real danger, but it is impossible to draw that conclusion at the present time because of the inadequacy of the accumulated scientific data.

The current worldwide political effort to force massive new reductions in CO2 emissions is not based on conclusive, or even convincing, scientific proof of human-caused global warming because at present there is none. Absent such proof, advocates have turned to propaganda to achieve their goals, replete with the suppression of evidence, the stifling of debate, the demonization of opponents, and the distortion of data.

The climate of personal destruction of any scientist who dares counter the so-called scientific consensus on global warming is well-documented. Typical is an email sent by Michael T. Eckhart, president of the environmental group the American Council on Renewable Energy (ACORE), who wrote to Marlo Lewis, senior fellow at the Competitive Enterprise Institute (CEI) on July 13, 2007: "It is my intention to destroy your career as a liar. If you produce one more editorial against climate change, I will launch a campaign against your professional integrity. I will

---

523 Environmental Protection Agency," 40 CFR Chapter 1, page 1 http://74.125.47.132/ search?q=cache:fWgUA2OsBcAJ:www.epa.gov/climatechange/endangerment/ downloads/FinalFindings.pdf+%22carbon+dioxide%22+%22epa%22+%22pollutant% 22+%22final+findings%22&cd=1&hl=en&ct=clnk&gl=us

call you a liar and charlatan to the Harvard community of which you and I are members."[524]

The Politics of Global Warming Science

Those who dare criticize global warming theories, are routinely vilified as "holocaust deniers" or similar pejoratives. A sampling of quotes and headlines:

- British Prime Minister Gordon Brown says global warming skeptics are "flat-earthers" and "anti-science."[1]
- Al Gore on 60 minutes in 2008, referring to global warming skeptics: "I think that those people are in such a tiny, tiny minority now with their point of view. They're almost like the ones who still believe that the moon landing was staged in a movie lot in Arizona and those who believe the earth is flat."[2]
- "RFK, Jr. on global warming skeptics: 'This is treason. And we need to start treating them as traitors'" (July 8, 2007)
- "Nuremberg-Style trials proposed for global warming skeptics" (October 11, 2006)
- "Skeptics called 'climate criminals' who are committing 'terracide' (killing of planet earth)" (July 25, 2007)
- "Skeptical state climatologist in Oregon has title threatened by governor" (February 8, 2007)
- "Canadian environmentalist David Suzuki calls for skeptical leaders to be thrown 'into jail.'" (February 10, 2008)
- "U.N. official says it's 'completely immoral' to doubt global warming fears" (May 10, 2007)[3]

---

1   *London Telegraph*, December 4, 2009, by James Kirkup and Louise Gray http://www.prisonplanet.com/universally-reviled-unelected-prime-minister-gordon-brown-calls-global-warming-skeptics-flat-earthers.html
2   Al Gore's New Campaign," March 30, 2008 http://www.cbsnews.com/stories /2008/03/27/60minutes/main3974389.shtml?tag=contentMain;contentBody
3   EPA Chief Vows to Probe E-mail Threatening to Destroy Career of Climate Skeptic," July 27, 2007 http://epw.senate.gov/public/index.cfm?FuseAction=Minority.Blogs& ContentRecord_id=04373015-802A-23AD-4BF9-C3F02278F4CF

True scientists are a patient lot who systematically apply the rigors of the scientific method, following wherever the evidence leads them. But some of the most influential climate change scientists have exchanged scientific principles for the pursuit of preconceived conclusions, personal gain and

---

524   EPA Chief Vows to Probe E-mail Threatening to Destroy Career of Climate Skeptic," July 27, 2007 http://epw.senate.gov/public/index.cfm?FuseAction=Minority.Blogs&ContentRecord_id=04373015-802A-23AD-4BF9-C3F02278F4CF

political power. They have made absolutist claims unsupported by the scientific record, staining the reputation of the scientific community.[525]

Americans have grown justifiably skeptical of scientists and politicians who attempt to cut off debate and who demand that immediate, drastic action must be taken to avert worldwide calamity. According to a December 2009 Rasmussen poll, only 25 percent of Americans believe that most scientists agree on the subject of global warming. Shortly before the report was issued, White House spokesman Robert Gibbs, said, "I don't think ... [global warming] is, quite frankly, among most people, in dispute anymore."[526]

The November 2009 leak of thousands of emails exchanged between leading global warming scientific organizations, dubbed "Climategate" by global warming critics, exposed the corrupt underbelly of the global warming agenda. In mid-November 2009, a cache of more than a thousand emails and technical documents from the Climate Research Unit (CRU) at East Anglia University in Britain were made available for download off the Internet. The emails paint a disturbing portrait of a small group of extremely politicized scientists consumed with petty bickering, personal attacks and the corrupt manipulation of data.

In perhaps the most circulated of the emails, CRU'S Phil Jones admitted to colleagues in 1999 that he had used "Mike's Nature trick" to "hide the decline" that inconveniently appears after 1960 in one set of temperature records. Steven Hadley, with the American Enterprise Institute, writes:

> (D)ozens of other messages, while less blatant than 'hide the decline,' expose the scandalously unprofessional behavior. There were ongoing efforts to rig and manipulate the peer-review process that is critical to vetting manuscripts submitted for publication in scientific journals. Data that should have been made available for inspection for other scientists and outside critics were released only grudgingly. Perhaps more significant, the email archive also reveals that even inside this small circle of climate scientists ...

525 "The Science and Politics of Climate Change," December 2, 2009, by Mike Hulme http://online.wsj.com/article/SB10001424052748704107104574571613215771336.html

526 http://www.rasmussenreports.com/public_content/politics/current_events/environment_energy/americans_skeptical_of_science_behind_global_warming. "Americans Skeptical of Science Behind Global Warming," December 3, 2009.

there was considerable disagreement, confusion, doubt, and at times acrimony over the results of their work.[527]

Far from being settled science, climate change is an extremely politicized field of research so compromised as to preclude reasonable persons and governments from making major policy decisions based thereon, at the very least until a thorough housecleaning and investigation is conducted. But the administration's tone-deaf march toward climate change legislation, in spite of the huge array of red flags, betrays a commitment not based on science but on an ideology and an appetite for power.

The whitehouse.gov website calls for "immediate action to reduce the carbon pollution that threatens our climate and sustains our dependence on fossil fuels."[528] In July 2009 the Obama administration issued a required climate status report that contained the most urgent warnings ever to come from the White House, including predictions of rising sea levels, possible extinction of plant species, heavier downpours and deeper droughts. "There are in some cases already serious consequences," report co-author Anthony Janetos told The Associated Press. "This is not a theoretical thing that will happen 50 years from now. Things are happening now." The report warned that world temperatures could rise by as much as 11.5 degrees by the end of the century, with the U.S. average temperature possibly rising by an even greater amount.[529]

After the November emails exposed the manipulation, falsification, and suppression of scientific data, the Obama administration doubled down on its expressed confidence in the evidence for global warming. Carol Browner, the assistant to the president for energy and climate, denounced opposing voices as "a very small group of people," and "a couple of naysayers." Rep. John Shadegg, (R- AZ) responded, "Anyone who thinks that those emails are insignificant, that they don't damage the credibility of the entire movement is naïve. ... "[530]

---

527 Source: "Scientists Behaving Badly," by Steven Hadley, December 14, 2009, Volume 015, Issue 13 http://www.weeklystandard.com/Content/Public/Articles/000%5C000%5C01 7%5C300ubchn.asp?pg=1

528 http://www.whitehouse.gov/issues/energy-and-environment

529 White House Climate Change Report Issues Dire Warning on Worsening Situation," June 16, 2009, by Seth Borenstein http://www.huffingtonpost.com/2009/06/16/white-house-climate-chang_n_216534.html

530 Political Punch: White House Pushes Back on Climate Change Email Controversy," December 3, 2009, http://blogs.abcnews.com/politicalpunch/2009/12/white-house-pushes-back-on-climate-change-email-controversy.html

President Obama's science czar, Dr. John Holdren, appeared before the House Select Committee on Energy Independence and Global Warming on December 2, 2009. He dismissed the disputed data as a "very small part of the immense body of data and analysis on which our understanding of climate change exists."[531] Holdren failed to acknowledge the obvious: that the scandal casts severe doubt on the larger body of data and analysis. East Anglia University's Climate Research Unit serves as the main data collector for both the United Nations and the Environmental Protection Agency, and its data is the basis for virtually all peer-reviewed literature.[532] He attempted to pass off the controversy as "not all that uncommon in science," and, incredibly, touted the scandalized peer review process as curative of such controversies.[533]

When a Congressman asked Holdren if there was evidence of scientific fascism in the NOAA (National Oceanic and Atmospheric Administration), he responded, "I am not even sure exactly what that term would mean. …"[534] Holdren certainly understood what the term meant in 1977, when he co-authored a science textbook that discussed various involuntary fertility control measures, including putting sterilants in public drinking water and subjecting women to forced abortions.[535] Holdren's office issued a statement to Foxnews.com in July 2009 that contradicted several statements made in the book: "Dr. Holdren has stated flatly that he does not now support and has never supported compulsory abortions, compulsory sterilization, or other coercive approaches to limiting population growth."[536]

The book, titled *Ecoscience: Population, Resource, Environment,* also considered the idea of a "planetary regime" that would regulate human population levels and natural resources to protect the planet.[537] According

---

531 Political Punch: White House Pushes Back on Climate Change Email Controversy," December 3, 2009, http://blogs.abcnews.com/politicalpunch/2009/12/white-house-pushes-back-on-climate-change-email-controversy.html

532 Political Headlines, "Special Report with Brett Baier," December 7, 2009 http://findarticles.com/p/news-articles/international-wire/mi_8131/is_20091207/political-headlines/ai_n50991279/

533 Political Punch: White House Pushes Back on Climate Change Email Controversy," December 3, 2009, http://blogs.abcnews.com/politicalpunch/2009/12/white-house-pushes-back-on-climate-change-email-controversy.html

534 IBID

535 The Truth-O-Meter Says: Glenn Beck claims…," http://www.politifact.com/truth-o-meter/statements/2009/jul/29/glenn-beck/glenn-beck-claims-science-czar-john-holdren-propos/

536 Obama's Science Czar Considered Forced Abortions, Sterilizations as Population Growth Solutions," by Joseph Abrams, July 21, 2009 http://www.foxnews.com/politics/2009/07/21/obamas-science-czar-considered-forced-abortions-sterilization-population-growth/

537 IBID

to the U.S. Bureau of the Census, the U.S. population in 1977 was approximately 220 million; in 2009 it was approximately 308 million, an increase of 88 million people.[538]

In 1986, Holdren predicted that global warming would kill about one billion people by 2020. When asked about the prediction at his March 2009 confirmation hearing, Holdren replied, "It is a possibility, and one we should work energetically to avoid."[539]

For global warming activists and many environmentalists, overpopulation has long been and continues to be a major concern, since humans are blamed for the alleged rise in earth's temperature. Just five days after Holdren's comments, Diane Francis, Editor-at-large for one of Canada's largest national newspapers, published a column advocating coercive population control modeled after China's one-child policy.[540]

In *Ecoscience*, Holdren and his co-authors were more charitable; they made the case for a governmentally mandated two-child limit:

> In today's world, however, the number of children in a family is a matter of profound public concern. The law regulates other highly personal matters. For example, no one may lawfully have more than one spouse at a time. Why should the law not be able to prevent a person from having more than two children?[541]

Population growth, like global warming, is a legitimate area of concern, research and appropriate response. But Americans must demand that our government officials demonstrate, in word and action, an unwavering commitment to basic constitutional rights and to *honest research*. Otherwise, the government will use fraudulent means to scare the public into accepting coercive means as "necessary."

Columnist H.L. Mencken once wrote, "The whole aim of practical politics is to keep the populace alarmed – and hence clamorous to be led to safety – by menacing it with an endless series of hobgoblins, all of

---

538 http://www.census.gov/statab/hist/HS-01.pdf http://www.census.gov/population/www/popclockus.html

539 Obama's Science Czar Considered Forced Abortions, Sterilizations as Population Growth Solutions," by Joseph Abrams, July 21, 2009 http://www.foxnews.com/politics/2009/07/21/obamas-science-czar-considered-forced-abortions-sterilization-population-growth/

540 The Real 'inconvenient truth': the whole world needs to adopt China's one-child policy," by Diane Francis, December 8, 2009 http://www.financialpost.com/story.html?id=2314438

541 http://zombietime.com/john_holdren/ (citing Ecoscience: Population, Resource, Environment, p. 838)

them imaginary."[542] And so goes the permanent campaign of propaganda and indoctrination being waged at the highest levels of the United States government today.

542 http://www.quotationspage.com/quote/33072.html

10

Health Care: Unhealthy Process, Unconscionable Bill

In 2009, 140 U.S. banks and thrifts failed; a five-fold increase over 2008. The U.S. unemployment rate soared to a 25 year high of 10.2 percent. The federal deficit exceeded the record $455 billion 2008 deficit by almost a trillion dollars. The national debt soared above a record $12 trillion, or over $111,000 per taxpayer.

Common sense suggests that the government should seek ways to reduce the deficit during a financial crisis, but the Obama White House refused to let record levels of federal debt deter it from pursuing a grossly expensive, patently unconstitutional, and chillingly intrusive health care bill. On March 21, 2010, after more than ten months of political jockeying, Congress passed the health care reform bill. Thirty-four Democrats joined the unanimous Republican opposition to the bill, which passed by a seven-vote margin.[543] Two days later, Obama ignored his campaign promise to secure a sixty percent majority of Congressional votes on health care legislation and signed the bill into law.[544]

---

543 "H.R. 3590: Patient Protection and Affordable Care Act," GovTrack.us. http://www. govtrack.us/congress/bill.xpd?bill=h111-3590. Internet; accessed 29 April 2010. Pear, Robert and Herszenhorn, David M. "Obama Hails Vote on Health Care as Answering 'the Call of History,'" New York Times. http://www.nytimes.com/2010/03/22/health/policy/22health.html. Internet.

544 While Obama's eagerness to sign the legislation is understandable, he violated his campaign promise to allow five days for public comments before signing a bill. Politifact rated this promise as broken. "Barack Obama Campaign Promise No. 234," Politifact.com. http://www.politifact.com/truth-o-meter/promises/promise/234/allow-five-days-of-public-comment-before-signing-b/. Internet. Stolberg, Sheryl Gal and Pear, Robert. "Obama Signs Health Care Overhaul Bill, With a Flourish," New York Times. http://www.nytimes.com/2010/03/24/health/policy/24health.html. Internet. One week later, Obama signed the health care reconciliation bill, which fixed the problems House Democrats had with the bill they had just passed. "H.R. 4872: Health Care and Education Reconciliation Act," GovTrack.us. http://www.govtrack.us/congress/bill.xpd?bill=h111-4872). Internet. The House passed the Senate's version of the bill, resolving to fix it afterwards, because Senate Democrats had lost their filibuster proof 60-seat majority in January 2010, when Republican Scott Brown won the Massachusetts' U.S Senate seat previously held by Ted Kennedy. Since the House's health care reconciliation fix ostensibly only dealt with budget issues, Senate rules allowed its passage with only a majority vote.

To say that there was a lack of broad consensus on health care reform would be an understatement. The only bipartisanship in the Senate or House was in opposition to the bill. For months, virtually every public poll indicated that a solid majority of the American public opposed the health care bill. In fact, a few days after its passage, a Rasmussen poll showed that 55 percent of Americans favored repealing the legislation, including 46 percent who strongly favored repeal.[545]

Obama's health-care legislation, unveiled by the White House in February 2010 in an effort to break congressional stalemate over competing Senate and House plans, included hundreds of billions of dollars in new taxes, such as the first-ever Medicare tax on capital gains, a tax on high-end health benefits, and a 2.9 percent assessment on income from interest, dividends, annuities, royalties, and rents for individuals earning more than $200,000 annually or families with incomes over $250,000. Obama's plan imposed $10 billion in additional fees on the pharmaceutical industry starting in 2011, $67 billion in fees on the insurance industry from 2014 through 2024, and a $20 billion excise tax on medical devices makers starting in 2013. Though Obama touted health care reform as an effort to bring quality health care to all Americans, his plan targeted premium employer-provided plans with a 40 percent excise tax.[546]

The health care legislation Obama signed into law is a

> ### That Depends on What the Meaning of "Shall" Shall Be...
>
> Representative Tom McClintock, (R-CA), noted on the floor of the House of Representatives that one version of the health care bill included the word "shall" more than 3,400 times, a staggering statistic for those who prefer to make their own health care decisions.[1] The legislation lists 1,607 instances in which the Secretary of HHS is given the power to interpret the terms of the bill.[2]
>
> ---
>
> 1 "3,400 Shalls," McClintock.House.gov. http://mcclintock.house.gov/2009/11/3400-shalls-1.shtml. Internet.
> 2 Ferrechio, Susan. "HHS would become federal giant under Senate plan," Washington Examiner. http://www.washingtonexaminer.com/politics/HHS-would-become-federal-giant-under-Senate-plan-8586777-73718162.html. Internet.

---

545 "55% Favor Repeal of Health Care Bill," Rasmussen Reports. http://www.rasmussenreports.com/public_content/politics/current_events/healthcare/march_2010/55_favor_repeal_of_health_care_bill. Internet.
546 The premium, or "Cadillac," plans are employer-provided plans with premium costs that exceed $10,200 for singles and $27,500 for families. Donmoyer, Ryan J. and Gaouette, Nicole. "Obama Endorses New Wealth Taxes, More Drugmaker Fees (Update4)," Bloomberg BusinessWeek. http://www.businessweek.com/news/2010-02-22/obama-endorses-new-medicare-tax-more-drugmaker-fees-update1-.html. Internet.

betrayal of the voters' trust: thousands of government mandates, along with new entitlements, taxes and bureaucracies hidden in thousands of pages of legislative jargon. The bill's path to passage illustrates how the Obama administration employs deceitfulness, positioning and fear-mongering to achieve government expansion and radical social change.

Health Care Case Study of Disingenuous Tactics

On Transparency and the Legislative Process: As part of his pledge to deliver the most open and transparent administration ever, Obama repeatedly promised that health care reform would be negotiated publicly.

> I'm going to have all the negotiations around a big table. We'll have doctors and nurses and hospital administrators. Insurance companies, drug companies…We'll have the negotiations televised on C-SPAN, so that people can see who is making arguments on behalf of their constituents, and who are making arguments on behalf of the drug companies.[547]

Obama abandoned his commitment to open negotiations after taking office. When questioned about the broken promise, Gibbs pointed to town hall meetings as proof that "this president has demonstrated more transparency than any president."[548] Politifact.com, on the other hand, categorized Obama's promise as "broken"[549] because most of the critical negotiations took place away from the media.[550]

---

547 "Barack Obama Campaign Promise No. 517," Politifact.com. http://www.politifact.com/truth-o-meter/promises/promise/517/health-care-reform-public-sessions-C-SPAN/. Internet.

548 Lightman, David and Talev, Margaret. "Obama campaign vow of public debate on health care fading," McClatchy Newspapers. http://www.mcclatchydc.com/251/story/71584.html. Internet.

549 "Barack Obama Campaign Promise No. 517," Politifact.com. http://www.politifact.com/truth-o-meter/promises/promise/517/health-care-reform-public-sessions-C-SPAN/. Internet.

550 Lightman, David and Talev, Margaret. "Obama campaign vow of public debate on health care fading," McClatchy Newspapers. http://www.mcclatchydc.com/251/story/71584.html. Internet. Senate Finance Committee Chairman Max Baucus acknowledged that the first two major deals – industry agreements to cut drug and hospital costs – were negotiated in private. In June 2009 Baucus and the pharmaceutical industry made a weekend announcement of a deal to cut drug costs for senior citizens. The next month Vice President Joe Biden announced that leading hospital groups would accept $155 billion in cuts to government programs. When reporters attempted to question Biden and the hospital executives, they declined, leaving the public to wonder about the details of the arrangement.

C-SPAN CEO Brian Lamb called Obama's hand in January 2010 when he wrote to Congressional leaders, urging them to open "all important negotiations, including any conference committee meetings," to televised coverage. In the letter he pledged C-SPAN's network resources to cover the sessions "live and in their entirety."

> President Obama, Senate and House leaders, many of your rank-and-file members, and the nation's editorial pages have all talked about the value of transparent discussions on reforming the nation's health care system ... we respectfully request that you allow the public full access, through television, to legislation that will affect the lives of every single American.[551]

Congressional leadership and the White House maintained that the health care legislative process was being conducted in a transparent manner. "There has never been a more open process for any legislation in anyone who's served here's experience," said Pelosi.[552] Finally, in late January 2010, Obama acknowledged the lack of transparency. "The health care debate as it unfolded legitimately raised concerns not just among my opponents, but also amongst supporters that we just don't know what's going on. And it's an ugly process and it looks like there are a bunch of back room deals."[553] The prevalence of such "back room deals" became apparent when news broke that several senators pledged support for the legislation only

---

551 "C-SPAN Challenges Congress to Open Health Care Talks to TV Coverage," FoxNews. com. http://www.foxnews.com/politics/2010/01/05/c-span-challenges-congress-open-health-care-talks-tv-coverage/. Internet. In response to Lamb's request, Obama called Republican and Democrat leaders together for a six hour health care debate on C-SPAN, during which Democrats and the President monopolized approximately two-thirds of the allotted time. Obama told Republicans that he took responsibility for failing to work out the "logistics" of having a central place for the meetings that had taken place after the process moved out of committees. Curl, Joseph. "At summit, Obama mostly hears Obama," Washington Times. http://www.washingtontimes.com/news/2010/feb/26/obama-listens-at-health-summit-but-mostly-hears-fr/. Internet.

552 "C-SPAN Challenges Congress to Open Health Care Talks to TV Coverage," FoxNews. com. http://www.foxnews.com/politics/2010/01/05/c-span-challenges-congress-open-health-care-talks-tv-coverage/. Internet.

553 "President Obama: Lack of transparency a 'mistake,'" Politico.com. http://www.politico. com/news/stories/0110/31990.html. Internet.

after special deals that saved their respective states hundreds of millions of dollars were inserted into the bill.[554]

The process turned even uglier as Pelosi scrambled to drum up votes to pass the health care bill. To give House Democrats political cover, Democrat leaders formulated a "deem-and-pass" strategy, which relied on a procedural rule that simply deemed the Senate bill to have been passed by the House – without an actual vote – once the House approved legislation amending the Senate bill. When asked to comment on the unorthodox strategy, Obama deferred: "So you've got a good package, in terms of substance. I don't spend a lot of time worrying about what the procedural rules are in the House or in the Senate."[555] Amidst a rising tide of criticism, the House leadership abandoned the plan.

Obama refused to admit that procedural tactics such as deem and pass and the lack of information about the House's pass-it-then-fix-it reconciliation bill muddled the allegedly transparent process. "By the time the vote has taken place, not only I will know what's in [the bill], you'll know what's in it because it's going to be posted and everybody's going to be able to evaluate it on the merits."[556]

When Congress passed the health care bill, it also ended a 45 year old program which allowed banks and other financial institutions to loan money to college students, with the government assuming virtually all the default risk. The new law provides for the government to take over the student loan business, providing direct federal loans to students. Under the new law, all student loans will be funded directly through the federal government as of July 1, 2010. Congressional budget analysts estimated savings of $61 billion over 10 years. The law expands the public sector at the expense of the private sector. It also makes it easier for the government to regulate what kinds of classes or careers would be eligible for student loans. The measure was quietly attached to the reconciliation bill which

---

554 The Senate eventually withdrew a provision, known as the "Cornhusker Kickback," that would have subsidized Nebraska's cost burden under the expansion of Medicare mandated by the bill. Senator Mary Landrieu (D-La) bargained for the insertion of $300 million of Medicaid funds targeted to her state, and potentially to other states struck by natural disasters in the future, in exchange for her vote. Republicans attacked the provision as a corrupt payoff. Democrats defended it as an appropriate response to the devastation of Hurricane Katrina. Fabian, Jordan. "Obama healthcare plan nixes Ben Nelson's 'Cornhusker Kickback' deal," The Hill. http://thehill.com/blogs/blog-briefing-room/news/82621-obama-healthcare-plan-nixes-ben-nelsons-cornhusker-kickback-deal. Internet.

555 "President Barack Obama Talks to Bret Baier About Health Care Reform Bill," FoxNews.com. http://www.foxnews.com/story/0,2933,589589,00.html. Internet.

556 Ibid.

was posted online just three days before Congress approved the bill, with virtually no debate and very little media coverage.[557]

Obama did not want transparency because the polls reflected that the more the American people knew about the health care bill, the less they liked it; that is the reason for the middle-of-the-night secret negotiations, the back room deals, the rush-mode mentality, the holiday votes, the broken promises, and Obama's inability to credibly defend the abhorrent legislative process. Congress and the President were determined to pass their health care bill, process and public opinion be damned.

On Honesty: Obama pledged to head the most ethical administration in history. He called for "honest debate" on health care reform,"[558] but the health care bills were built for deception. Consider the length of the Senate version of the bill: 2,457 pages, including the 383 page Manager's Amendment. Add to that the 153 page reconciliation bill, and the health care reform legislation totaled a mind-numbing 2,993 pages. The length rendered the legislation effectively inaccessible to the public and provided cover for Congress and Obama; health care reform proponents could deny public criticism of the bill knowing that the public would have neither the time nor resources to refute their denials. Obama regularly sought refuge under the complexity cover when facing questions about abortion funding, health care access, and changes to the current system.

Obama spent the summer of 2009 pushing for immediate passage of the bill even while demonstrating his ignorance of its details. In a conference call with bloggers, Obama was asked about a section of the House legislation, which an *Investor's Business Daily* editorial had claimed would effectively outlaw private insurance. Obama replied, "You know, I have to say that I am not familiar with the provision you are talking about."[559] His unfamiliarity with certain provisions did not stop him from urging bloggers to keep pressuring Congress to pass the bill, or from promising during the conference call, "If you have health insurance, and

557 Anderson, Nick and MacGillis, Alec. "Obama's student loan plan moving forward with health bill," Washington Post. http://www.washingtonpost.com/wp-dyn/content/article/2010/03/18/AR2010031802289.html. Internet.
558 Superville, Darlene. "Obama Wants Honest Health Care Debate," ABCNews.com http://abcnews.go.com/Politics/wireStory?id=8388414. Internet.
559 Stein, Sam. "Obama Calls on Bloggers to Keep Health Care Pressure on Congress," Huffington Post. http://www.huffingtonpost.com/2009/07/20/obama-calls-on-bloggers-t_n_241570.html. Internet.

you like it, and you have a doctor that you like, then you can keep it. Period."[560]

Obama was not the only healthcare reform proponent unfamiliar with the bill. *Newsweek* reported that most Democrats voted for a version of the bill without first reading the proposed legislation.[561]

> The effort to jam the bill through Congress made the public dubious. Most Democrats voted for a version of the bill on the first round without having read, let alone digested, its thousands of pages. As the Christmas Eve vote approached, desperate last-minute stocking stuffers appeared in the small print, such as a $1.2 billion payoff to the state of Nebraska that secured Sen. Ben Nelson's reluctant vote. Obama had promised us a transparent "Google Government," but now we know what Obama government actually looks like: ambitious and generous, perhaps, but also secretive, Chicago-style, and way too complicated. Fewer than half of voters now support the legislation, murky as it still is to them.[562]

When House Republicans demanded that Representatives actually read the bill before voting on it, Congressman John Conyers (D-MI) expressed indignation: "I love these members -- they get up and say, 'Read the bill.' What good is reading the bill if it's a thousand pages and you don't have two days and two lawyers to find out what it means after you read the bill?"[563] The length and complexity of the legislation is indeed an outrage, which Conyers only magnified by his gall. Though he found reading the 1990 page bill too much of a bother, he had no problem voting "yes" to a bill he admits he did not read and would not understand if he did.

On Fear-mongering: In 2008, political pundits overwhelmingly agreed that, if he was elected, Obama's health care overhaul would be a near-certain casualty of the market meltdown. The pundits reasoned that no rational government embarks upon a massively expensive new entitlement program when the economy is cratering and the national debt is exploding out-of-control, but Obamacare defies reason.

---

560 "Obamacare: You Will Lose Your Current Insurance. Period. End of Story,"The Foundry. http://blog.heritage.org/2009/07/20/obamacare-you-will-lose-your-current-insurance-period-end-of-story/. Internet.

561 Fineman, Howard. "Obama's Health-Care Gamble," Newsweek. 11 January 2010.

562 Ibid.

563 Ballasy, Nicholas. "Conyers Sees No Point in Members Reading 1,000-Page Health Care Bill--Unless They Have 2 Lawyers to Interpret It for Them," CNSNews.com. http://www.cnsnews.com/news/print/51610. Internet.

Administration officials knew that health care reform would not gain traction with the public if it increased the deficit, so officials preyed on the public's fears and argued that the government could only gain control of the deficit through health care reform. The administration cultivated a health care crisis, claimed that government intervention into health care would save money, and exploited its self-made crisis to rush legislation through Congress.[564] Peter Orszag, director of the White House Office of Management and Budget, came out swinging with an article in the *Wall Street Journal*:

> To transform our health-care system so that it improves efficiency and increases value, we need to undertake comprehensive health-care reform, and the president is committed to getting that done this year. Once we do, we will put the nation on a sustainable fiscal path and build a new foundation for our economy for generations to come.[565]

Based on the CBO's estimate, "Obamacare" will cost $871 billion over the next decade, while reducing the debt by $132 billion and extending coverage to 31-36 million insured Americans.[566] The report seems to support Orszag's argument at first blush, but the problem with this calculation is that the CBO must accept Congress' cost assumptions, no matter how fanciful or purposely misleading. Both the House and Senate bills used accounting gimmicks and utterly unrealistic fiscal assumptions in an unsuccessful attempt to dupe the American public.[567]

The health care bill frontloaded revenue collection but delayed the payment of most benefits until 2014, skewing the numbers by using ten years of income to pay for six years of benefits. It also assumed a future Congress

---

564 "(I)f we don't pass it, here's the guarantee: That the people who are watching tonight, your premiums will go up, your employees are going to load up more costs on you … and the federal government will go bankrupt, because Medicare and Medicaid are on a trajectory that are unsustainable…" "Obama: Unanticipated job losses, difficult war decisions," USA Today. http://content.usatoday.com/communities/theoval/post/2009/12/obama-surprising-job-losses-difficult-war-decisions/1. Internet.

565 Orszag, Peter. "Health Care Costs are the Real Deficit Threat," Wall Street Journal. http://online.wsj.com/article/SB124234365947221489.html. Internet.

566 Associated Press. "House and Senate look to final health care costs," MSNBC.com. http://www.msnbc.msn.com/id/34602095/ns/politics-health_care_reform/. Internet.

567 Both bills front-loaded payments into the system, in the form of taxes and premiums, but back-loaded the vast majority of coverage and benefits (costs). Both bills claimed hundreds of billions of dollars in Medicare savings, (including deep payment cuts to doctors, which most people agree will not be implemented). Doug Holtz-Eakin, former Congressional Budget Office Director under George W. Bush, about the health bill, said of the health bills, "I don't know a budget gimmick that's out there that hasn't been used." David, Pete. "Doug-Holtz-Eakin on Health Reform," Capital Fains and Games. http://www.capitalgainsandgames.com/blog/pete-davis/1269/doug-holtz-eakin-health-reform. Internet.

will accept a trillion-dollar tax on high-cost health care plans; counted a new $72 billion trust fund for long-term care as a cost savings, even though the money will eventually be paid out; and included an automatic 21 percent cut in payments to doctors treating Medicare patients that Congress never intended to become reality. The cuts are routinely removed from the budget each year through the so-called "doc fix".

Less than three months after passage of the health care bill, Obama cynically blasted Republicans who sought to pay for the doc fix by cutting spending elsewhere, charging that they were "willing to walk away from the needs of our doctors and our seniors."[568] According to the CBO, inclusion of the doc fix in the health care bill would have cost $208 billion over the next decade, increasing the deficit by $59 billion.[569]

Universal Health Scare

Are you scared yet? No? Well, you should be! Without his health care reform, Obama wants you to know that your doctor might extract a body part just for fun and profit:

> Right now doctors a lot of times are forced to make decisions based on the fee schedule that's out there. So if they're looking - and you come in and you've got a bad sore throat, or your child has a bad sore throat, or has repeated sore throats, the doctor may look at the reimbursement system, and say to himself, you know what, I make a lot more money if I take this kid's tonsils out.[1]

Already had your tonsils out, you say? Hold onto your feet!

> Let's take the example of something like diabetes ... Right now ... if a family care physician works with his or her patient to help them lose weight, modify diet, monitors whether they're taking their medication in a timely fashion, they might get reimbursed a pittance. But if that same diabetic ends up getting his foot amputated, that's 30,000, 40-50,000 dollars immediately, the surgeon is reimbursed.[2]

The sheer absurdity of the President's rhetoric on health care is jarring. Obama should realize that every excursion into such nonsense only further diminishes his already-crashed credibility.

---

1   "The White House: News Conference by the President, July 22, 2009," WhiteHouse. gov. http://www.whitehouse.gov/the_press_office/News-Conference-by-the-President-July-22-2009/. Internet.
2   "The White House: Remarks by the President in Health Insurance Reform Town Hall," WhiteHouse.gov. http://www.whitehouse.gov/the-press-office/remarks-president-town-hall-health-insurance-reform-portsmouth-new-hampshire. Internet.

---

568   "Obama and GOP bicker over doctors' Medicare pay," by Charles Babington, Associated Press Writer, June 13, 2010 www.news.yahoo.com/s/ap/us_obama_medicare/print
569   Congressional Budget Office letter to Congressman Paul Ryan dated March 19, 2010 www.cbo.gov/ftpdocs/113xx/doc11376/RyanLtrhr4872.pdf

On Positioning – Taxes: Obama promised "no new taxes" for families making under $250,000 on the campaign trail. The health care legislation includes several provisions that will reduce disposable income among middle class families. The individual mandate in the legislation requires all Americans to purchase health insurance or pay an excise tax. If a family earning less than $250,000 opts against purchasing an insurance plan, they will be hit with an excise tax.

When ABC's George Stephanopoulos pressed Obama to admit that the individual mandate was a tax increase, Obama said, "I absolutely reject that notion."[570]

That was six months *before* passage of the health care reform bill. Less than two months *after* the bill became law, the Obama administration filed a motion in federal court in defense of the law, arguing that the individual mandate *is a tax*.[571]

Similarly, the employer mandate requires employers who do not provide health care coverage to pay an additional non-deductible tax for all full-time employees if at least one employee qualifies for a health tax credit. Though small business owners pay their business taxes on their personal income tax returns, the bill does not carve out an exemption for employers making less than $250,000. The legislation even targets flexible spending accounts, (FSAs), which allow employees to divert pre-tax income into an account designated for health care expenses within a specified calendar year. Under Obama's health plan, FSAs will be limited to $2500 per year. Families with special needs children, who relied on the previously uncapped, tax-free FSAs to afford special needs education, will be hit hardest.[572]

On Positioning - Medical Benefits for Illegal Immigrants: Medical benefits for illegal immigrants took center stage in the health care debate when Representative Joe Wilson (R-SC) shouted "You lie!" during Obama's speech to a joint session of Congress, in reaction to Obama's claim that illegal immigrants would not be covered under health care reform.[573]

---

570 "Obama's Nontax Tax," September 21, 2009 http://online.wsj.com/article/SB10001424 05297020448830457442529402938738.html
571 "Obama Admin. Argues in Court That Individual Mandate Is a Tax," by Philip Klein, June 17, 2010 http://spectator.org/blog/2010/06/17/obama-admin-argues-in-court-th
572 Kartch, John. "No New Taxes, Mr. Obama?" FoxNews.com. http://www.foxnews.com/ opinion/2010/02/23/john-kartch-health-care-obama-taxes-family/. Internet.
573 "Rep. Wilson shouts, 'You lie' to Obama during speech," CNN.com. http://www.cnn. com/2009/POLITICS/09/09/joe.wilson/. Internet.

At the time of the speech, Obama's statement was not technically inaccurate; the House bill contained language disallowing coverage for illegal aliens. A section of the bill titled, "No Federal Payment for Undocumented Aliens," read, "Nothing in this subtitle shall allow federal payments for affordability credits or subsidies on behalf of individuals who are not lawfully present in the United States."[574] After Republicans protested that the section was unenforceable because the Democrats had twice defeated GOP proposals that would have enabled the federal government to verify citizenship, Senate leaders said they were looking at ways to include citizenship verification into their version of the bill.[575] The same day the White House, for the first time, sent out talking points that said "verification will be required when purchasing health insurance on the exchange."[576]

Obama could afford such positioning on the health care bill because he had another mechanism in mind for ensuring health care coverage for illegal immigrants; less than a week after the Senate passed its health care bill, the *Baltimore Sun* and the *Los Angeles Times* reported that the White House was gearing up to pass an immigration amnesty bill in 2010 for the estimated 12 million illegal aliens living in America.[577]

On Positioning - Abortion: Obama not only repeatedly denied that the health care bill would allow federal funding of abortions, he invoked Scripture in accusing opponents of lying: "There are some folks out there who are, frankly, bearing false witness. You've heard that this is all going to mean government funding of abortion. Not true. These are all fabrications ..." [578]

Obama told Planned Parenthood in 2007 that his public option health insurance plan would "provide all essential services, including reproductive

---

574 "Fox: Rep. Joe Wilson Talks 'You Lie!' and Health Care," Washington Post. http://www.washingtonpost.com/wp-dyn/content/article/2009/09/13/AR2009091301559.html. Internet.

575 Condon, Stephanie."Senate Revisits Illegal Immigrant Health Care Question," CBSNews.com. http://www.cbsnews.com/blogs/2009/09/11/politics/politicalhotsheet/entry5303572.shtml. Internet.

576 Viqueira, Mike. "WH on Health Care, Illegal Immigrants," MSNBC.com. http://firstread.msnbc.msn.com/archive/2009/09/11/2065287.aspx. Internet.

577 Nicholas, Peter. "Obama Readying Immigration Overhaul Despite Political Risks," The Baltimore Sun. http://www.disinfo.com/2010/01/obama-readying-immigration-overhaul-despite-political-risks/. Internet.

578 "President Barack Obama: *40 Minutes for Health Care Reform* on BlogTalkRadio," August 19, 2009 http://blog.blogtalkradio.com/government/president-obama-enlists-faithful-healthcare-reform-i-spread-facts-speak-truth/

services,"[579] but Obama told a joint session of Congress in 2009, "Under our plan, no federal dollars will be used to fund abortions."[580]

At the time Obama addressed Congress, the statement was categorically false; the House bill explicitly authorized the federal government to pay for abortions under the public option and to subsidize abortions through private insurance plans.[581] The Capps Amendment to H.R. 3200, adopted by the House Energy and Commerce Committee two months before Obama's joint session address, stated that abortions provided under Medicaid shall be provided under the public option plan. The amendment gave the Secretary of HHS discretion regarding coverage of other abortions.[582]

The enacted health care bill opens the door to federal abortion funding through federally administered and subsidized abortion plans, through at least $18 billion dollars in direct appropriations not covered by abortion restrictions, and through a massive array of provisions granting authority to the Secretary of HHS, some of which could be exercised in the future to issue pro-abortion mandates.[583] Indeed, information released by Maryland's State Health Insurance Plan revealed that Maryland will receive $85 million

579 "Obama's Public Option Dance," Accuracy in Media. http://www.aim.org/don-irvine-blog/obamas-public-option-dance/. Internet.

580 President Obama said he wanted to maintain the "status quo" on abortion in the health bill. Current law known as the Hyde amendment, put in place in 1977 and affirmed by the Supreme Court, along with similar provisions passed later, prohibits the U.S. government from funding abortion in any federal health program., except in cases of rape, incest, or danger to the life of the woman.

581 Subsequently, in order to gain enough votes for passage, the House accepted an amendment introduced by Senator Bart Stupak, (D-MI), that maintained the status quo by preventing the public health insurance option and private plans receiving federal subsidies from covering abortion services. Federally subsidized beneficiaries could use their own money to pay for a supplemental policy to cover abortion. Similarly, persons purchasing insurance from the newly created health insurance exchange could use their own money to buy a policy that covered abortion. The final Senate bill did not include the Stupak language; instead, it included language added by Senator Ben Nelson (D-NE), which relied on an accounting gimmick to give the illusion that tax-dollars would not fund abortions. "House Vote 884 – H.R. 3962: On Agreeing to the Amendment Stupak of Michigan Amendment," New York Times. http://politics.nytimes.com/congress/votes/111/house/1/884. Internet.

582 "Nothing in this Act shall be construed as preventing the public health insurance option from providing" abortion services that would not be covered under Medicaid. 2009 "Abortion: Which Side is Fabricating?" Factcheck.org. http://factcheck.org/2009/08/abortion-which-side-is-fabricating/. Internet; accessed 29 April 2019.

583 "March 19, 2010 Letter from the National Right to Life Committee to Members of the U.S. House of Representatives. http://www.nrlc.org/AHC/NRLCToHouseOnHealthBill.pdf. Internet. Michigan Congressman Bart Stupak and other "pro-life" Democrats switched their votes to yes on the final health bill at the eleventh hour after President Obama promised to issue an Executive Order that would "reiterate" the President's "strong belief" that the "bill maintains the status quo."

from the federal government for the state's federally mandated high-risk insurance pool, which will cover abortions. Pennsylvania had previously made a similar announcement.[584]

On Positioning - Rationing Health Care: Americans spent months debating whether Obamacare would lead to rationing after former Alaska Governor Sarah Palin accused Obama of wanting to set up "death panels." The death panel discussion erupted after Dr. Ezekiel Emmanuel, the OMB Special Advisor for Health Policy tasked with reorganizing healthcare delivery and reimbursement systems for the reform bill, proposed implementing a "complete life system" priority curve to determine how health care should be allocated under the new system. Ezekiel's complete life system affords more substantial healthcare to patients between the ages of 15 and 40: "Even if 25-year-olds receive priority over 65-year-olds, everyone who is 65 years now was previously 25 years. Treating 65-year-olds differently because of stereotypes or falsehoods would be ageist; treating them differently because they have already had more life-years is not."[2585]

Actually, the complete life system advocates discriminating against older Americans precisely because of their age – which is the definition of ageism.[586]

The Obama administration and Congress want the American people to believe that health care reform will secure health care coverage for tens of millions of currently uninsured persons, cut hundreds of billions of dollars from Medicare, and prevent insurance companies from denying coverage for pre-existing conditions without rationing services or increasing the federal deficit. Even a second grader can figure out that the math does not work.

Of course the government will ration health care; no sentient person seriously disputes this. Health care reform proponents make a fledgling effort at dismissing such talk, but, if pushed, they respond that the current system already rations health care according to ability to pay. Some argue that they

584 "Maryland Becomes Second State to Offer Federally Funded Abortions Under ObamaCare," by Matt Cover, July 18, 2010 http://newsbusters.org/blogs/matt-cover/2010/07/18/maryland-becomes-second-state-offer-federally-funded-abortions-under-oba

585 Persad, Gavin, Wertheimer, Alan and Emmanuel, Ezekiel. "Principles for allocation of scarce medical interventions," Lancet. http://www.ncpa.org/pdfs/PIIS0140673609601379.pdf. Internet

586 The American Heritage Dictionary of the English Language defines ageism as "discrimination based on age, especially prejudice against the elderly." Ageism: "The American Heritage Dictionary of the English Language, Fourth Edition," Copyright 2009 by Houghton Mifflin Company http://dictionary.reference.com/browse/ageism

are just trying to level the playing field, but when a government bureaucracy wields control over an individual's ability to receive potentially life-saving medical care, one thing is certain: the field is anything but level.

On Positioning - Redistribution of Wealth: The health care legislation will redistribute resources among Americans. The federal government will provide coverage for those who cannot afford it, using tax revenue from those who need health insurance least, (young adults), and those who can afford it most, (the wealthy).

Close to $900 billion will be allocated from 2014 to 2019 to help American families earning up to 400 percent of the federal poverty level (about $88,000 for a family of four). This redistribution will be effected by means of new, refundable tax credits toward the purchase of private health insurance. In addition, there will be a significant expansion of Medicaid and the Children's Health Insurance Program for very low-income families.[587]

The individual mandate section of the bill is a thinly-disguised confiscation and redistribution of property from one group of citizens to another. The bill requires that Americans secure expensive, government-approved health insurance plans that may cost up to $15,000 for a typical family, or pay tax penalties for failing to do so.[588]

The purpose of this compulsory contract, coupled with the arbitrary price ratios and controls, is to require some people to buy artificially high-priced policies as a way of subsidizing coverage for others and for an industry saddled with the costs of other government regulations. Rather than appropriate funds for higher federal health-care spending, the sponsors of the current bills are attempting, through the personal mandate, to keep the forced wealth transfers entirely off budget.[589]

Dr. Donald Berwick, a July 2010 recess appointment of Obama to head Medicare and Medicaid, is on record acknowledging, "Excellent health care is by definition redistributional."[590]

587 Rinehardt, Uwe E. "Christmas in the Senate," Today's Economist. http://economix.blogs. nytimes.com/2009/12/23/christmas-in-the-senate/. Internet.

588 Barnett, Randy, Stewart, Nathaniel and Gaziano, Todd. "Why the Personal Mandate to Buy Health Insurance is Unprecedented and Unconstitutional," HeritageFoundation. org. www.heritage.org/Research/LegalIssues/lm0049.cfm. Internet.

589 Ibid.

590 Gibbs Evades Question of Whether Obama Agrees With His Medicare Director That Health-Care System Must Redistribute Wealth," by Fred Lucas, July 8, 2010 http://www.cnsnews.com/news/article/69149

On Positioning - Loss of Current Insurance Coverage and Choice of Doctor: In pushing the new bill through, Obama repeatedly promised, "No matter how we reform health care, I intend to keep this promise: If you like your doctor, you'll be able to keep your doctor."[591] But the healthcare reform legislation introduced a host of government-imposed changes that will directly impact insurance companies and doctors, such as changing the conditions under which doctors are reimbursed and mandating coverage for pre-existing conditions. Virtually everyone except Obama acknowledges that some insurers will either be driven out of business or stop offering certain policies. Many employers, faced with massive new expenses for providing employer-based health insurance, will drop coverage for employers. Many doctors will stop accepting Medicare and Medicaid to avoid new bureaucratic requirements and reduced fee schedules, forcing patients to find new healthcare providers. According to a 2009 poll, 65 percent of doctors opposed the health care legislation, while 45 percent of doctors "would consider leaving their practices or taking an early retirement" to avoid government-controlled healthcare.[592]

Less than four months after passage of Obamacare, the *New York Times* reported that large insurers were pushing plans that limited choice of doctors:

> Prominent officials like Mr. Obama and Hillary Rodham Clinton learned to utter the word "choice" at every turn as advocates of overhauling the system. But choice -- or at least choice that will not cost you – is likely to be increasingly scarce as health insurers and employers scramble to find ways of keep (sic) premiums from becoming unaffordable. [593]

591 The White House Blog, " A Town Hall, and a Health Care Model, in Green Bay," June 11, 2009 http://www.whitehouse.gov/blog/A-Town-Hall-and-a-Health-Care-Model-in-Green-Bay/
592 Jones, Terry. "45% of Doctors Would Consider Quitting if Congress Passes Health Care Overhaul," Investors.com. http://www.investors.com/NewsAndAnalysis/Article.aspx?id=506199. Internet.
593 "Insurers Push Plans That Limit Choice of Doctor," by Reed Abelson, July 17, 2010

On Positioning - Government Takeover of Health Care: Obama has publicly stated that he favors a single-payer, universal healthcare system,[594] but he denied that the public option was a step toward a single-payer system during the healthcare debate. Addressing the American Medical Association in 2009, Obama said, "The public option is not your enemy; it is your friend... When you hear the naysayers claim that I'm trying to bring about government-run health care, know this – they're not telling the truth."

Promoting the Public Option

Despite Obama's claims that he did not campaign on a public option, his statements on the campaign trail tell a different tale.

- Obama told Planned Parenthood activists in 2007 that he wanted to set up "a public plan that all persons and all women can access if they don't have health insurance."[1]
- Obama told union activists in 2007 that he wanted "those who can go through their employer to access a federal system" and, over a period of 10-15 years, to "eliminate employer coverage."[2]
- Obama's campaign website said that his plan for health care included "a new public insurance program..."[3]
- Obama responded to a 2008 *Washington Post* questionnaire promising, "For those without health insurance I will establish a new public insurance program, and provide subsidies to afford care for those who need them."[4]
- The *New York Times* reported in May 2007: "In the biggest domestic policy proposal so far of his presidential campaign, Mr. Obama ... would create a public plan for individuals who cannot obtain group coverage through their employers or the existing government programs, like Medicaid."[5]

In a letter dated June 3, 2009 from Obama to Senators Edward Kennedy and Max Baucus, Obama wrote, "I strongly believe that Americans should have the choice of a public health insurance option alongside private plans."[6]

---

1 "Obama's Public Option Dance," Accuracy in Media. http://www.aim.org/don-irvine-blog/obamas-public-option-dance/. Internet.
2 "Public Option Was in Obama's Health Plan," Politifact.com. http://www.politifact.com/truth-o-meter/statements/2009/dec/23/barack-obama/public-option-obama-platform/. Internet.
3 "The Obama Plan," BarackObama.com. http://www.barackobama.com/issues/healthcare/. Internet.
4 "Public Option Was in Obama's Health Plan," Politifact.com. http://www.politifact.com/truth-o-meter/statements/2009/dec/23/barack-obama/public-option-obama-platform/. Internet.
5 Toner, Robin. "Obama Calls for Wider and Less Costly Health Care Coverage," New York Times. http://www.nytimes.com/2007/05/30/us/politics/30obama.html. Internet.
6 Benen, Steve. "Obama Wants a Public Option," Washington Monthly. http://www.washingtonmonthly.com/archives/individual/2009_06/018466.php. Internet.

---

594 In 2003, Obama said, "I happen to be a proponent of a single-payer, universal health care system. ... But as all of you know, we may not get there immediately because first we've got to take back the White House and we've got to take back the Senate." "Obama in '03 uncut: I'd like to see a 'single payer health care plan,'" Breitbart.tv. http://www.breitbart.tv/obama-in-03-id-like-to-see-a-single-payer-health-care-plan/. Internet.

While Obama refused to admit it, other Democrats lauded the public option as a tool for crippling the current healthcare system and enabling the single-payer system. Jan Schachowsky, (D-IL), told Health Care for America Now about an insurance company representative who argued that the public option would stifle, and ultimately smother, private health insurance competition. Schachowsky heralded the duplicity of using the public option as a stepping stone to the single-payer system, exclaiming, "He was right! The man was right!"[595]

A single-payer system is the Holy Grail for progressives. It represents a complete government takeover of health care. Arguing that the health care legislation is not a government takeover because it does not include a single payer or public option is misleading; the government will control the health care system through an elaborate labyrinth of new rules and regulations, fines and taxes, fee schedules and coverage requirements, civil and criminal penalties, and boards and bureaucracies. The government will dictate who must have insurance, how much profit insurance companies will be allowed, which medical treatments will be covered, and how much your doctor will be paid.

595 "Still not convinced the public option is a Trojan horse for single payer?" The Foundry. http://blog.heritage.org/2009/08/03/still-not-convinced-the-public-option-is-a-trojan-horse-for-single-payer/. Internet.

PART 3

OLD BILL OF RIGHTS, NEW BILL OF GOODS

*"Without Freedom of Thought there can be no such Thing as
Wisdom; and no such Thing as Publick Liberty, without Freedom
of Speech; which is the Right of Every Man, as far as by it, he does
not hurt or control the Right of another: And this is the only Check
it ought to suffer, and the only Bounds it ought to know.
This sacred Privilege is so essential to free Governments, that the
Security of Property, and the Freedom of Speech always go together;
and in those wretched Countries where a Man cannot call his
Tongue his own, he can scarce call any Thing else his own. Whoever
would overthrow the Liberty of a Nation, must begin by subduing
the Freeness of Speech, a Thing terrible to Publick Traytors."*
– Benjamin Franklin, "Silence Dogood, No 8," The New-
England Courant, July 9, 1722[596]

---

596 Franklin, Benjamin. "Silence Dogood, No. 8," The New England Courant. July 9, 1722.

11

Freedom of Expression:
A Core Principle

Freedom of expression is a key component of America's unique success. The founders envisioned a vigorous marketplace of ideas and, true to that vision, the United States has afforded more protection to free speech than any country in history. In its First Amendment rulings, the Supreme Court has stringently protected political speech in order to sustain the exchange of ideas.

> The most important 'marketplace' in which ideas are contested is the political realm. In a democracy, free debate about public issues, government policy and candidates for office is essential to self-governance because it informs citizens, inculcates public values, and provides a forum for criticism of the government. Protection of political speech is, therefore, at the core of the First Amendment, even if it does not define its entire scope.[597]

The founders considered the free press to be a pillar of American politics. Jefferson, in a letter to Dr. James Currie dated January 28, 1786 minced no words in affirming this truth: "Our liberty depends on the freedom of the press, and that cannot be limited without being lost."[598] The founding fathers recognized the critical role that a free press played in preventing governmental abuse of power:

> To watch the progress of such endeavors is the office of a free press. To give us early alarm and put us on our guard against encroachments of power. This then is a right of utmost importance,

---

597 Feinman, Jay M. Law 101, 2nd Ed. Oxford: Oxford University Press, 2006.
598 "Thomas Jefferson to James Currie, January 28, 1786," The Thomas Jefferson Papers Series 1. General Correspondence. 1651-1827. http://memory.loc.gov/cgi-bin/ampage?collId=mtj1&fileName=mtj1page005.db&recNum=0215. Internet.

one for which, instead of yielding it up, we ought rather to spill our blood.[599]

Jefferson and others of his day trusted a free press to responsibly exercise its freedom, to seek out and publish truth. By vigilantly pursuing the truth, a free press provides citizens with a safeguard against tyranny. A free press can shed light on the government's actions and help hold public officials accountable, particularly important functions in post-New Deal America.

To preserve freedom, citizens must have access to primary source data, especially as it relates to actions of the federal government. The Freedom of Information Act (FOIA), adopted in 1966, is a valuable tool in protecting Americans' access to information from the United States government, but presidents have tried to limit FOIA's reach.[600]

Shortly after the 9/11 terrorist attacks, George W. Bush signed Executive Order 13233, limiting access to presidential records of former officeholders.[601] As part of his Executive Order 13489, signed January 21, 2009, Obama revoked George W. Bush's executive order.[602] George W. Bush also signed into law the "OPEN Government Act of 2007," a modest attempt to reduce agency backlogs in complying with FOIA requests.[603] On December 29, 2009, Obama issued Executive Order 13526, which "prescribes a uniform system for classifying, safeguarding, and declassifying national security information…." Section 1.7 (d) of the Order, however, allows the federal government to retroactively reclassify certain types of information as exempt from an FOIA request, on the basis of national security. In other words, even if an FOIA request meets current criteria for availability under FOIA, the federal government can reject the request if it determines that it should have classified the requested information as unavailable to the public.[604]

---

599 Coffman, Steve, Ed. Founders v. Bush. http://www.scribd.com/doc/12706506/Founders-v-Bush-Founding-Fathers-Quotes. Internet.

600 "The Freedom of Information Act," 5 U.S.C. § 552, as amended by P.L. No. 104-231, 110 Stat. 3048.

601 "Executive Order 12233 – Further Implementation of the Presidential Records Act," The National Archives. http://www.archives.gov/about/laws/appendix/13233.html. Internet.

602 "Executive Order 13489," The National Archives. http://edocket.access.gpo.gov/2009/pdf/E9-1712.pdf. Internet.

603 Hodes, Scott A. "FOIA Facts: The Impact of the OPEN Government Act of 2007," LLRX.com. http://www.llrx.com/columns/foia47.htm. Internet.

604 "Executive Order – Classified National Security Information," WhiteHouse.gov. http://www.whitehouse.gov/the-press-office/executive-order-classified-national-security-information. Internet.

The size of the U.S. federal government has grown dramatically since the early 1900s, resulting in centralized power and a lack of accountability. Annual federal spending has increased more than a thousand-fold since 1930; expenditures increased nearly two and one-half times between the years 2000-2009 alone.[605] Even armed with investigative tools such as the FOIA, the establishment media's historical role as government watchdog has dimmed to that of pet puppy as the size and power of the federal government has exploded in recent years. Much has been written about the failure of the media to adequately examine the facts connected to the Bush administration's prosecution of the war in Iraq and the issues related to the 2008 presidential campaign.

The advent of the 24/7 cable news cycle and the Internet brought massive changes to media, increasing competitive pressures and putting a premium on the entertainment value of news, often at the expense of its informational value. The increasingly partisan tone of Washington politics has also taken root in the mainstream media. The debate still rages about the media's liberal or conservative leanings. Anyone seeking conservative commentary or liberal commentary can easily find either. The media is ubiquitous; indeed it is hard to avoid its reach.

When Ted Turner's Cable News Network (CNN) launched in 1980, it became the first all-news television network in the U.S., providing 24-hour coverage.[606] Other networks followed CNN with competing 24/7 news-focused channels, and the world entered a new era of news reporting and constant commentary. The Internet only intensified the never-ending news and information cycle. Yet one thing is harder to find than ever before: straight, objective news reporting. Today's media establishment has

605 Office of Management and Budget. "President's 2011 Fiscal Budget, Historical Tables," WhiteHouse.gov. http://www.whitehouse.gov/omb/budget/Historicals/. Internet. In the 1910s, real federal government per capita expenditures (2000 dollars) were approximately $129. In 2004, the federal government spent $7100 per capita. Garrett, Thomas A. and Rhine, Russel M. "On the Size and Growth of Government," Review. http://docs.google.com/viewer?a=v&q=cache:rvbB1gfHaH4J:research.stlouisfed.org/publications/review/06/01/GarrettRhine.pdf+%22size+of+the+federal+government%22+%22historical+analysis%22&hl=en&gl=us&pid=bl&srcid=ADGEESgNSkNHZorjCRzbQRY8AqZ4gAWgcvkJLefAWutQNPYe9548DGbPlsg1-5_JrU6pKBk4-JHKyiF4vSO7Cx-Tf4qhzS74RSv3wBCwBr68E7N7y-BFzlYj09iLlPIZ2uFXo0LmxqLYb&sig=AHIEtbThiBHNACStp-WeAW7jop3SP4yBdA. Internet. Federal spending grew 221% in real (inflation-adjusted) dollars between 1970 and 2007, nearly nine times faster than median income. "2009 Federal Revenue and Spending Book of Charts," Heritage.org. http://www.heritage.org/research/features/BudgetChartBook/Federal-Spending-Grew-Seven-Times-Faster-Than-Median-Income.aspx. Internet.
606 Kiesewetter, John. "In 20 years, CNN has changed the way we view the news," Enquirer.com. http://www.enquirer.com/editions/2000/05/28/loc_kiesewetter.html. Internet.

abandoned its search for the truth in favor of an agenda-driven template. Even the façade of objectivity is missing from most modern American media. The media is in a meltdown. In *The Audacity of Hope*, Obama summarized the implications:

> The absence of even rough agreement on the facts puts every opinion on equal footing and therefore eliminates the basis for thoughtful compromise. It rewards not those who are right, but those -- like the White House press office -- who can make their arguments most loudly, most frequently, most obstinately, and with the best backdrop.
>
> Today's politician understands this. He may not lie, but he understands that there is no great reward in store for those who speak the truth, particularly when the truth may be complicated. The truth may cause consternation; the truth will be attacked; the media won't have the patience to sort out all the facts and so the public may not know the difference between truth and falsehood.[607]

The FTC's Ideas for More Government Control of Media

Technological advances have unleashed a major period of transition in media and its various forms. Free market forces are reshaping media, rewarding enterprises that offer timely news, and offering consumers unprecedented access to information via the Internet. Traditional forms of media such as newspapers are in decline, but new, financially viable media forms are emerging. News organizations which earn the public trust by establishing a track record for accuracy, insight and journalistic balance are gaining market share, while those that filter news through an establishment media, agenda-driven template are faltering.

The crisis in the mainstream media is a crisis of integrity. The establishment media has lost the trust of the populace. Government intervention can only drive trust in media even lower, exacerbating its problems.

Nonetheless, in May 2010 The Federal Trade Commission issued a working paper on ways to "reinvent" journalism that would surely signal the death knell of a free press in America should its ideas be implemented. Among the FTC's disturbing and dangerous suggestions: a new tax on news-aggregator websites such as the Drudge Report; a new five percent tax on consumer electronics; new fees on "telecom users, television and radio broadcast licenses, or Internet service providers"; tax exemptions for newspapers; a national fund for local news organizations; and a new journalism division within AmeriCorps.[1]

---

1   "Putting Watchdogs on the Payroll," June 12, 2010 by Theodore Dawes, American Thinker
    http://www.americanthinker.com/2010/06/putting_the_watchdogs_on_the_p.html

---

607 Obama, Barack. The Audacity of Hope. New York : Crown Publishers, 2006.

American media doesn't need the government's "help"; indeed, it cannot afford it. The unifying theme of the FTC's ideas is government control of media through new taxes and federal subsidies. Putting journalists on a government payroll, or subsidizing favored media outlets, or punitively taxing disfavored media forms, is antithetical to a free press because it makes the media beholden to government for its financial viability. Application of the FTC's ideas would increase the power of federal bureaucrats at the expense of consumers and would constitute a blatant conflict-of-interest.

Reporters, including news anchors and bureau chiefs, should seek out the truth wherever it leads and report the news without allowing their own bias to enter into the process or the results. Obama attributes the media's deficit of in-depth, factual reporting to a lack of patience, but clearly the problem runs much deeper. The media's failure to hold politicians accountable to facts has created a contentious environment for the truth-seeking citizen, who has to work much harder to ferret out facts and to reach cohesive, well-reasoned positions. The 24/7 media cycle is infected by factual inaccuracies, distortions and omissions; events reported without credible corroboration; critical context edited out purposely or for sound-bite effect; opinion disguised as fact; and bloviated banter mixed with news reporting.

Politicians often hide behind the wall of noise created by today's information glut, a wall built higher by the media's fact-finding deficiencies. If a politician is in hot water due to an ill-considered or ill-received statement, he or she may choose simply to deny having ever made the remark. The denial stands a good chance of working in the politician's favor because no one knows whom to trust anymore. Consequently, people are more apt to simply disregard a report if it contradicts their personal views or biases.

In *Journalistic Fraud*, Bob Kohn explains how *The New York Times* methodically misinforms readers to pursue a leftist agenda. By dissecting actual news stories from the *Times* he shows how the once-proud newspaper manipulates rather than informs, distorting headlines, leads, and facts. He exposes various manipulative tricks the *Times* employs, such as expressing opinion as fact, misleading with polls, and slanting news through labels and loaded language. Calculated misrepresentations like those the *Times* employs are now standard fare across the dominant news media. Objective reporting is out; agenda-driven distorting is in. The mainstream media's coverage of the nationwide tea party movement protests is a case in point.

In the first months of 2009, the Internet buzzed with details of hundreds of planned tea party events across America. Fox News became the consummate promoter for the events. A study by the liberal media watchdog Media Matters claimed that from April 6 to April 13, Fox News featured twenty segments on the tea party protests, supplemented by 73 "in-show and commercial promotions" for its planned April 15 coverage of the events.[608] Fox commentators were keynote speakers at several of the most prominent protests. Sean Hannity's nightly television show broadcast live from the Atlanta tea party for the full hour of its April 15, 2009 broadcast. Fox commentators Glenn Beck, Greta van Susteren, and Neil Cavuto were keynote speakers at other tax day tea parties. Fox reporter Megyn Kelly advised viewers: "You can join the tea party action from your home if you go to thefoxnation.com, that's thefoxnation.com. We've got all day tea party coverage for you, and a virtual tax day tea party, where you can sound off on your feelings on it online, if you like."[609]

Aside from the conservative Fox News, network and cable news stations barely mentioned the events prior to April 15, unless it was to disparage them. For example, in his April 13 preview of the planned protests, MSNBC anchor David Shuster offered twelve separate oral-sex double entendres.[610] Bias turned to bile as a few well-known reporters openly ridiculed the tea party participants and engaged in crude sexual banter. Most of America had no idea that the term "tea-bagging" is an oral sex slang term, at least until the networks unleashed their odious offensive. MSNBC's Rachel Maddow and her guest, Air America's Ana Maria Cox, combined to use the term "teabag" at least 51 times in thirteen minutes. Smitten by her own cleverness, Cox said there's "a lot of love in tea-bagging."[611]

In an NBC segment, reporter Lee Cowan reported that "organizers insist today's 'tea parties' were organic uprisings of like-minded taxpayers from both parties," but "some observers suggest not all of it was as home-grown as it may seem." NBC News Political Director Chuck Todd intoned,

608 "Hosting the party: Fox aired at least 20 segments, 73 promos on 'tea party' protests – in just 8 days," MediaMatters.org. http://mediamatters.org/research/200904150033. Internet.
609 "Fox's Kelly: 'You can join the tea party action from your home if you go to the FoxNation.com... a virtual tax day tea party,'" MediaMatters.org. http://mediamatters.org/mmtv/200904150017. Internet.
610 "Bozell: 'Now the News Isn't Just Biased, It's R-Rated. MSNBC and CNN Owe the Public An Apology," Media Research Center. http://www.mrc.org/press/2009/press20090416.asp. Internet.
611 Ibid.

"A lot of the sentiment is about organizing anti-Obama rallies, getting conservatives excited about the conservative movement again."[612] On ABC World News, Charles Gibson reported, "These self-styled 'tea parties' were aimed squarely at President Obama and the democratic leaders in Congress and aimed at garnering media attention as well."[613] The Associated Press distorted their lead and the facts, used loaded language and expressed opinion as fact – all in one lead sentence: "Whipped up by conservative commentators and bloggers, tens of thousands of protestors staged 'tea parties' to tap into the collective angst fueled by a bad economy, while President Barack Obama vowed 'a simpler tax code that rewards work and the pursuit of the American dream.'"[614]

The Rise of Talk Radio

Each area of media has its own unique mix of programming. Television offers extensive conservative commentary on Fox News (i.e. *Hannity, Glenn Beck Show, The O'Reilly Factor*). However, with the exception of Fox, televised reporting reflects an obvious liberal bias. Major-market newspapers are also dominated by liberal bias, led by the *New York Times, Washington Post, Los Angeles Times,* and *USA Today.* The same is true of most major weekly magazines, such as *Time* and *Newsweek.*

In the last twenty years, talk radio and the Internet have filled the void left by television and print media. Talk radio has become dominated by conservative radio personalities such as Rush Limbaugh, Sean Hannity and Glenn Beck, who command a combined weekly audience of approximately 39 million listeners.[615] Talk radio is not solely occupied by conservative commentators; state public radio and taxpayer-subsidized national public radio (NPR) each have carved out niche audiences.

Conservative radio programming, however, has been far more profitable than liberal programming. Air America, the liberal talk radio network that began operations in 2004, filed for bankruptcy after two years. It remained on the air and underwent a series of management changes, but faltered due to a lack of advertising, investors, and listeners. In February 2010,

612 Baker, Brent. "ABC, CBS and NBC Try to Discredit 'Tea Party' Protests," Newsbusters.org. http://newsbusters.org/blogs/brent-baker/2009/04/16/abc-cbs-nbc-try-discredit-tea-party-protests. Internet.
613 Ibid.
614 Associated Press. "Anti-tax 'tea parties' being held across U.S.," MSNBC.com. http://www.msnbc.msn.com/id/30227452/. Internet.
615 "The Top Talk Radio Audiences," Talkers. http://talkers.com/online/?p=71. Internet.

Air America filed for Chapter 7 bankruptcy protection.[616] Currently there are fewer than 100 U.S. commercial radio stations carrying liberal talk programs. Rush Limbaugh, by contrast, is carried on nearly 600 stations.[617] In response to market demands, the majority of unsubsidized talk radio is dedicated to conservative and Christian programming.

A brief history of the government's role in the regulation of radio and television helps explain the rise of talk radio. In 1934, Congress created the Federal Communications Commission (FCC) to oversee the allocation of broadcast outlets, issue licenses, and to regulate the airwaves in the public interest.[618]

In 1949, the FCC established the Fairness Doctrine, in "an attempt to ensure that all coverage of controversial issues by a broadcast station be balanced and fair."[619] The Fairness Doctrine required broadcast licensees to "afford reasonable opportunity for discussion of contrasting points of view on controversial matters of public importance."[620] A central consideration in the promulgation of the doctrine was the scarcity of broadcast outlets at the time. In 1949, there were 2881 radio and 98 television stations. By 1960, 4,309 radio and 569 television stations existed and by 1989, the numbers had mushroomed to more than 10,000 radio stations and nearly 1,400 television stations.[621]

The Fairness Doctrine was constitutionally problematic from its inception because it put a government bureaucracy in charge of judging programming content. Politicians and special interests used the doctrine to harass or manipulate broadcast stations, which were tasked with the impossible mission of pleasing all sides with a perfect balance of

---

616 "Radio network Air America is bankrupt, to dissolve," Reuters. http://www.reuters.com/ article/idUSN0317292120100203. Internet.

617 "The Rush Limbaugh Show." http://www.rushlimbaugh.com/home/menu/rush.guest. all.html. Internet.

618 "The Fairness Doctrine: Unfair, Outdated and Incoherent," Senate Republican Policy Committee. http://docs.google.com/viewer?a=v&q=cache:KKvQbjQgpbIJ:rpc.senate. gov/public/_files/072407FairnessDoctrinePL.pdf+%221949%22+%22number+of+bro adcast+outlets%22&hl=en&gl=us&pid=bl&srcid=ADGEESh1_cav92x_xDmJLQ8qV HiTb79EsyCUDsy8Dbtqj4hPMXd163JO3etxQNpl-0nGqDVO7ECJLkjL97Kbhi3fj3 wwhOzsKNQcB57rH5qXPZolBuNYe6rgiRqFYKCgY9Zzq_qUj863&sig=AHIEtbTD yBXjQ1rODTbeKIhDd2erASoyBA. Internet.

619 "Fairness Doctrine: U.S. Broadcasting Policy," Museum.tv. http://www.museum.tv/ eotvsection.php?entrycode=fairnessdoct. Internet.

620 Gattuso, James. "Back to Muzak? Congress and the Un-Fairness Doctrine," Heritage.org. http://www.heritage.org/Research/Reports/2007/05/Back-to-Muzak-Congress-and-the-Un-Fairness-Doctrine. Internet.

621 Thierer, Adam. "Why the Fairness Doctrine is Anything But Fair," Heritage.org. http:// www.heritage.org/research/regulation/em368.cfm. Internet.

programming. Bill Ruder, Democratic campaign consultant and Assistant Secretary of Commerce in the Kennedy administration, recalls manipulating the Fairness Doctrine for political gain: "Our massive strategy was to use the Fairness Doctrine to challenge and harass right-wing broadcasters and hope the challenges would be so costly to them that they would be inhibited and decide it was too expensive to continue."[622]

In 1969, the Supreme Court upheld the constitutionality of the Fairness Doctrine based on the scarcity of broadcast frequencies.[623] By the mid-eighties, with the explosion of thousands of new radio broadcast frequencies, it became clear that the Fairness Doctrine was no longer needed. In 1987, the FCC abolished the Fairness Doctrine, noting that the Doctrine restricted journalistic freedom and inhibited the discussion of controversial issues.[624]

The demise of the Fairness Doctrine in 1987 cleared a pathway for the ascent of the AM talk radio format. Until then, the Fairness Doctrine precluded broadcast stations from effectively carving out an ideological niche based on their own content choices in relation to the specific audience characteristics of a geographical market; the government's Fairness Doctrine had stifled free market forces. AM music stations were in need of a lifeline at the time. FM stations held a competitive edge because they can broadcast in stereo, which provides far superior musical quality. A talk format eliminates the advantage since the spoken word does not require high fidelity. Critics and fans alike credit Rush Limbaugh for launching the talk radio format to prominence.

> More or less on the heels of the Fairness Doctrine's repeal came the West Coast and then national syndication of *The Rush Limbaugh Show* through Mr. McLaughlin's EFM Media. Limbaugh is the third great progenitor of today's political talk radio partly because he's a host of extraordinary, once-in-a-generation talent and charisma – bright, loquacious, witty, complexly authoritative –

---

622 Jesse Walker, "Tuning out Free Speech," The American Conservative. http://www. amconmag.com/article/2007/apr/23/00021/. Internet.

623 Red Lion v. FCC, 395 U.S. 367, (1969)

624 "Heritage: Fairness Doctrine 2.0," Deep Thoughts and Incoherent Ramblings." http:// chrissteffen.blogspot.com/2008/12/heritage-fairness-doctrine-20.html. Internet. The FCC's decision was prompted by a federal court ruling that the FCC was not obligated to enforce the Fairness Doctrine. The Supreme Court never overturned Red Lion, but technological advances have made its scarcity rationale for upholding the constitutionality of the Fairness Doctrine moot.

whose show's blend of news, entertainment, and partisan analysis became the model for legions of imitators.[625]

The Fairness Doctrine had been laid to rest for twenty years when, in 2007, conservative talk radio led a revolt against immigration legislation favored by George W. Bush and the newly minted Democratic Congress. Conservative commentators urged listeners to flood the Capitol Hill switchboards with comments about the amnesty provisions in the bill and the lack of border security measures. The response was overwhelming and the Comprehensive Immigration Reform Act of 2007 was abandoned without a full vote.[626]

After the immigration reform debacle, several politicians and bureaucrats suggested a Fairness Doctrine revival. Pelosi led the charge, complaining that "hate radio" had hijacked political discourse.[627] Others, including Mark Lloyd, Obama's FCC Chief Diversity Officer and General Counsel, opposed reinstating the Fairness Doctrine because it would not be radical enough.

In 2007, Lloyd co-authored a report for the Center for American Progress entitled "The Structural Imbalance of Political Talk Radio."[628] Lloyd's report detailed his recommendations for shifting programming on privately-owned talk radio stations from profitable conservative and Christian programs to less commercially viable liberal programs. Lloyd proposed a variety of tactics to force stations to remove successful programs from the air, including shortened broadcast license terms, diversity mandates, and punitive fees for broadcast owners who fail to abide by "public interest obligations."[629] Lloyd knows that the Fairness Doctrine is

---

625 Wallace, David Foster. "Host." Atlantic. 2006

626 "Pelosi: 'Hate Radio Hijacked Political Discourse with 'Xenophobic, Anti-Immigrant' Rhetoric," ThingProgress.org. http://thinkprogress.org/2007/06/28/pelosi-talk-radio/. Internet.

627 Ibid.

628 Halpin, John, et al. "The Structural Imabalance of Talk Radio," Center for American Progress. http://www.americanprogress.org/issues/2007/06/talk_radio.html. Internet.

629 The public obligations inherent in the Fairness Doctrine are still in existence and operative, at least on paper. It is worth noting that Lloyd's suggestions closely track Obama's goals for talk radio. During the 2008 campaign, Obama spokesman Michael Ortiz offered this statement regarding Obama's view on the Fairness Doctrine. "[Obama] considers this debate to be a distraction from the conversation we should be having about opening up the airwaves and modern communications to as many diverse viewpoints as possible... That is why Sen. Obama supports media-ownership caps, network neutrality, public broadcasting, as well as increasing minority ownership of broadcasting and print outlets." "Obama Truth Campaign," Accuracy in Media. http://www.aim.org/aim-column/pelosi-support-return-of-fairness-doctrine/. Internet.

not the most effective tool for furthering a big government, command-and-control agenda. Instead of reinstating the Fairness Doctrine, Lloyd wants to use "localism" to control broadcast content.

Localism is a nebulous FCC regulatory policy that requires broadcast stations to meet the needs of the local community in order to acquire and maintain broadcast licenses. Since telling broadcasters what to broadcast is inappropriate, Lloyd proposes that government, through outrageous fees, fines and fiats, indirectly control content by confiscating conservative problem stations and facilitating their subsequent sales to liberal-friendly entities.

Because the bureaucracy cannot act alone to take over the airwaves, Lloyd's strategy would use liberal community leaders to file FCC localism complaints against conservative broadcasters. Under his plan for the FCC, commercial broadcasters who violate FCC regulations, including localism requirements, would be fined up to $250 million dollars. The proceeds of such fines would "directly support local, regional and national public broadcasting." In other words, the money would be confiscated from conservative broadcasters and redistributed to liberal, government-financed radio.

Just in case Lloyd's sin tax on conservative radio is insufficient to ensure a liberal talk radio takeover, Lloyd has a backup plan to charge broadcasters annual license fees equaling 100 percent of their annual operating budgets, the revenues from which would be used to fund and expand traditionally liberal public radio. Any station that cannot pay the license fee would lose its license and be sold to new owners. Obama, Lloyd, and FCC Commissioner Michael Copps have all expressed a determination to increase minority ownership of radio stations and Lloyd's fee plan provides a mechanism for achieving that goal.

Certain Democratic members of Congress are joining with a coalition of minority broadcast owners to ensure that the high cost of annual license fees, as envisioned by Lloyd, would not be a problem for minority owners. In May 2009, House Majority Whip James Clyburn (D-SC), along with Financial Services Committee Chairman Frank, Ways and Means Committee Chairman Charles Rangel (D-NY) and Oversight Committee Chairman Edolphus Towns (D-NY) wrote Geithner requesting help for minority broadcasters in the form of a minority broadcaster support program, bridge funding, or government-backed loans. Two months later, the broadcasters' coalition issued a formal request to Geithner for a bailout akin to the one provided to the auto industry. "Minority-owned broadcasters are close to becoming an extinct species," the letter said. "Even in better economic times, minority broadcasters have historically had difficulties accessing the capital markets."[630] Groups that signed on to the letter included the National Association of Black Owned Broadcasters, the Inner City Broadcasting Coalition, and the Spanish Broadcasting System.[631]

It is no wonder that Obama and Lloyd are opposed to reinstating the Fairness Doctrine; if Lloyd's strategy succeeds, they would not want to be constrained by a balanced content requirement.

The Internet: Media 2.0

In addition to talk radio, concerned citizens are turning to the Internet to supplement their daily news intake. While bloggers, interest groups and Internet news sites may have ideological agendas, the function of a free press has always rested, most of all, on the free flow of information within a framework of basic integrity.

The establishment media's abandonment of even an ideal of objectivity is a disservice to the public, but robust, subjective and opinionated discussion, such as that found on talk radio and the Internet, is a vital part of the marketplace of ideas concept. The First Amendment guarantees the press freedom from governmental interference, not a nanny-state determination of objectivity, balance or fairness. The press is, and always has been, an untamed beast.[632]

The Internet has forever changed the way Americans learn about, research and review news and opinion by diversifying available information sources. Now, every citizen is a potential reporter with the possibility of gaining a mass audience. Matt Drudge is a prime example. Drudge was unknown before he started the Drudge Report, a conservative news aggregation web site that began in 1994 as an e-mail newsletter focused on entertainment gossip. By March 1995, the Drudge Report boasted 85,000 email subscribers. As the newsletter's popularity grew, Drudge shifted to the web as the primary distribution vehicle. Drudge's ability to scoop the establishment media on major news stories - he announced Jack Kemp would be Bob Dole's running mate in 1996 and broke news of the

---

630 Johnson, Fawn. "Minority Broadcasters Seek Federal Aid," Wall Street Journal. http://online.wsj.com/article/SB124752187967935029.html. Internet.
631 Ibid.
632 Allen, W.B., ed. "1807 Review of the Pamphlet on the State of the British Constitution Reference," Works of Fisher Ames, vol. 1 (183-184).

Monica Lewinsky scandal, among others - brought him national attention and hyper-boosted his popularity. Today, the Drudge Report boasts nearly eight billion annual web visits.[633]

The founders' idea of a free marketplace of competing ideas has never been more alive in America than it is on the Internet. The Web effectively leverages the power of the people. Because millions of citizens use the Internet as a platform for their views, virtually every viewpoint is represented. Eyewitnesses become reporters and any citizen can share his or her research with the world.

Establishment media and certain government officials warn that swimming in the Web's ocean of information risks falling prey to disinformation sharks. Certainly, the Web is a buyer-beware world of raw free speech in action, its wonders and warts alike in prominent display. Yet the determined truth-seeking citizen can, by cross-referencing various news accounts and commentaries over a period of time, (and especially by using primary source data, such as congressional records, Supreme Court opinions and transcripts of speeches and interviews whenever possible), garner facts and discern which sources are the most credible. Though the Internet must be navigated cautiously, it does afford fingertip access to information unavailable to past generations. Using a seemingly infinite number of websites, citizens can probe below the surface of political half-truths and lies that infect discussion of legislative and policy initiatives. For the fading traditional media, informed citizen-reporters are a threat which must be marginalized.

Politicians, with a few exceptions, share this elitist perspective. Politicians and bureaucrats have quickly come to fear the power of the Internet to expose government duplicity, waste, fraud, and abuse. To the very extent that the Web empowers people, it frightens the politically powerful, including Obama.

Liberty and the Law

Along with life and the pursuit of happiness, liberty is identified in the Declaration of Independence as one of the core unalienable rights of all people, a right endowed by the Creator. Freedom of expression, which encompasses freedom of the press and freedom of speech, is a core component of any comprehensive definition of liberty. Dictionary.com

---

633 Drudge Report. http://www.drudgereport.com. Internet.

defines liberty broadly as "the condition of being free from restriction or control," and more specifically as "the right and power to act, believe, or express oneself in a manner of one's own choosing."[634]

The First Amendment to the Bill of Rights declares that "Congress shall make no law … abridging the freedom of speech, or of the press, or the right of the people peaceably to assemble, and to petition the Government for a redress of grievances." The Fourteenth Amendment to the Constitution, enacted in 1868, declares no individual state can deny U.S. citizens the "privileges and immunities" they enjoy by virtue of their citizenship, nor "deprive any person of life, liberty or property, without due process of law," nor "deny to any person within its jurisdiction the equal protection of the laws." In *Gitlow v. People of State of New York* (1925), the Supreme Court applied the right to freedom of expression incorporated in the Bill of Rights to the States through the Fourteenth Amendment Due Process Clause.[635]

Notwithstanding the "Congress shall make no law" language of the First Amendment, freedom of expression has never been regarded as an absolute right in America because the abuse of such freedom has the potential to harm others by infringing upon their basic rights. Jefferson had this basic understanding in mind when in 1789 he suggested the following First Amendment language as a constitutional possibility: "The people shall not be deprived or abridged of their right to speak, to write or otherwise to publish anything but false facts affecting injuriously the life, liberty, property, or reputation of others or affecting the peace of the confederacy with foreign nations."[636] The Courts have generally agreed with Jefferson. For example, it is now settled law that the Bill of Rights does not confer the right to issue a death threat, to commit mail fraud, to plagiarize another author, to distribute child pornography, to engage in obscene speech, to commit perjury, or to defame anyone by libel or slander.

Eugene Volokh, professor of First Amendment law at UCLA School of Law, writes, "There was never a time when 'no law' meant 'no law' and all speech was protected."[637] Some kinds of speech are afforded more constitutional protection today than in earlier periods of American history. For instance, anti-government speech and anti-Christian speech were afforded

---

634 Liberty. Dictionary.com. Dictionary.com Unabridged. Random House, inc. http://dictionary.reference.com/browse/liberty (accessed 29 April 2010).

635 Gitlow v. People of State of New York (1925), 268 U.S. 652.

636 "Freedom of Expression – Speech and Press," Findlaw.com http://caselaw.lp.findlaw.com/data/constitution/amendment01/06.html#1. Internet.

637 Volokh, Eugene. "First Myths: Some on the right are getting the First Amendment wrong," National Review. http://www.nationalreview.com/comment/volokh200401050906.asp. Internet.

less protection by courts in the 1800s. Until the early 1800s, in many states truth wasn't accepted as a defense in criminal libel prosecutions.[638]

The Supreme Court has played a necessary role in establishing principles for interpreting the First Amendment rights to freedom of the press and of speech in the context of specific cases. The Court has held that a law restricting speech is unconstitutional if it is so vaguely written that the average person must guess at its meaning and application. Similarly, the Court will strike down a law if it is "so broadly written as to prohibit protected speech as well as unprotected speech."[639] The same rationale guides the Court for both vague and overly broad laws: they both chill speech, causing citizens to fear exercising their constitutional speech rights for fear of punishment by the government. The Court almost always strikes down any attempt to impose a prior restraint on speech or publication, recognizing that it would severely limit or permanently deny specific expressions.[640]

The Court will consider any law that discriminates based on the content of a message presumptively unconstitutional. Applying the principle of strict scrutiny, the Court will permit the speech regulation only if it "is narrowly tailored to further a compelling government interest, and there is no less restrictive alternative…Content-neutral regulation of the time, place, or manner of speech that does not interfere with the message being delivered and leaves adequate alternative channels of communication is permissible."[641]

Lawful regulation of speech varies depending on the category of speech. Properly tailored laws against obscenity and "fighting words" may also be held constitutional by the Court. In *Brandenburg v. Ohio*, (1969), the Supreme Court held that even speech advocating the use of force or of lawbreaking is constitutional, "except where such advocacy is directed to inciting or producing imminent lawless action and is likely to incite or produce such action."[642]

"Political speech receives the greatest protection under the First Amendment."[643] Laws regulating commercial speech are subject to an

---

638 Ibid.
639 Electronic Privacy Information Center. "Free Speech," EPIC.org. http://epic.org/free_speech/#Overview%20of%20Free%20Speech%20Protection. Internet.
640 Ibid.
641 "Glossary,"FirstAmendmentCenter.org.   http://www.firstamendmentcenter.org/about.aspx?item=glossary/ Internet.
642 Brandenburg v. Ohio, (1969), 395 U.S. 444.
643 Hudson, David L., Jr. "Hate Speech Online: Overview," FirstAmendmentCenter.org. http://www.firstamendmentcenter.org/speech/internet/topic.aspx?topic=internet_hate_speech. Internet.

intermediate level of scrutiny; any regulation must be carefully tailored to achieve a substantial government interest, and must be in proportion to the interest.[644]

Rodney Smolla, Dean of the University of Richmond School of Law, gives an insightful analysis of why America, in its constitutional law and in its people, has "powerfully internalized" freedom of speech as a prized societal value.

> Free speech is an indispensable tool of self-governance in a democratic society. Concurring in *Whitney v. California* (1927), Justice Louis Brandeis wrote that 'freedom to think as you will and to speak as you think are means indispensable to the discovery and spread of political truth.'[645]
>
> Optimistic Americans additionally believe that, over the long run, free speech actually improves our political decision-making. Just as Americans generally believe in free markets in economic matters, they generally believe in free markets when it comes to ideas, and this includes politics.
>
> On an individual level, speech is a means of participation, the vehicle through which individuals debate the issues of the day, cast their votes, and actively join in the process of decision-making that shape the polity...
>
> Freedom of speech is also an essential contributor to the American belief in a government confined by a system of check and balances, operating as a restraint on tyranny, corruption and ineptitude.[646]

Cass Sunstein's Big Brother World

Obama-appointee Cass Sunstein argues that America's version of free speech is too free. Sunstein believes speech rights emanate not from God or natural law, but from government. According to Sunstein, the American

---

644 Electronic Privacy Information Center. "Free Speech," EPIC.org. http://epic.org/free_ speech/#Overview%20of%20Free%20Speech%20Protection. Internet. The relative ease in most cases of identifying speech that has an expressly commercial purpose and content arguably provides a reasonable foundation for discriminating between commercial and political speech.
645 Smolla, Rodney. "Speech: Overview," FirstAmendmentCenter.org. http://www. firstamendmentcenter.org/speech/overview.aspx. Internet.
646 Ibid.

idea of an unregulated free speech marketplace is a myth because it fails to acknowledge or account for the effect of property laws and rules that underlie that marketplace. In his view, the real issue is how to regulate speech, using restrictions that maximize constitutional aspirations of free speech. Sunstein proposes displacing America's historic understandings of free speech, well-summarized by Smolla, with a New Deal regulatory paradigm. He prefers a big government command-and-control concept to the marketplace of ideas construct.

Obama anointed Sunstein as his "Regulatory Czar," formally known as the Administrator of the Office of Information and Regulatory Affairs (OIRA) in the Office of Management and Budget, a position created in 1980 and requiring Senate confirmation. As Regulatory Czar, Sunstein exercises oversight of thousands of regulations for the federal agencies.[647] According to the White House website, "OIRA reviews all collections of information by the federal government. OIRA also develops and oversees the implementation of government-wide policies in several areas, including information quality and statistical standards in addition to reviewing draft regulations under Executive Order 12866."[648]

Sunstein, a long-time close confidant of Obama, is widely praised for his analytical skills and creativity, but many of his views are extreme.[649] The Wall Street Journal described the breadth of Sunstein's post at OIRA:

Although obscure, the post wields outsize power. It oversees regulations throughout the government, from the Environmental Protection Agency to the Occupational Safety and Health Administration. Obama aides have said the job will be crucial as

---

647 The OMB defines a regulation as "a general statement issued by an agency, board, or commission that has the force and effect of law. ... Federal regulations specify the details and requirements necessary to implement and to enforce legislation enacted by Congress." "Regulations and the Rulemaking Process," RegInfo.gov. http://www.reginfo.gov/public/jsp/Utilities/faq.jsp. Internet.

648 "About OIRA," Whitehouse.gov. http://www.whitehouse.gov/omb/inforeg_administrator/. Internet. Executive Order 12866, signed by President Clinton in 1993, established uniform standards for the nation's regulatory system. "Executive Order 12866 of September 30, 1993," Archives.gov. http://www.archives.gov/federal-register/executive-orders/pdf/12866.pdf. Internet. The regulation established principles for rulemaking, including consideration of alternatives and cost-benefit analysis, and describes OIRA's role in the rulemaking process. Source: "Regulatory Review," RegInfo.gov. http://www.reginfo.gov/public/. Internet.

649 Sunstein has won support from UCLA professor Volokh, a self-described "moderate conservative" quoted earlier, as well as from Peter Van Doren, editor of the Cato Institute's Regulation magazine. Mak, Tim. "Who is Cass Sunstein?," FrumForum.com. http://www.frumforum.com/who-is-cass-sunstein. Internet.

the new administration overhauls financial-services regulations, attempts to pass universal health care and tries to forge a new approach to controlling emissions of greenhouse gases. [650]

Sunstein Says...

Sunstein has made his fair share of radical comments, including:

- Everything depends on whether and to what extent the animal in question is capable of suffering. If rats are able to suffer, then their interests are relevant to the question of how, and perhaps even whether, they can be expelled from houses.[1]
- We could even grant animals a right to bring suit without insisting that animals are persons, or that they are not property. A state could certainly confer rights on a pristine area, or a painting, and allow people to bring suit on its behalf, without therefore saying that area and that painting may not be owned.[2]
- Without taxes there would be no property. Without taxes, few of us would have any assets worth defending ... There is no liberty without dependency. That is why we should celebrate tax day.[3]
- In a nutshell, the New Deal helped vindicate a simple idea: No one really opposes government intervention. Even the people who most loudly denounce government interference depend on it every day.[4]

---

1 Sunstein, Cass R. and Martha C. Nussbaum ,Martha C. Animal Rights: Current Debates and new Directions. New York:Oxford University Press, 2004.
2 Sunstein, Cass R. and Martha C. Nussbaum ,Martha C. Animal Rights: Current Debates and new Directions. New York: Oxford University Press, 2004.
3 Holmes, Stephan Holmes and Sunstein, Cass. Sunstein, "Why We Should Celebrate Paying Taxes," The Chicago Tribune. http://home.uchicago.edu/~csunstei/celebrate.html. Internet.
4 Sunstein, Cass R. The Second Bill of Rights: FDR's Unfinished Revolution and Why We Need it More Than Ever. New York: Basic Books, New York, 2004.,

---

The wide-ranging scope of oversight Sunstein has as OIRA Administrator can be seen from a cursory look at a government website that details regulations currently under review by OIRA. For example, on February 28, 2010, OIRA's website, www.reginfo.gov/public/, listed 91 pending actions, including eighteen by the Environmental Protection Agency, nine by the Department of Agriculture, eight by the Department

---

650 Weisman, Jonathan and Bravin, Jess."Obama's Regulatory Czar Likely to Set a New Tone," Wall Street Journal. http://online.wsj.com/article/SB123138051682263203. html. Internet.

of Transportation, seven by HHS, seven by Department of Labor, and three by the DOJ[651]

Sunstein's Nudge: "Gently Force People"

In recent years, Sunstein has collaborated with behavioral economists such as Richard Thaler. Their 2008 book, *Nudge: Improving Decisions about Health, Wealth, and Happiness,"* advocates the application of empirical findings regarding human behavior to steer people's decisions in the direction government determines is best.

Sunstein and Thaler have coined the term, "choice architect" to describe their philosophy of government intervention in people's lives. According to the authors, government should use applied behavioral science to construct regulations that "help" people make improved choices (*Hi, we're from the government and we're here to help you*).

Trusting a mammoth government bureaucracy to "nudge" citizens into making improved decisions is like trusting a bull in a china shop to "nudge" a rare vase into the corner of the storefront window, only worse; unlike a vase, a person possesses both rights and feelings.

Applying New Deal Principles to the First Amendment

In his position at OIRA, Sunstein has the potential to impact constitutional rights across a spectrum of issues. Sunstein has written prolifically about free speech, and has advocated a wholesale restructuring of First Amendment principles:

> In light of astonishing economic and technological changes, we must doubt whether, as interpreted, the constitutional guarantee of free speech is adequately serving democratic goals. It is past time for a large-scale reassessment of the appropriate role of the First Amendment in the democratic process.[652]

Specifically, Sunstein advocates a reformulation of First Amendment law, relying in large part on what he terms the "Madisonian criteria for evaluating the system of free expression." He identifies these criteria as "the depth and breadth of attention to public issues and the degree of diversity of view." "The overriding goal of the reformulation is to reinvigorate

---

651 "Regulatory Review," RegInfo.gov. http://www.reginfo.gov/public/jsp/EO/eoDashboard.jsp?main_index=0&sub_index=0#. Internet.

652 Sunstein, Cass. Democracy and the Problem of Free Speech. New York: Simon and Schuster, 1995.

processes of democratic deliberation by ensuring greater attention to public issues and greater diversity of view."[653]

Sunstein proposes the application of "New Deal" economic regulatory principles in the constitutional law of free speech. He cites a host of New Deal regulatory reforms that restricted free speech in the area of commerce: Security and Exchange laws that restrict what people can say when they sell stocks and bonds, the FCC's public interest standard, the Food and Drug Administration's labeling requirements, the National Labor Relations Board restrictions on what may be said by employees, employers, and unions; and the Federal Trade Commissions' regulations related to unfair or deceptive trade practices.[654] Sunstein then concludes:

> The New Dealers conspicuously rejected the view that speech was absolutely immune from government control. Many of their agencies were a response to the perception that in light of the existing distribution of rights and entitlements, legal controls on speech may actually turn out to promote a well-functioning system of free expression. … We should not be so reflexively opposed to 'government regulation.' Speaker autonomy, made possible as it is by law, may not promote constitutional purposes. … With respect to freedom of expression, I think that American constitutionalism has failed precisely to the extent that it has not taken the New Deal reformation seriously enough.[655]

Sunstein's analysis is fundamentally flawed. According to Sunstein, law, a function of government, makes the very existence of an individual's free speech rights possible. Implicit in Sunstein's writings is a rejection of America's core foundational concept that certain rights are unalienable, given to every person by the Creator. Among these are "life, liberty, and the pursuit of happiness." These rights are not gifts of government, but of God alone. Government has no right to take away what it has not given.

Sunstein further argues that "speaker autonomy may not serve constitutional purposes," but since speaker autonomy, or a personal right of free speech, *is* a core constitutional purpose, Sunstein's statement is self-contradicting. It is one thing to argue that a person does not promote constitutional purposes when he or she abuses a constitutional right; it

---

653 Ibid.
654 Ibid.
655 Ibid.

is quite another to contend that the right itself does not promote such purposes.

The core of Sunstein's argument is that New Deal commerce-related speech restrictions show how government can legally exert control over speech in order to improve the functionality of the free speech system. The views espoused by Supreme Court Justices Lewis Brandeis and Oliver Wendell Holmes, who served on the Court in the first half of the twentieth century, have helped shaped modern free speech jurisprudence. Each argued that government could not ban political speech merely because the speech was dangerous. In his famous dissent in *Abrams v. United States* (1919), Holmes advocated a marketplace metaphor for evaluating free speech issues.[656] The metaphor has since served as the Court's pole star, but Sunstein rejects it outright in favor of government regulation of speech, purportedly to advance ideals of deliberative democracy.

> A New Deal for speech would draw on Justice Brandeis' insistence on the role of free speech in promoting political deliberation and citizenship. It would reject Holmes' 'marketplace' conception of free speech, a conception that disserves the aspirations of those who wrote America's founding document.[657]

Sunstein relies heavily on what he terms Justice Brandeis's "greatest opinion," given in *Whitney v. California* (1927). Brandeis concluded that the founders did not "exalt order at the cost of liberty" or "fear political change." The antidote to noxious speech was always more speech, not less, except in the case of a clear and present danger of an imminent threat: an emergency in which an evil would befall before an opportunity for discussion could operate to avert the evil.[658] Sunstein turns Brandeis' opinion on its head, concluding: "There is no market metaphor here. Brandeis does not speak of 'free trade.' Brandeis's opinion emphasizes not all speech, but the distinctive properties of political discussion and political debate."[659]

Far from rejecting the metaphor, Brandeis praised the indispensable, truth-generating role freedom of thought and speech plays in the political process. But Sunstein wants to reshape the framework of American free

---

656 Abrams v. United States (1919) 250 U.S. 616.
657 Sunstein, Cass. Democracy and the Problem of Free Speech. New York: Simon and Schuster (1995).
658 Whitney v. California, 274 U.S. 357 (1927).
659 Sunstein, Cass. Democracy and the Problem of Free Speech. New York: Simon and Schuster (1995).

speech jurisprudence by scrapping the marketplace of ideas construct in favor of Brandeis' supposed elevation of deliberative political debate over other political speech that the government deems less deliberative. In the name of strengthening America's political system, Sunstein wants to exert more government control of speech. He fails to make the case. The views of both Holmes and Brandeis actually undermine Sunstein's conclusion.

For example, SEC laws regulating what can be said in the buying and selling of stocks illustrate the justices' prerequisite that, in light of First Amendment protections, only a clear and present, imminent danger of harm can justify the regulation of speech. The stock market moves with lightning speed. Insider trading laws operate to secure the free and timely flow of pertinent information. Absent such laws, corporate insiders and their privileged friends could take unfair advantage of market-relevant company news before releasing the information to other stockholders. Insiders could move first in the market, instantly harming other stockholders, and thus nullifying the potential curative effect of more speech (i.e., once the news reached the rest of the shareholders, it would be too late for them to act.) Similarly, false information, once disseminated, does immediate and irreparable harm to stock traders who rely upon it. There is no time for more speech to remedy the immediate harm of the noxious speech.

Political speech operates in a different realm. Damage to a politician's reputation from defamatory speech can be immediate, but, unlike the loss from a stock transaction, the politician has a host of legal and practical remedies, including rebutting the charges, demanding a retraction, and threatening or filing a lawsuit. Time and more speech are potentially curative.

Similarly, misleading or false information regarding an issue of public concern can have an immediate effect on public opinion or upon the prospects for proposed legislation, but the political process is deliberative by design. There is time for more speech to overcome the noxious speech; therefore, under Brandeis' framework more speech, not regulations restricting speech, is the constitutional remedy.[660] Before becoming law, a bill must pass both chambers, be reconciled into one bill, pass another vote, and receive presidential approval. There is time for the marketplace

---

660 Politicians attempt to short-circuit the deliberative political process by cultivating a climate of fear and crisis. They call for votes on bills before the public has an opportunity even to read the bill; even before the politician has read the bill. The public is rarely fooled. When citizens see such brazen disregard for the process and for the public, they voice their concerns and demand a fuller airing of the issue. The health care bill is a perfect example.

of ideas to work. Sunstein's extrapolation from the economic marketplace to the political marketplace fails to account for this disparity in time frames. Furthermore, insider trading laws are narrowly tailored to prevent insiders from exploiting private company information in a way that gives them an unfair competitive advantage. The context of political speech is not analogous to the narrow context of securities law.

With regard to other speech restrictions that were a part of FDR's New Deal program, some, such as the FTC's regulations on deceptive trade practices, functioned to prevent a fraud from being perpetrated on the public. Con artists, whether individuals or businesses, have never found First Amendment cover for bilking unsuspecting victims. Further, the specific context of each example prevents generalization to speech as a broad category.

A Two-Tier First Amendment?

Finally, Sunstein advocates a constitutional preference for certain kinds of political speech, again drawing upon his misreading of Brandeis' theory of free speech. As support for his radical proposition, he points to the Court's existing, two-tiered approach, restricting certain kinds of harmful speech and affording greater protection to political speech than to commercial speech.

> The law now faces new constitutional problems raised by campaign finance laws, hate speech, pornography, rights of access to the media and to public places, and government funds accompanied by conditions on speech. These problems have shattered old alliances, and they promise to generate new understandings of the theory and practice of freedom of expression.[661]

Specifically, Sunstein believes government should "place a special premium on attention to public issues and exposure to diverse political views."[662] Under Sunstein's two-tiered free speech theory, government would regulate in favor of certain subcategories of political speech, such as diverse speech, local speech, and other speech that promotes constitutional aspirations, as determined by the government. Political speech that fell outside of the government-favored categories, as determined by legislation,

---

661 Sunstein, Cass. Democracy and the Problem of Free Speech. New York: Simon and Schuster,(1995).
662 Ibid.

regulation, or judicial fiat, would receive a lower level of First Amendment protection. In this scheme, unelected government regulators, such as Sunstein, would determine whether a particular expression of speech met the new standards for preferential First Amendment protection.

Unfortunately, Sunstein fails to keep paramount the true core of the First Amendment guarantee: the unalienable right of humans to live free by making their own life choices, including the right of what to say and what to hear. He views personal autonomy as just one of many social goals that might be emphasized in developing a free speech theory and concludes that the value of speech in supporting democratic ideals determines whether it deserves heightened government protection:

> I have suggested that a two-tier First Amendment will be superior to the alternatives ... We might emphasize autonomy, self-development, or the many other social goals likely to be promoted by the free speech guarantee. But of all the possible standards for distinguishing between forms of speech, I suggest that an emphasis on democracy and politics is best ... For present purposes I mean to treat speech as political when it is both intended and received as a contribution to public deliberation about some issue.[663]

Sunstein's proposal is radical. Neither the language of the Constitution nor Supreme Court precedent offers support for such active government meddling in citizens' free speech rights. The government has no constitutional basis for artificially establishing preferred categories of political speech. Even Sunstein's proposed standard for determining what constitutes political speech is ill-conceived, if not nonsensical: since when does speech have to be welcomed by the listener as a "contribution to public deliberation" for it to count (or even to be allowed)? Most political speech is inherently adversarial, and is typically not warmly embraced by members of the opposing political party.

The Supreme Court is already highly protective of political speech, and rightly so, in light of its importance to the functioning of a constitutional republic. Sunstein himself acknowledges that "political speech never falls within [the categories of speech that are less protected or not protected at all] by the Supreme Court."[664] Ironically, in the name of promoting a better system for protecting free expression, Sunstein puts political speech, and all other kinds of speech, at risk. This is because he advocates government

663 Ibid.
664 Ibid.

intervention through regulation as the remedy, as his advocacy of a so-called New Deal for free speech makes clear.

Sunstein's two-tiered approach is both impractical and imprudent. In order to categorize speech in this way, government officials will first have to evaluate its content. There will always be the temptation for the government to protect political speech it deems favorable to itself; this is precisely what the Constitution forbids. Sunstein's government-mandated and administered political speech hierarchy would open the door to partisan manipulation and abuse by unelected government bureaucrats.

Sunstein cautions against using "the existence of an unjust status quo" to apply affirmative action principles to the area of free speech, since "(t)here is a serious risk that judicial or legislative decisions about the relative power of various groups, and about who is owed redistribution, will be biased and unreliable." He argues that "(i)nstead of allowing restrictions, we should encourage efforts to promote a better status quo," [665] but Sunstein's free speech theory, at least as applied, facilitates the very sorts of restrictions and redistributions he purports to reject. For example, FCC Chief Diversity Officer Mark Lloyd has openly lamented the conservative bent of most talk radio. In 2005, he addressed the issue of diversity at a conference on media reform and racial justice.

> We have really, truly good white people in important positions. And the fact of the matter is there are a limited number of those positions. And unless we are conscious of the need to have more people of color, gays, other people in those positions, we will not change the problem [applause]. But we're in a position where you have to say, "Who is going to step down so someone else can have power?"[666]

For Lloyd, diversity and localism, (subcategories of political speech Sunstein suggests should receive top-tier constitutional protection) are thinly-disguised artifices for silencing conservative talk radio hosts.

The marketplace of ideas metaphor may not be a perfect framework for a system of free speech, but it is far superior to Sunstein's heavy-handed substitute. The marketplace metaphor protects the dignity of the human spirit by recognizing that free speech is an unalienable right; it gives free

---

665 Ibid.
666 "FCC 'Diversity Czar': Few Things Frighten Americans More Than Dark Skin Black Men." http://www.breitbart.tv/fcc-%E2%80%98diversity-czar%E2%80%99-few-things-frighten-americans-more-than-%E2%80%98dark-skin-black-men%E2%80%99/.

speech space to pursue truth and advance self-governance; and it preserves free speech as a tool for citizens to check the encroachment of government power. Sunstein's two-tiered proposal makes speech merely a vehicle for government to use, or abuse, in advancing its definition of the public's interest. It increases government power and burdens citizens with more governmental restriction of their personal autonomy.

Sunstein's examples of how his proposal might impact various issues give weight to this conclusion. For example, he argues that in *Buckley v. Valeo* (1976), the Court was wrong in holding unconstitutional a limit on independent corporate expenditures in support or opposition to a candidate, but as the Court stated in *Buckley*, "the concept that government may restrict the speech of some elements of our society in order to enhance the relative voice of others is wholly foreign to the First Amendment."[667] In a decision consistent with *Buckley*, the Court in *Citizens United v. Federal Election Commission*, decided January 21, 2010, invalidated a provision of the 2002 McCain-Feingold law which barred corporations and unions from using their treasury funds to purchase "electioneering communications."[668] The Court has consistently declared that constitutional speech rights extend to corporations, and both cases safeguard political speech under the Court's strict scrutiny principle. Sunstein would instead allow the government to limit disfavored political speech according to its determination of the public interest.

In the area of hate speech, Sunstein writes, "A subject matter restriction on unprotected speech should probably be upheld if the legislature can plausibly argue that it is counteracting harms rather than ideas." This is a shockingly weak level of protection against government subject-matter restriction of speech. "Hate" and "plausible harm" are inherently malleable terms.

Sunstein even writes in favor of government subsidies to newspapers "that agree to cover substantive issues in a serious way." [669] Of course, such federal financial input would open wide the door to the government's control of any media on the receiving end of such taxpayer-funded subsidy.

---

667 Ibid; Buckley v. Valeo, 424 U.S. 1 (1976)
668 Citizens United v. Federal Election Commission (2010) No. 08-205, decided January 21, 2010.
669 Ibid.

Sunstein's Spine-Chilling Propaganda Proposal

Cass Sunstein's plans go far beyond regulatory efforts to chill speech which bureaucrats deem false or harmful. In 2008, while at Harvard Law School, Sunstein co-authored a paper in which he advocates that government "engage in cognitive infiltration of the groups that produce conspiracy theories ..."[670]

Sunstein unabashedly argues that the best way to increase citizens' faith in government officials is for the government to actively deceive Americans, in both cyber-space and real space. He suggests that government agents covertly disseminate propaganda in "chat rooms, online social networks, or even real-space groups." in order to undermine the credibility of government-alleged conspiracists. If Sunstein were to have his way, a citizen would have sound reason to wonder if the person he is communicating with online, or the person next to him at church or at a tea party gathering or a political meeting, was actually an undercover government agent.[671] In Sunstein's Orwellian world, even the truthfulness of a conspiracy may not inoculate its disseminators against a covert government disinformation campaign; he concedes only that "as a general rule, true accounts should not be undermined."[672]

In the name of quashing conspiracy theories, Sunstein advocates conspiratorial conduct on the part of the federal government. He defines a conspiracy theory as an effort to explain some event or practice by reference to the machinations of powerful people, who have also managed to conceal their role."[673] He acknowledges that some conspiracies are true, but assumes a "well-motivated government that aims to eliminate conspiracy theories ... if and only if social welfare is improved by doing so."[674] Sunstein explicitly – and conveniently – disavows any attempt to define the meaning of "social welfare." He implicitly trusts that government bureaucrats, and their paid covert agents, will exercise their anonymously exercised powers of deception for the good of the American people. The government will decide which conspiracies are false, which merit government response,

---

670 Harvard University Law School, Public Law & Legal Theory Research Paper Series, University of Chicago Law School Public Law & Legal Theory Research Paper Series, Paper No. 199, "Conspiracy Theories," by Cass R. Sunstein and Adrian Vermeule, preliminary draft, January 15, 2008, page 14 Link found at http://www.salon.com/news/opinion/glenn_greenwald/2010/01/15/sunstein
671 IBID, page 22
672 IBID, page 5
673 IBID, page 4
674 IBID, page 15

what the response will be, and who must sacrifice their rights for the supposed good of society.

In assuming a "well-motivated," or well-intentioned, government, Sunstein surrenders his entire argument; the whole genius of the U.S. Constitution is its system of *limited government,* which safeguards individual rights and protects against governmental abuses of power. Government is made up of people. People are not always well-intentioned. Even well-intentioned government officials, if given unchecked power, are capable of inflicting great personal harm upon the citizens of the United States.

In the working paper, Sunstein champions a broad implementation of his infiltration proposal.

> First, responding to more rather than fewer conspiracy theories has a kind of synergy benefit: it reduces the legitimating effect of responding to any one of them, because it dilutes the contrast with unrebutted theories. Second, we suggest a distinctive tactic for breaking up the hard core of extremists who supply conspiracy theories: cognitive infiltration of extremist groups, whereby government agents or their allies (acting either virtually or in real space and either openly or anonymously) will undermine the crippled epistemology of those who subscribe to such theories. They do so by planting doubts about the theories and stylized facts that circulate within such groups... .[675]

Given the current, understandable pervasiveness of public dissatisfaction and distrust of government, Sunstein's army of regulatory zealots would stay busy under his proposals. The virulent anti-citizen rhetoric that emanated from the halls of Congress and the White House in 2009 against the tea party movement and town hall attendees served as ample notice of government's desire to squelch dissent.

The range of governmental responses to conspiracy theories that Sunstein envisions is even more frightening.

> What can government do about conspiracy theories? ... We can readily imagine a series of possible responses. (1) Government might ban conspiracy theorizing. (2) Government might impose some kind of tax, financial or otherwise, on those who disseminate such theories. (3) Government might itself engage in counterspeech, marshaling arguments to discredit conspiracy

---

675 IBID, page 15

theories. (4) Government might formally hire credible private parties to engage in counterspeech. (5) Government might engage in informal communication with such parties, encouraging them to help. Each instrument has a distinctive set of potential effects, or costs and benefits, and each will have a place under imaginable conditions. However, our main policy idea is that government should engage in <u>cognitive infiltration of the groups that produce conspiracy theories</u>, which involves a mix of (3), (4) and (5) (*emphasis in original*).[676]

Aside from his Kafkaesque infiltration proposals, Sunstein believes there is a place in America, "under imaginable conditions," for spitting on the First Amendment by making it illegal even to develop a theory that explains an event or practice by the under-the-radar actions of powerful people. Not that Sunstein wants more government transparency; in the paper he argues for a diminished role generally for the courts in invoking statutes such as the Freedom of Information Act to force government disclosure of information related to a conspiracy theory. He concludes "there is little reason to believe that judges can improve on administrative choices in these situations."[677] Sunstein's conclusions rest on an entire panoply of illogical or disingenuous assumptions (that government bureaucrats withholding information are always well-intentioned, that plaintiffs who sue for release of information always do so to *rebut* a conspiracy theory, that the conspiracy theory is false, etc.).

The sure casualty of Sunstein's vision is *truth*. Sunstein imagines a world where a government-knows-best bureaucracy wields power to ban speech it deems harmful, even if it is true, and to disseminate speech it deems beneficial, even if it is false. Sunstein is well aware that governments are among the most persistent purveyors of false conspiracy theories; nevertheless, he is comfortable with government controlling the flow of, and response to, information related to all conspiracy theories, regardless of their origin. "(W)e note that real-world governments can instead be purveyors of conspiracy theories. ... But this would just be another case of a conspiracy theory circulating in the population, which might or might not be worth responding to ..."[678]

Sunstein ignores the elephant in the room: who monitors the government?

---

676 IBID, page 14
677 IBID, page 15
678 IBID, page 16

Writing at Salon.com, columnist Glenn Greenwald details the similarities of Sunstein's proposal with the Bush administration's recruitment of former generals to pose as "independent analysts" in the media while coordinating their statements with the Pentagon, or the administration's hiring of certain columnists to advocate pro-Bush policies without disclosing their contracts, or its hiring of a company to plant pro-U.S. articles in newspapers in Iraq while pretending the articles came from Iraqi citizens. He also cites the Obama administration's undisclosed payments of hundreds of thousands of dollars to MIT Professor Jonathan Gruber to provide consultation on the President's health care plan. Gruber played a major public relations role for the administration in advocating the health care plan, and both the media and the White House falsely held out Gruber as an "independent" or "objective" authority.[679]

Greenwald concludes that "there is a very strong case to make that what Sunstein is advocating is itself illegal under long-standing statutes prohibiting 'propaganda' within the U.S., aimed at American citizens..." Conservatives and liberals alike should heed his prescient warning:

> Covert government propaganda is exactly what Sunstein craves. ….
> What is most odious and revealing about Sunstein's worldview is his condescending, self-loving belief that 'false conspiracy theories' are largely the province of fringe, Internet masses and the Muslim world….
>
> The reason conspiracy theories resonate so much is precisely that people have learned – rationally – to distrust government actions and statements. Sunstein's proposed covert propaganda scheme is a perfect illustration of why that is. In other words, people don't trust government and 'conspiracy theories' are so pervasive precisely because government is typically filled with people like Cass Sunstein, who think that systematic deceit and government-sponsored manipulation are justified by their own Goodness and Superior Wisdom."[680]

---

679 "Obama confidant's spine-chilling proposal," by Glenn Greenwald, January 15, 2010
http://www.salon.com/news/opinion/glenn_greenwald/2010/01/15/sunstein
680 "Obama confidant's spine-chilling proposal," by Glenn Greenwald, January 15, 2010
http://www.salon.com/news/opinion/glenn_greenwald/2010/01/15/sunstein

Sunstein's "Excellent Idea": Chill Internet Speech

Regulatory Czar Sunstein may believe his "New Deal" regulatory approach will enhance important social goals and provide a unified theory of free speech, but powerful political figures undoubtedly see political opportunity – a mechanism for suppressing dissent and increasing governmental power. What does this portend for the future of the Internet? In his 2001 book, *Republic.com*, Sunstein contends that the Internet may weaken democracy because it easily allows citizens to network and communicate with others who share their own views and experiences. Yet the right to freely associate with others for the purpose of engaging in free speech is itself constitutionally protected. In *NAACP v. Alabama ex rel. Patterson* (1958), the Supreme Court held that the freedom to associate for the advancement of beliefs and ideas is constitutionally protected because it is inseparable from the First Amendment freedom of speech.[681]

Nonetheless, in Sunstein's view the new web-based social networking phenomenon poses a great danger to the Republic. He fears that by networking with others who share their views and opinions, people reinforce and cement their own biases, misconceptions, and false beliefs. Citing the harm done by the rapid spread of damaging information via the Internet, Sunstein warns of a future in which "people's beliefs are a product of social networks working as echo chambers in which false rumors spread like wildfire."[682]

A common theme running through Sunstein's writings is a keen distrust of the citizenry. The Internet has greatly enhanced the ability of citizens to communicate with other persons of varying races, nationalities, backgrounds and perspectives. It has also enabled persons to associate with like-minded individuals and groups. Sunstein views the latter not as a freedom to be celebrated but as a threat to be regulated:

> Democracy does best with what James Madison called a "yielding and accommodating spirit," and that spirit is at risk whenever people sort themselves into enclaves in which their own views and commitments are constantly affirmed ... Such sorting should not be identified with freedom, and much less with democratic self-government.[683]

---

681 NAAACP v. Alabama ex rel. Patterson, 357 U.S. 449 (1958).
682 Sunstein, Cass R. On Rumors: How Falsehoods Spread, Why We Believe Them, What Can Be Done. New York: Farrar, Straus, and Giroux (2009).
683 Sunstein, Cass R. Republic 2.0. Princeton: Princeton University Press (2007).

Sunstein views freedom of association as an oxymoron. His proposals go beyond narrowly tailored efforts to help existing laws function effectively in the web world. Sunstein wants new government regulations on free speech to elevate the level of Internet discourse. One such law, if passed, would chill free speech on the Internet. Sunstein believes that "whether you're a blogger or the *New York Times* or a Web hosting service – you should be held responsible even for what your comments say."[684] Web hosting services enable individuals and organizations to serve content to the Internet through their own web sites. Sunstein proposes a "notice and take down" law that would require bloggers and hosting services to "take down falsehoods upon notice."[685]

The long-standing, current libel standard requires proof of actual malice by those who write about public figures. Sunstein questions the wisdom of the current libel standard; his new Internet law would not require proof of libel. If, in the cyberspace regulator's opinion, a Web post was false, a "take down" notice would issue. If the accused did not remove the cited content, the matter would eventually be resolved in court.

For example, in the 2008 election Vice Presidential candidate Sarah Palin accused Barack Obama of "palling around with terrorists;" it was widely reported on the Internet. Under Sunstein's plan, a new bureaucracy in charge of cyberspace regulation would determine the veracity of the statement. Anyone who cannot recognize the limitless potential for governmental abuse posed by such a law is too trusting of government. One thing seems certain: lawyers would have a field day. Already overloaded courts would be buried beneath an avalanche of new cases.

The contentious and protracted health care debate highlights the problems implicit in Sunstein's proposed "notice and take down" Internet regulation. The administration and congressional representatives offered the public little more than a blizzard of half-truths and deceptions. Opponents of health care legislation repeatedly accused Congress and/ or the president of deceiving the public regarding the contents of the legislation, buried in thousands of pages of legalese. In return, Obama repeatedly accused critics of lying.

Sunstein's idea that government bureaucrats act as truth arbitrators is folly. The federal government cannot be trusted to tell the truth, much less act as the official truth moderator for the entire Internet. Determining what

---

684 Sunstein, Cass R. On Rumors: How Falsehoods Spread, Why We Believe Them, What Can Be Done. New York: Farrar, Straus, and Giroux (2009).
685 Ibid.

constitutes a legal falsehood would be problematic; those willing to host or post on the Internet under the Sunstein plan would shrink dramatically because Sunstein would hold Internet hosting services responsible for the content of the data sent through its servers (potentially billions of web pages). Every person with access to the Internet would pose a legal liability of the company.

Bloggers would perhaps suffer the most under such a law. Sunstein would argue that blogs could still blog, web hosting services could still host, media organizations and web sites could still provide community forums for public comment – they would just have to do so more responsibly. The policing burden imposed by such a law, along with the limitless potential for lawsuits, would have a devastating effect on free speech. Web forums would disappear faster than background information on Obama administration czars and radical political connections. Comment sections would be closed faster than GM dealerships. Bloggers would be forced to choose their words more carefully than White House press secretary Robert Gibbs (and with a much greater regard for the truth).

In *On Rumors*, Sunstein contemplates the positive social effects of increased regulation of Internet speech:

> We could also imagine a future in which those who spread false rumors are categorized as such, discounted and marginalized ... In such a future, people approach rumors skeptically even when they provide comfort and fit their own biases and predilections.[686]

Sunstein thinks chilling free speech is an "excellent idea"[687] because, as previously noted, he does not trust the 'marketplace of ideas' concept widely revered since the country's founding:

> It is true that the risk of a chilling effect has to be taken seriously. It is also true that on the Internet, you can try to correct a false rumor in an instant. But even in the age of the Internet, the marketplace of ideas can fail to produce truth; the social mechanisms explored here ensure that any marketplace will lead many people to accept destructive falsehoods. In extreme cases, such falsehoods can create contempt, fear, hatred, and even violence. Some kind of chilling

---

686 Ibid.
687 Ibid.

effect on damaging rumors is exceedingly important ... to ensure the proper functioning of democracy itself.[688]

The constitutional right to freedom of expression is fundamental to every form of freedom and a critical safeguard against government oppression. "The right of freely examining public characters and measures, and of free communication among the people thereon... has ever been justly deemed the only effectual guardian of every other right."[689]

Without a free press and a citizenry free to communicate with others of their own choosing, without threat of government sanction or censure, America would no longer be a free society.

---

688 Ibid.
689 Madison, James."Virginia Resolutions 24 December 1798." Documents of American History, Commmager, vol. 1 (182).

12

Freedom of Religion, Civil Liberties, and Antidiscrimination Law

"Congress shall make no law respecting an establishment of religion, or prohibiting the free exercise thereof, or abridging the freedom of speech, or of the press, or the right of the people peaceably to assemble, and to petition the Government for a redress of grievances."
-- Amendment 1, United States Constitution

Contrary to the thrust of much modern legal interpretation, the Constitution does not mandate the removal of Christianity, or any religion, from the public domain; historical evidence shows that the framers of the Constitution repudiated such a viewpoint. "The First Amendment has often been understood to limit religious freedom in ways never imagined by the late eighteenth dissenters who demanded constitutional guarantees of religious liberty."[690]

The concept of a "wall of separation between Church and State" appears nowhere in the Constitution. It entered the American historical record more than a decade after the Constitution was ratified, as an obscure phrase in a personal letter written by Jefferson to the Danbury Baptist Association.[691] It took nearly nine decades for the phrase to first enter the lexicon of Supreme Court jurisprudence, and it was mentioned only once until Justice Black, writing in *Everson v. Board of Education* (1947), made Jefferson's separation metaphor the lynchpin of modern Establishment Clause jurisprudence.[692] Many of the founders emigrated here to gain religious freedom; religious statements or pronouncements by political figures in early America were commonplace and accepted.

---

690 Hamburger, Philip. Separation of Church and State. Cambridge: Harvard College (2002).
691 Ibid.
692 Ibid. See also Everson v. Board of Education, 330 U.S. 1 (1947)

The vast majority of the founders were devout Christians who believed that the general principles of Christianity were vital to the American system of government. The American concept of religious freedom is rooted in the belief that each person has a right to practice his faith and express his beliefs in society. As such, the founders were united in their commitment to establish a government that protected the individual's freedom of religion. The modern view that the First Amendment ensures freedom from religion grossly distorts the legislative intent of the Amendment. In fact, Jefferson openly scoffed at the notion of freedom from religion: "The legitimate powers of government extend to such acts only as are injurious to others. But it does me no injury for my neighbour to say that there are twenty gods or no god. It neither picks my pocket nor breaks my leg."[693]

Criminalizing Christianity

In 2008, the American Civil Liberties Union (ACLU) filed a lawsuit on behalf of two Florida students against Santa Rosa County Schools and Pace High School Principal Frank Lay alleging that school employees "persistently and persuasively promote their personal religious beliefs in the public schools and at school events." The School Board settled out of court with the ACLU and agreed to prohibit its employees from promoting or sponsoring prayers during school events.[1]

In January 2009, U.S. District Judge M. Casey Rodgers entered a 90 day injunction prohibiting school employees from promoting or appearing to promote religion in school-related activities. Under Rodgers's order, school officials:

- may not advance, endorse, participate in, or cause prayers;
- must prohibit non-student third parties from offering a prayer, invocation, benediction, or religious remark during, or in conjunction with, a school event;
- must instruct speakers at school events that their messages must exclude prayer; and
- shall not offer a prayer, recite a prayer alongside or with students, or posture in a manner that is likely to be perceived as an endorsement of the prayer, (e.g. bowing their heads, kneeling, or folding their hands).

In 2009, Lay and Pace High School Athletic Director Robert Freeman were charged with criminal contempt for willfully violating the court order after Freeman said grace at a booster luncheon at Lay's request. The criminal charges carried up to a $5000 fine and six-month jail term.

---

1   Duin, Julia. "School Prayer Charges Stir Protests." *Washington Times,* August 14, 2009.

---

693 Bassani, Luigi Marco. "Life, Liberty, and...:Jefferson on Property Rights." Journal of Libertarian Studies 1, no. 18 (2004): 31-87. Ludwig von Mises Institute.

After a seven hour trial and $500,000 in legal fees, Rodgers ruled that Lay and Freeman were not guilty because they had not intentionally violated the court order.[2]

It is a sobering day for the American justice system when a defendant avoids jail because his prayers lacked criminal intent.

2   "Florida high school officials' prayer did not violate court order, judge rules." *Catholic News Agency*, September 19, 2009.

To safeguard religious freedom, the framers passed two separate clauses which make up the first sixteen words of the First Amendment: "Congress shall make no law respecting an establishment of religion; or prohibiting the free exercise thereof." The first clause is known as the "Establishment Clause" and the second as the "Free Exercise Clause."[694] There has been much debate regarding the interpretation of these clauses, with a general break between two camps: those who emphasize the Establishment Clause to advocate a strict wall of separation between church and state, and those who emphasize the Free Exercise Clause to advocate state accommodation of a person's right to freely practice her faith without interference from government. The error in these interpretations is that the two clauses were never intended to work in isolation from, or in opposition to, one another; they were explicitly adopted so that together they would protect religious freedom in America.

Madison, who chaired the House conference committee on the Bill of Rights, originally proposed the following text for the First Amendment in a 1789 speech in the House: "The civil rights of none shall be abridged on account of religious belief or worship, nor shall any national religion be established, nor shall the full and equal rights of conscience be in any manner, or on any pretext infringed."[695]

Madison wanted the First Amendment to prohibit the federal government from establishing a national religion, and he even suggested in House debate the insertion of the word "national" in order to "point the amendment directly to the object it was intended to prevent."[696] He also intended for the amendment to secure freedom of conscience so that each citizen could freely define her religious convictions, beliefs and practices. Madison objected to the appropriation of federal funds "for the use and

694   "Constitution of the United States," Amendment I.
695   "FindLaw for Legal Professionals: Religion," Findlaw.com. http://caselaw.lp.findlaw.com/data/constitution/amendment01/01.html
696   Ibid.

support of religious societies," as a violation of the Establishment Clause, as demonstrated in his presidential veto of an 1811 bill which granted a parcel of land for a church in Salem, Massachusetts.[697]

Jefferson wrote in 1808 that he believed the federal government was prohibited from "intermeddling with religious institutions, their doctrines, discipline, or exercises." As support he cited both the First and the Tenth Amendments, concluding, "Certainly, no power to prescribe any religious exercise or to assume authority in any religious discipline has been delegated to the General [federal] Government. It must then rest with the States."[698]

Originally the First Amendment applied only to the federal government. Though the idea seems unfathomable now, the First Amendment did not prohibit states from establishing state churches, and several of them did – often with severe penalties for noncomformists.[699] Cognizant of this inglorious history, the framers sought to secure protection against the establishment of a national church or religion. Some arguably also viewed it as a safeguard to prevent discrimination among Christian sects.[700] Though they did not extend First Amendment protections to state law, they did intend to prevent the federal government from using its power to force religious orthodoxy upon the citizens.

> Whilst we assert for ourselves a freedom to embrace, to profess and to observe the Religion, which we believe to be of divine origin, we cannot deny an equal freedom to those whose minds have not yet yielded to the evidence, which has convinced us. If this freedom

---

697 Ibid.

698 Barton, David. Original Intent: The Courts, the Constitution, and Religion. Aledo: WallBuilder Press (1997).

699 Levin, Mark. Men in Black: How the Supreme Courtis Destroying America. New York: Regnery (2006). In colonial Massachusetts (Puritan church, later Congregationalist), Virginia (Anglican church), and Connecticut (Congregationalist church), the state established church used the power of law to force its religious orthodoxy upon all citizens. Such laws varied from state to state, but typically included payment of taxes to support the established church and other religiously discriminatory policies. For example, in Connecticut, penalties were imposed for failure to attend church on Sunday or to observe public fasts and thanksgivings. Clergy of other denominations faced numerous restrictions and their parishioners, as well as other dissenters, were prevented from holding public office. In Virginia, "a series of anti-Quaker laws passed in the late 1600s criminalized the refusal of Quakers to baptize their children, prohibited their assembly, and provided for their execution if they returned after expulsion."

700 Wallace v. Jaffree, 472 U.S. 38 (1985)

be abused, it is an offence against God, not against man: To God, therefore, not to man, must an account of it be rendered.[701]

The founders never intended that general encouragement of religion by government, without financial support, automatically constitute an establishment of religion, but whether intended or not, the practical effect of Supreme Court decisions over the past fifty years has been hostility towards Christianity. David Barton, in *Original Intent: The Courts, the Constitution, and Religion,* concludes that even Jefferson and Franklin, two founders oft-cited for holding beliefs outside of orthodox Christianity, believed the principles of Christianity were a critical support to government: "The strongest civil code is impotent against malicious behavior unless the heart itself can be restrained, and even Benjamin Franklin joined Thomas Jefferson (two of the least religiously orthodox founders) in believing that the teachings of Christianity best accomplished that goal."[702]

The 1853-1854 House and Senate Judiciary Committee Reports further addressed the establishment issue. The House Judiciary Committee's report noted that establishment of religion must have a creed, rites, ordinances and ministers, while the Senate Judiciary Committee argued that framers intended to prohibit a state-funded religious establishment like the Church of England.[703] Of the two committees, the Senate's came much closer to the mark than the House's in expressing the intentions of the framers, but both correctly expressed the framers' aversion to the idea that the First Amendment be used against religion itself, or to "war against Christianity."

Based on Jefferson's language in the Declaration of Independence and the influence of concepts of natural law upon the founders, some scholars ground constitutional ideas of human freedom in Jefferson's concept of "Nature's God." Judge Andrew P. Napolitano makes the case for natural law as the primary philosophy underpinning the Constitution:

> That freedom comes not from government, not from the consent of the governed, not from the community, but from God and is inherent to our humanity has profound effects on modern jurisprudence. It means that our basic freedoms – such as freedom of the press, freedom of speech, freedom of religion, freedom of association, freedom to travel, and freedom from arbitrary

---

701 Madison, James. "Memorial and Remonstrance Against Religious Assessments." http://www.firstfreedom.org/PDF/Memorial_Remonstrance.pdf
702 Barton, David. Original Intent: The Courts, the Constitution, and Religion. Aledo: WallBuilder Press (1997).
703 Ibid.

restraints - cannot be taken away by the government unless we are convicted of violating Natural Law, and the government can only convict us if it follows what is called "procedural due process. [704]

Though he perhaps stretches the limits of what can historically or logically be attributed to natural law, Napolitano's most basic assertion is sound: the founders sought to protect America from positivistic encroachments against fundamental rights by grounding those rights not in government, but in God.

Jefferson's wall was a not a boundary between government and religion; instead, "Jefferson placed the federal government on one side of his wall and state governments and churches on the other."[705] Though the Supreme Court first misinterpreted the phrase in an 1879 criminal appeal ruling,[706] the metaphor made its modern debut in a 1947 Establishment Clause challenge to a New Jersey program that used state tax dollars to reimburse parents of Catholic schoolchildren for transportation to parochial schools.[707]

By the 1960s, the Court was using the wall of separation metaphor to keep prayer out of schools. The Court banned government-composed, voluntary prayer at the beginning of the school day in 1962,[708] eliminated a designated minute of silence "for meditation or silent prayer" in 1985,[709] and ruled in 1992 that a prayer offered by a clergy member at a public school graduation ceremony violated the Establishment Clause.[710] In 2000, the Supreme Court decided that a school district policy permitting student-led, student-initiated prayer at football games violated the Establishment Clause.[711]

---

704 Napolitano, Andrew J. The Constitution in Exile: how the federal government has seized power by rewriting the supreme law of the land. Nashville: Nelson Current (2006).

705 Dreisbach, Daniel L. "The Mythical "Wall of Separation": How a Misused Metaphor Changed Church–State Law, Policy, and Discourse," Heritage.org. http://www.heritage.org/Research/PoliticalPhilosophy/fp6.cfm#_ftnref3

706 Reynolds v. United States. 98 U.S. 145 (1878)

707 Everson v. Board of Education, 330 U.S. 1 (1947). The Court found that the program did not breach the wall of separation between church and state because it was a "general program to help parents get their children, regardless of their religion, safely and expeditiously to and from accredited schools."

708 Engel v. Vitale, 370 U.S. 421 (1962).Proscribed a law requiring use of government-composed, nonsectarian prayer at beginning of school day, even if pupils are allowed to remain silent or be excused while prayer is being read.

709 Wallace v. Jaffree 472 U.S. 38 (1985) Held: Alabama statute authorizing a 1-minute period of silence in all public schools "for meditation or silent prayer" violated the Establishment Clause. Rationale: "The First Amendment requires that a statute must be invalidated if it is entirely motivated by a purpose to advance religion."

710 Lee v. Weisman, 505 U.S. 577 (1992) Held: "Including clergy who offer prayers as part of an official public school graduation ceremony is forbidden by the Establishment Clause."

711 Santa Fe Independent School District v. Doe, 530 U.S. 290 (2000).

The Establishment Clause, created to prevent the religious majority from using the government to force its beliefs upon others, is now used as justification for government discrimination against persons of faith, particularly Christians. For example, the 2009 stimulus bill, which included billions of dollars for use in higher education, included a provision that banned funds from being used for the "modernization, renovation, or repair" of facilities that allow "sectarian instruction, religious worship or a school or department of divinity."[712] Rather than prohibiting the use of funds for the purpose of supporting religion, the bill goes further by pointedly denying funds for the repair or maintenance of any facility that allows religious instruction or worship. The language of the bill is hostile to religion and arguably prohibited by the Free Exercise clause.[713]

In October 2009 Obama signed into law a hate crimes bill that added gender identity and sexual orientation as protected classes of minorities under existing federal hate crime laws. Similar legislation in Europe and Canada has resulted in the short-term jailing of Christian pastors for expressing the view that homosexual acts are in violation of biblical standards.[714]

The Supreme Court's ruling in *Christian Legal Society v. Martinez*, decided June 28, 2010, is a serious setback to Americans' historic freedoms of religion, speech, and association. In that case, the Hastings College of Law, a school within the University of California public school system, rejected an application in 2004 by the Christian Legal Society (CLS) to become a registered student organization because CLS required that its members affirm and abide by certain religious beliefs, in violation of the school's nondiscrimination policy. Registered groups are allowed to meet on university grounds and to access multiple channels of communication (posting messages on designated bulletin boards, sending mass emails to students, distributing information through the Student Information Center, etc.). Registered groups may also apply for limited funds, which amount to less than $85 per registered group.

Hastings had more than 60 registered groups during the 2004-2005 school year, including the Hastings Jewish Law Students Association, the Hastings Association of Muslim Law Students, the Black Law Students

---

712 Corbin, Christina."Republican Senator Proposes Amendment to Overturn Ban on Cash for Schools that Host Faith Forums," FoxNews.com. http://www.foxnews.com/ politics/2009/02/05/republican-senator-calls-provision-stimulus-attack-religion/

713 Good News Club v. Milford Central School, 533 U.S. 98 (2001)

714 "Obama signs hate crimes bill into law," by Jon Ward, October 29, 2009 http:// www.washingtontimes.com/news/2009/oct/29/obama-signs-hate-crimes-bill-into- law/?page=1

Association, and the Clara Foltz Feminist Association. Many of the registered groups were dedicated to expressing a particular message or viewpoint.

In a dissent joined by Justices Scalia and Thomas, Justice Alito noted that at the time of the school's rejection, "Hastings routinely registered student groups with bylaws limiting membership and leadership positions to those who agreed with the groups' viewpoints." Hastings used its nondiscrimination policy as a pretext for discriminating against religious viewpoints with which it disagreed, as Alito explained:

> As Hastings stated in its answer, the Nondiscrimination Policy 'permit[ted] political, social, and cultural student organizations to select officers and members who are dedicated to a particular set of ideals or beliefs.' App. 93. But the policy singled out one category of expressive associations for disfavored treatment: groups formed to express a religious message. Only religious groups were required to admit students who did not share their views. An environmentalist group was not required to admit students who rejected global warming. An animal rights group was not obligated to accept students who supported the use of animals to test cosmetics. But CLS was required to admit avowed atheists. This was patent viewpoint discrimination."[715]

Discrimination against religious groups is not confined to the Courts, Congress and college campuses. According to the Alliance Defense Fund (ADF), a legal alliance founded in 1994 by Christian leaders to defend religious freedom in America's courts, more than 750 public facilities across the country have policies that restrict or ban access to public meeting rooms for religious purposes. In June 2010, ADF sent letters to 151 governmental entities, primarily public libraries and school districts, urging them to amend the policies. ADF Senior Legal Counsel Joel Oster summarized the constitutional basis for the letter:

> Christians shouldn't be excluded and restricted from using public meeting rooms and other facilities simply because they plan to express a Christian viewpoint. The Constitution prohibits the government from deciding who can and cannot use space based upon which viewpoints are being discussed during those meetings. Public officials can't give preferential treatment to some views over others."[716]

---

715 *Christian Legal Society v. Martinez* (2010) http://www.supremecourt.gov/opinions/09pdf/08-1371 .pdf
716 Alliance Defence Fund, June 8, 2010, http://www.adfmedia.org/News/PRDetail/4065

The historical record shows that the First Amendment was designed to set boundaries between the federal government and religious institutions, but it did not erect an impenetrable wall of separation, a legal fiction that has led the Court to sanction discrimination against Christian individuals and groups seeking to exercise First Amendment rights. By contrast, the Court has not applied the wall of separation rhetoric to individuals and groups whose belief systems are hostile to Christianity, such as atheism and secular humanism. The so-called wall of separation between church and state is a "misleading metaphor" that has been abused to marshal a judicial attack against religion never intended by the founders. Rehnquist, dissenting in *Wallace v. Jaffree*, 472 U.S. 38 (1985) explains:

> It is impossible to build sound constitutional doctrine upon a mistaken understanding of constitutional history, but unfortunately the Establishment Clause has been expressly freighted with Jefferson's misleading metaphor for nearly 40 years. Thomas Jefferson was of course in France at the time the constitutional Amendments known as the Bill of Rights were passed by Congress and ratified by the States. His letter to the Danbury Baptist Association was a short note of courtesy, written 14 years after the Amendments were passed by Congress. He would seem to any detached observer as a less than ideal source of contemporary history as to the meaning of the Religion Clauses of the First Amendment.[717]

After the Civil War, the states ratified the Fourteenth Amendment to ensure that former slaves were afforded the full protection of the laws of the land. It read in part, "no state ... shall deprive any person of life, liberty, or property without due process of law...." In 1947 the Supreme Court appropriated the Due Process Clause of the Fourteenth Amendment to declare the Establishment Clause applicable to state action as well as federal action.

Over the last 65 years, the Supreme Court has drifted away from the founders' intent on religious freedom issues. The Court frequently struggles to find neutral ground in religious freedom cases, neither interfering with religious exercise nor promoting religion. The notion of neutrality has proved to be, at its core, a myth. The First Amendment was never designed to require neutrality on the part of government between religion

---

717 Wallace v. Jaffree, 472 U.S. 38 (1985).

and secularism, or between religion and irreligion.[718] Unfortunately, the Supreme Court has used the Establishment Clause to neuter the Free Exercise Clause, resulting in anti-Christian discrimination and alarming government restrictions on the free exercise of religion.

Complicating matters is the drastic change in the relationship between government and education over the last 200 years. At America's inception, Christian instruction was the primary purpose of education. The founders believed that education, including instruction in virtue, was indispensable.[719] David Limbaugh, author of *Persecution: How Liberals are Waging War Against Christianity*, writes:

> To the extent that we can imagine public schools being endorsed by the founders, we can be certain that they would not have objected to religious instruction, but would have insisted on it. If the founders could have anticipated that our schools would become a government near-monopoly and that the Establishment Clause would be stretched beyond recognition to prohibit Christian instruction, I think it's safe to say they would have opposed public education altogether.[720]

Public schools today are caught in the crossfire of a raging cultural battle. Since public education is funded through both federal and state monies, courts have become disturbingly immersed in the minutiae of public school life. In some public schools the mere mention of the word "God" prompts First Amendment alarms among educators and activists. Those who use strict separation of church and state as a weapon against every public expression of Christianity ignore the irony that there is no more invasive state intermeddling into the personal religious lives of citizens than that which exists today. For public school teachers and city, county, state, and federal employees especially, their free exercise of religion protection has been nullified by the Court's contorted interpretation of the Establishment Clause.

---

718 Wallace v. Jaffree, 472 U.S. 38 (1985).
719 Barton, David. Original Intent: The Courts, the Constitution, and Religion. Aledo: WallBuilder Press (1997). Perhaps the best historical proof of this is found in the Northwest Ordinance, which set forth the requirements of statehood for prospective territories. Approved by the same Congress that drafted the First Amendment, it states in part: "Religion, morality, and knowledge, being necessary to good government and the happiness of mankind, schools and the means of education shall forever be encouraged."
720 Limbaugh, David. Persecution, Regenery Publishing, Washington, D.C., Copyright 2003 by David Limbaugh. Page xii

The Islam Experiment

In 2006, seventh-graders in a California public school participated in a three-week indoctrination in the religion of Islam using an interactive educational module. The "Student Guide" portion of the module, titled, "Islam: A simulation of Islamic history and culture," included the following instruction to students:

> From the beginning, you and your classmates will become Muslims. You will be a member of a caravan starting from a trading center based around an Islamic city. The task of each caravan group is to be the first group to complete a pilgrimage to Mecca, the holiest of Islamic cities ... This pilgrimage or 'haij' is a requirement of all faithful Muslims once in their lifetime.[1]

As part of the simulation, the teacher read Muslim prayers and the Qur'an to the class and required students to recite a line from a Muslim prayer, such as "In the name of God, Most Gracious, Most Merciful," before leaving class each day. Concerned parents filed a lawsuit, and the case went to the United States District Court for the Northern District of California.[41] The Court issued a summary judgment in favor of the school district, concluding: "Students did not perform the actual five pillars of faith in their class .... Role-playing activities which are not in actuality the practice of a religion do not violate the Establishment Clause."[2]

The infamously liberal Ninth Circuit Court of Appeals upheld the ruling and the U.S. Supreme Court refused to hear the appeal. It is difficult to escape the conclusion that the Supreme Court has endorsed a double standard, exposing the tiniest hint of Christian influence to the strictest scrutiny while endorsing the coercion of students into the essential tenets of Islam, including praying to Allah.

---

1   Eklund v. Byron Union School District. http://www.blessedcause.org/protest/Islam%20 Ruling%2012-05-03.pdf In its ruling filed December 5, 2003, the Court described a number of undisputed facts, including the following: The teacher distributed copies of the "Student Guide" portion of the Islam module to students. Students were encouraged to choose a Muslim name to facilitate role-playing. For the first two pillars of the Muslim faith, the teacher read Muslim prayers and portions of the Qu'ran aloud in class and required student groups to recite a line from a Muslim prayer on their way out of class each day, such as 'In the name of God, Most Gracious, Most Merciful,' and make banners, some of which included the prayer. The teacher required the students to fulfill the third and fourth pillars of the Muslim faith, which consisted of fasting and fulfilling the Muslim requirement of Zakaat by performing community service. To fulfill the fifth pillar of the Muslim faith, the students were required to participate in a simulated pilgrimage to Mecca by responding to informational fact cards categorized as "trivia, truth, or fiction." Truth cards contained statements of Muslim belief, such as "The Holy Qu'ran is God's Word as revealed through the prophet Muhammed through archangel Gabriel," without any prequalification such as "Muslims believe." The students were encouraged to dress up in Arabic style clothing for the group presentations.

2   Ibid.

Neither teachers nor students are required by the Constitution to shed their religion before stepping on public school property. The Constitution's Free Exercise Clause exists to guarantee Americans the right to freely exercise their religion; nowhere does it limit that freedom to the private sphere. It is absurd to hold that the Establishment Clause is triggered whenever teachers reference their faith or give a history lesson that references God or religion (though First Amendment issues *are* raised by the kind of intense, coercive indoctrination described in the preceding sidebar). It is even more absurd to hold that *students* act as de facto agents of the government in violation of the Establishment Clause whenever they pray or converse about God in a public school setting.

In the name of church-state separation, the majority of public school textbooks have eliminated most or all of America's rich religious history. School districts, fearful of legal action from anti-Christian activists, adopt absurdly restrictive policies that effectively intimidate teachers into silence regarding anything that dares mention God or religion. Thus, by omission, students are led to believe the lie that America's founders were either atheists or apathetic about religious matters.

A Judeo-Christian Heritage

Even Obama acknowledges that many of America's ideals are founded upon Judeo-Christian principles. Those principles have historically been applied in a fashion far from perfect. Christian political leaders have at times twisted Scripture and reason in pursuit of unjust ends. Christian educators have often failed to exhibit sensitivity for the feelings and rights of persons with differing backgrounds and religious views. In responding to religious discrimination against them, Christians have too often responded in an unchristian manner, forgetting Jesus' admonition to "love one another as I have loved you."

And yet, those who long for a day when the public venue will be free of Christianity may come to rue that day, if and when it arrives, for it is those same Judeo-Christian values that were instrumental in the establishment of the First Amendment freedoms Americans enjoy. The founders believed that an America set adrift from those principles would eventually succumb to tyranny.

At the core of those principles is simply this: that every person is a unique creation of a Sovereign Creator. Therefore, every person, regardless of ethnicity, gender, income, status, disability, sexual orientation, religious belief or anything else, is a person of sacred worth, entitled to the basic unalienable rights that define freedom. Believers and unbelievers alike suffer when government, under the rubric of collectivism, progressivism, utopianism, or any other -ism, tramples individual liberties for the so-called greater good.

The Declaration of Independence documents the founders' understanding of the supportive role of religious belief in America's system of governance. Jefferson grounded Americans' fundamental rights in God. The founding fathers flatly rejected any assertion that government bestowed rights upon citizens according to its discretion. The framers were apprehensive of the inherent dangers of state endorsement of any one religion, but they never intended for the First Amendment to be used as a pretext for intimidating persons of faith into silence.

The Supreme Court has failed in its purported attempts to promote state neutrality of religion. The "neutrality" standard distorts the founder's intent of protecting and promoting freedom of religion. The effect of the recent line of Supreme Court rulings has been to cultivate a climate of religious intolerance. In a 2000 dissenting opinion, Chief Justice Rehnquist summarized the Court's stance: "[The majority opinion] bristles with hostility to all things religious in public life."[721] The Court's position mirrors an escalating intolerance of Christianity in American society. A majority of the Court appears oblivious to the explicit language of the First Amendment, which protects the free exercise of religion for every American. The expression of faith is integral to every facet of an individual's life, an inseparable aspect of one's identity. No one can detach their belief system from their public life. The First Amendment means nothing if it does not enable religious followers to live out the tenets of their faith, so long as in doing so they do not deny others the same rights.

Constitutional scholar and commentator Mark Levin writes in *Men in Black*, "The establishment clause was never intended to ban the invocation of God in public forums or the voluntary participation in 'ceremonies or rites that recognized God.'"[722] Persons of faith cannot and should not put a lid on their faith, reducing it to Sunday morning and their own private sphere. In spite of what many today believe, the framers did not intend for the First Amendment to guarantee freedom from religion. It is absurd to quell the free exercise of religion in the name of religious freedom, but that is exactly what is happening in America today.

Anti-discrimination Laws vs. the First Amendment

The 1964 Civil Rights Act, which secured legal protection against discrimination for minorities, was a positive turning point for race relations in the United States. In the South, especially, an abhorrent web of law and

---

721 Good News Club v. Milford Central School, 533 U.S. 98 (2001).
722 Levin, Mark. Men in Black: How the Supreme Courtis Destroying America. New York: Regnery (2006).

custom had relegated African Americans to something akin to a lower caste than whites. Righting matters, activists argued, required federal laws banning discrimination not only by state and local governments, but also by large private employers and business proprietors. Other groups received protection from the 1964 Civil Rights act by piggybacking on the moral authority of the African American freedom struggle.[723]

Within a few years of enactment, the Civil Rights Act virtually eliminated exclusion and segregation in motels, restaurants and other places of public accommodation. Equally important, the Act helped change attitudes. According to polls at the time, the percentage of citizens who believed that black Americans should have the same job opportunities as other Americans rose from a woeful 42 percent in 1944 to 87 percent in 1966.

Since the 1970s, numerous groups -- such as senior citizens, gays, and the disabled - have successfully used the Civil Rights Act to gain special protection through an expansion of anti-discrimination laws, often at the expense of First Amendment rights. Constitutional protections for speech, assembly and religion were crucial to the ultimate success of the Civil Rights Movement, but speech, assembly and freedom of religion have been limited in the name of civil rights progress. As the justification for anti-discrimination laws took on a more moralistic tone, enforcement of such laws took on more authoritarian traits, and bureaucratic structures to deal with discrimination proliferated.

> As the intense moralism of modern antidiscrimination ideology became entrenched in American politics and society, antidiscrimination advocates, especially those who worked for the enforcement bureaucracies, increasingly viewed civil liberties as, at best, competing rights to be balanced against efforts to wipe out bigotry. At worst, they saw civil liberties as inconvenient and unnecessary obstacles to a discrimination-free world. This had grave implications for the First Amendment. HUD, for example, consistently interpreted ambiguous provisions of the Fair Housing Act in ways that threatened freedom of expression. Meanwhile, many courts interpreted antidiscrimination laws broadly, at times absurdly so. ...
>
> By the mid-1980s, antidiscrimination laws had emerged as a serious threat to civil liberties. Courts found that these laws punished everything from refusing to cast a pregnant woman as a bimbo in a soap opera, to giving speeches extolling the virtues of stay-at-home mothers, to expressing politically incorrect opinions at work, to refusing to share one's house with a gay roommate, to refusing to fund heretical student organizations at a Catholic university.

723 Bernstein, David E. You Can't Say That. Washington D.C.: Cato Institute (2003)

Defendants protested that their First Amendment rights were being trampled on, but to no avail.[724]

Frivolous lawsuits brought by private individuals under civil rights legislation can exact a high cost on business owners. When vandals broke a bathroom mirror in a family-owned restaurant in California, for example, restaurant employees hung the replacement mirror two inches too high to meet disabilities regulations. Mike Piazza, the owner, immediately lowered the mirror once he was notified of the mistake; nonetheless, he was sued under the federal Americans with Disabilities Act for damages incurred during a total of 27 visits plaintiffs made to the restaurant prior to informing Piazza of the technical violation. [725]

Today, almost two-thirds of civil rights charges filed by the Equal Employment Opportunity Commission (EEOC) have nothing to do with race.[726] The conflict between antidiscrimination laws and constitutional civil liberties continues to pose a serious threat to First Amendment freedoms, though the Supreme Court has retreated somewhat in the last few years from the receptivity it had shown in the previous two decades to anti-discrimination based lawsuits.

A true violation of a person's civil rights flows from an abridgement of a right grounded in the Constitution or in other valid law. Modern antidiscrimination ideology has become so pervasive, however, that groups and politicians today often make charges of civil rights violations part of a political strategy for garnering sympathy and moving their particular cause forward, even if the charges have no legal basis. The Obama administration has apparently adopted this strategy on the contentious issue of illegal immigration. During a White House state visit May 19, 2010, Mexican President Felipe Calderon decried Arizona's new immigration law, SB1070, as discriminatory against Mexicans.[727]

In the weeks prior to Calderon's visit, the White House had not defended Arizona, which faced boycott threats from officials of other states. Instead, Obama charged that "if you are an Hispanic American in

---

724 Bernstein, David E. You Can't Say That. Washington D.C.: Cato Institute (2003)

725 "A bathroom mirror two inches too high drags family-owned restaurant into lawsuit," March 24, 2010 http://credigy.eu/credigy/a-bathroom-mirror-two-inches-too-high-drags-family-owned-restaurant-into-lawsuit/

726 U.S Equal Employment Commission, "Charge Statistics FY 1997 Through FY 2009," http://www.eeoc.gov/eeoc/statistics/enforcement/charges.cfm

727 "Obama, Calderon Blast Arizona Immigration Law During White House Visit," May 19, 2010, http://www.foxnews.com/politics/2010/05/19/mexicos-president-blasts-arizona-immigration-law-white-house-visit-1351636523/

Arizona ... now suddenly if you don't have papers, and you took your kid out to get ice cream, you're gonna be harassed."[728]

Were that the case, the lion's share of the blame would fall on the federal government, which has done an injustice to Hispanics who are legal immigrants or citizens. By failing to enforce federal immigration law, the government has allowed a flood of illegal immigrants to cast a shadow on those who have played by the rules.

But it is not the case; Obama mischaracterized the law, stoking the fears of the Hispanic community by engaging in fear-mongering. The Arizona law actually contains numerous safeguards to address legitimate racial profiling concerns. The new law bars investigation of complaints based on race, color, or national origin. Additionally, it authorizes police officers to verify a person's immigration status only after "any lawful, stop, detention, or arrest made by a law enforcement official" and only if "reasonable suspicion exists" – apart from any consideration of ethnicity – that the individual "is an alien and is unlawfully present in the United States."The Arizona law is patterned after a 58 year old federal law that makes it illegal to be in the U.S. without proper immigration papers.[729, 730]

The federal government's systematic failure to enforce federal immigration law has led to Arizona's desperate situation. Not surprisingly, the assistant secretary of homeland security for U.S. Immigration and Customs Enforcement (ICE) criticized the Arizona law and reportedly indicated that the agency will not necessarily process illegal immigrants referred to them by Arizona authorities. An estimated half-million illegal

---

728 "Palin to Obama: 'Do your job, secure our border,' May 16, 2010 http://www.cnn. com/2010/POLITICS/05/16/arizona.palin.brewer/index.html

729 "Courts Could Void Arizona's New Law," by Stuart Taylor, Jr., May 8, 2010 http://www. nationaljournal.com/njmagazine/or_20100508_1520.php

730 In an April 6, 2008 report entitled "Immigration Enforcement Within the United States," the Congressional Research Service (CRS) wrote: "The INA [Immigration and Nationality Act] includes both criminal and civil components, providing both for criminal charges (e.g., alien smuggling, which is prosecuted in the federal courts) and for civil violations (e.g., lack of legal status, which may lead to removal through a separate administrative system in the Department of Justice). Being illegally in the U.S. has always been a civil, not criminal, violation of the INA, and subsequent deportation and associated administrative processes are civil proceedings. For instance, a lawfully admitted nonimmigrant alien may become deportable if his visitor's visa expires or if his student status changes. Criminal violations of the INA, on the other hand, include felonies and misdemeanors and are prosecuted in federal district courts. These types of violations include the bringing in and harboring of certain undocumented aliens, the illegal entry of aliens, and the reentry of aliens previously excluded or deported." Should Overstaying a visa be considered a federal crime (vs. a civil offense)? http://immigration.procon.org/ view.answers.php?questionID=000781 Link to CRS report: http://immigration.procon. org/sourcefiles/ImmigrationEnforcementWithintheUnitedStates.pdf

immigrants are estimated to be living in Arizona, whose residents number an estimated 6.5 million.[731]

Arizona Governor Jan Brewer issued an executive order the day the law was passed which established training of law enforcement officials and agencies to assure they implement the law consistent with federal laws regulating immigration, and in a manner that protects the civil rights of all persons.[732]

Governor Brewer had strong words for the president, charging, "Our border is being erased, and the president apparently considers it a wonderful opportunity to divide people among racial lines for his personal political convenience."[733]

After Calderon spoke, Obama joined with the foreign leader in rebuking Arizona, which took action to protect its citizens from an intolerable level of violence, drug trafficking, and related problems stemming from years of federal dereliction of its constitutional responsibility to secure the border. Obama, who had previously called the Arizona law "irresponsible," again criticized the law as a "misdirected effort." He added, "We're examining any implications especially for civil rights because in the United States of America, no law abiding person -- be they an American citizen, illegal immigrant, or a visitor or tourist from Mexico -- should ever be subject to suspicion simply because of what they look like."[734] Obama's oxymoronic and incoherent description of a "law abiding … illegal immigrant" is proof that the issue is not about civil rights, even apart from his other distortions of the Arizona statute.

A few hours after Obama spoke, White House Press Secretary Robert Gibbs confirmed that the president had read the Arizona law.[735] Gibbs' awkward acknowledgment was necessitated not only by Obama's seeming unfamiliarity with the law, but by the fact that numerous other high-ranking administration officials who had criticized the Arizona law (including Attorney General Eric Holder, Jr., Secretary of Homeland

---

731 "Top Official Says Feds May Not Process Illegals Referred From Arizona," May 21, 2010 http://www.foxnews.com/politics/2010/05/21/official-says-feds-process-illegals-referred-arizona/ ICE has legal discretion in its processing decisions.

732 National Conference of State Legislatures, "Arizona's Immigration Enforcement Laws: An Overview of SB1070 and HB2162," http://www.ncsl.org/default.aspx?tabid=20263

733 IBID

734 "Obama, Calderon Blast Arizona Immigration Law During White House Visit," May 19, 2010, http://www.foxnews.com/politics/2010/05/19/mexicos-president-blasts-arizona-immigration-law-white-house-visit-1351636523/

735 "Obama has read Arizona immigration law," May 20, 2010, http://content.usatoday.com/communities/theoval/post/2010/05/obama-has-read-the-arizona-immigration-law/1

Security Janet Napolitano, and State Department Spokesman P.J. Crowley) later admitted that they had not read the Arizona statute.[736]

---

736 "Napolitano Admits She Hasn't Read Arizona Immigration Law in 'Detail,'" May 18, 2010   http://www.foxnews.com/politics/2010/05/18/napolitano-admits-read-arizona-immigration-law/

13

The Growing Threat to Private Property Rights

Self-labeled progressives view the concept of private property rights as a creation of law, subject to whatever restrictions and restraints government determines is best for the ordering of society, but the founders viewed property rights as fundamental human rights inseparable from the idea of liberty.

> For eighteenth-century Americans, property and liberty were one and inseparable, because property was the only foundation yet conceived for security of life and liberty: without security for his property, it was thought, no man could live or be free except at the mercy of another.[737]

Supreme Court Justice Potter Stewart, in *Lynch v. Household Finance Corporation* (1972), described the inseparable connection between property rights and personal liberty: "Property does not have rights. People do. ... In fact, a fundamental interdependence exists between the personal right to liberty and the personal right in property. Neither could have meaning without the other."[738]

In *The Second Treatise of Civil Government*, English philosopher John Locke advocated the individual's right to life, liberty, and property. When writing the Declaration of Independence, Jefferson modified Locke's language to assert that individuals are endowed by God with unalienable rights, including "life, liberty, and the pursuit of happiness." Those who argue that property rights are a creation of law often point to Jefferson's substitution of "life, liberty, and the pursuit of happiness" for Locke's "life, liberty, and estate" as evidence that Jefferson rejected the idea of property rights stemming from natural law. On the contrary, political documents from Jefferson's day show that the pursuit of happiness was

---

737 Bassani, Luigi Marco. "Life, Liberty, and...:Jefferson on Property Rights." Journal of Libertarian Studies 1, no. 18 (2004): 31-87. Ludwig von Mises Institute.
738 Lynch v. Household Finance Corp., 405 US 538 (1972).

seen as encompassing the natural rights of property. The Rights of Virginia (1776), the Constitution of Massachusetts (1780), the Constitution of Pennsylvania (1784), and the Constitution of New Hampshire (1784), all describe the right of property and the right to pursue happiness and safety within the familiar Lockean triad of unalienable rights deriving from natural law.[739] For example, the Rights of Virgina, penned by George Mason one month prior to the Declaration of Independence, states: "That all men are by nature equally free and independent and have certain inherent rights ... namely, the enjoyment of life and liberty, with the means of acquiring and possessing property, and pursuing and obtaining happiness and safety." [740]

Similarly, the Constitution of Massachusetts, drafted in 1780, states:

All men are born free and equal, and have certain natural, essential, and unalienable rights; among which may be reckoned the right of enjoying and defending their lives and liberties; that of acquiring, possessing, and protecting property; in fine, that of seeking and obtaining their safety and happiness.[741]

Jefferson's other writings prove that he considered the right to property among the unalienable rights of man.

Jefferson would continue to associate in terms of the Lockean triad throughout the rest of his writings, showing that the substitution by no means indicated an implicit purpose to exclude property from the catalog of natural rights. The terms 'life and property,' 'liberty, life and property,' and 'liberty and property' constantly recur throughout Jefferson's work, and are used in a manner fully consistent with the typical utilization and contextualization of the entire classical liberal tradition.[742]

In keeping with Jefferson's view of property rights, the Fifth Amendment right to due process guarantees a person the right to notice of legal proceedings and a hearing before being deprived of life, liberty or property. It further requires that government abide by certain identifiable standards of fairness. The Supreme Court has ruled that due process

---

739 Bassani, Luigi Marco. "Life, Liberty, and...:Jefferson on Property Rights." Journal of Libertarian Studies 1, no. 18 (2004): 31-87. Ludwig von Mises Institute.
740 Ibid.
741 Ibid.
742 Ibid.

includes both procedural and substantive components. Procedural due process deals with the legal process, or procedural rights, such as the right to proper notice of a lawsuit, the right to an attorney, and the right to obtain evidence. A fair process, however, does not guarantee a fair outcome if the underlying law itself is unjust. Thus, the principle of substantive due process "prohibits the government from infringing on fundamental constitutional liberties."[743] Despite these constitutional protections, both tangible and intangible property rights are under assault as never before in the history of America:

Net Neutrality and Property Rights

A modern example of the government's attack on intangible property rights is the danger of net neutrality. The Obama administration plans to reign in the Internet through a regulatory weapon called net neutrality, which will empower the government to micromanage the Internet. The FCC wants to use this concept as a basis for controlling how Internet service providers (ISPs) manage their networks. It argues, based on only scant – and anecdotal – evidence, that this regulatory control is needed to keep the Internet "open" and "free," and to prevent ISPs from engaging in discriminatory or unfair business practices. Opponents argue that the Internet is flourishing under free-market forces; it is not broken and will only suffer by government's heavy handed intervention.[744]

That oversimplified, in-a-nutshell summary deserves a more detailed explanation, which requires entering into techno-geek territory. The concept of net neutrality originated in the early days of the Internet as an engineering concept often called the "end-to-end" principle. The principle holds that the functionality of the network should be restricted to the ends of the network, where transmissions originate and are received. In order to reduce complexity and increase speed, data should be transmitted from end to end without intermediate processing. Often called the "First Amendment of the Internet," net neutrality was intended to be a guideline and was never codified as law.[745]

---

743 "Substantive Due Process," The Free Dictionary. http://legal-dictionary.thefreedictionary. com/Substantive+Due+Process
744 Lakely, James G. "Why Obama is Wrong about Net Neutality and His Scheme Must Be Defeated," BigGovernment.com. http://biggovernment.com/jlakely/2010/02/15/why-obama-is-wrong-about-net-neutrality-and-his-scheme-must-be-defeated/.
745 Gattuso, James. "Broadband Regulation: Will Congress Neuter the Net?" Heritage.org. http://www.heritage.org/Research/Regulation/bg1941.cfm.

The prominence of streaming media, such as audio or video transmissions, means Internet service providers (ISPs), especially smaller ones, can be taxed to the breaking point by large masses of data coming from multiple connections during peak periods. Broadband providers contend that they need the capability to engage in intermediate processing so as to allocate capacity efficiently and to maximize quality of service. These providers argue that net neutrality will prevent them from providing service plans well-tailored to meet specific consumer needs and demands, crush their ability to profitably expand and innovate, and negatively impact the customer experience generally, including slower and/or inconsistent internet transmission speeds.

In recent years net neutrality advocates, such as Google, Amazon, Facebook and Twitter, have argued that federal regulation is needed to prevent unfair competitive practices by ISPs; they want the government to restrict the ability of network providers to prioritize traffic based on a tiered pricing structure, or according to content or application. They also want to mandate uniformity of access across the entire internet spectrum.[746] In other words, net neutrality supporters want to the government to prevent ISPs from exerting control over the content and applications that flow through their networks.

Opponents, such as AT&T, Comcast and Verizon Communications, argue that while net neutrality seems reasonable on the surface, it is an unnecessary measure that would harm consumers, discourage investment, and reduce competition.[747] Bob Kahn, the most senior figure in the development of the Internet, strongly opposes network neutrality because it would stifle innovation.[748] The *Washington Post* echoes that view, criticizing FCC Chairman Julius Genachowski's proposal that the FCC prohibit ISPs from blocking, degrading, or prioritizing (favoring particular content or applications) lawful traffic over their networks. The Post concludes that such unnecessary micromanagement would "stifle further investments by ISPs."[749]

According to the Center for Individual Freedom (CIF), network neutrality will lead to federal price controls for companies offering Internet service. CIF calls net neutrality "corporate welfare of the worst order," arguing that it would artificially increase the cost of doing business in a way that would put smaller entrepreneurs in particular at risk:

746 Reardon, Marguerite. "Amazon, Facebook, and Google back FCC on Net neutrality," CNet.com. http://news.cnet.com/8301-30686_3-10378352-266.html
747 Ibid.
748 Orlowski, Andrew. "Father of internet warns against net neutrality," The Register. http://www.theregister.co.uk/2007/01/18/kahn_net_neutrality_warning/
749 "The FCC's Heavy Hand," Washington Post. http://www.washingtonpost.com/wp-dyn/content/article/2009/09/27/AR2009092703026.html.

'Net Neutrality' would begin regulating Internet Providers by forcing them to charge high-bandwidth sites such as Google the same that they can charge a low-bandwidth small website. Simply put, 'Net Neutrality' is anything but 'neutral,' as it substitutes government-mandated business models and pricing structures for free-market prices. [750]

David J. Farber, Professor of Computer Science and Public Policy at Carnegie Mellon University, is one of the most respected Internet visionaries and is a net neutrality opponent. A former chief technologist at the FCC, Farber fears net neutrality legislation will lead to harmful, unintended consequences, many of them unknown because the Internet is still in an early, fluid and dynamic life-stage. Phil Kerpen, Chairman of the Internet Freedom Coalition, warns that long-term, the government will make broadband Internet access another government entitlement at a time when the federal government is hemorrhaging red ink at unsustainable levels.[751]

The 2009 stimulus bill included $7.2 billion for grants to expand high-speed Internet access and allowed Congress one year to develop a plan for use of the money. In addition to the stimulus money, the FCC may also have use of an additional $15.5 billion from the Universal Service Fund, set up to provide affordable telecommunications services access for underserved communities.[752] Though the fund was set up to ensure that all Americans have access to basic telephone services, the FCC wants to tap into the fund to subsidize broadband and wireless networks.[753]

Congress directed the FCC to develop a National Broadband Plan for ensuring every American has "access to broadband capability."[754] Shortly before the March 2010 release of the plan, the FCC issued a statement asserting that one way of making broadband more affordable is to "consider use of spectrum for a free or a very low cost wireless broadband service."[755]

---

750 "'Net Neutrality' – Corporate Welfare and Price Controls Have a New Name," Center for Information Freedom. http://www.cfif.org/htdocs/legislative_issues/federal_issues/hot_issues_in_congress/technology/Net-Neutrality-.htm.

751 "Glenn Beck television program. October 20, 2009.

752 Puzzanghera, Jim. "FCC to propose nationwide expansion of high-speed Internet," Los Angeles Times. http://www.latimes.com/business/la-fi-broadband-plan16-2010mar16,0,6700849.story.

753 Tessler, Joelle. "FCC seeks to redirect subsidy to Internet," Dispatch.com. http://www.dispatch.com/live/content/business/stories/2010/03/08/fcc-seeks-to-redirect-subsidy-to-internet.html?sid=101.

754 "National Broadband Plan: Connecting America," Broadband.gov. http://broadband.gov/plan/executive-summary/

755 "U.S. considers some free wireless broadband service," Reuters. http://news.yahoo.com/s/nm/20100309/wr_nm/us_broadband_fcc_wireless

In the plan, the FCC set forth a goal: "Every American should have affordable access to robust broadband service, and the means and skills to subscribe if they so choose."[756] In short, since the beginning of the Obama administration, the financial and regulatory foundation for net neutrality has been constructed; Congress and the FCC appear to be rapidly moving to implement its regulatory framework.

Eminent Domain

While citizens of the Internet Age have become increasingly worried about their intangible property rights, the threat to tangible property rights remains an even greater concern. The right to purchase and possess private property is an indispensable feature of a free society.[757] A formidable threat to tangible property rights is the expansive use of eminent domain -- the government's sovereign power to appropriate private property for public use without the owner's consent. Definitively assessing the frequency, circumstances and impact of the use of eminent domain is problematic, since, as noted in a November 2006 U.S. Government Accountability Office (GAO) report to congressional committees, "no centralized or aggregate national or state data exist on the use of eminent domain."[758]

Eminent domain is a troublesome but necessary power of a sovereign nation. The founders recognized this, and sought to limit the government's power to prevent the abuse of individuals' private property rights. However,

---

756 "National Broadband Plan: Connecting America," Broadband.gov. http://broadband. gov/plan/executive-summary/

757 Eminent domain is by no means the only substantial government threat to tangible property rights. At the local level, government may exert pressure and control over the use of private property via too-stringent zoning regulations. Though reasonable zoning laws can positively impact land values, abuse of such laws can negatively impact property values and the rights of property owners. In the name of protecting wetlands, overzealous government bureaucrats in a variety of agencies exert pressure on landowners to comply with burdensome restrictions on land use, enforcing their rulings with fines and even jail sentences. Excessive taxation is still another way in which landowners' rights may be infringed by government. Corace, Don. Government Pirates.New York: Harper Paperbacks (2008). The Environmental Protection Agency has grown more powerful through the years, and recently gained its most potent regulatory weapon when it ruled that greenhouse gases pose a threat to public safety.

758 "Eminent Domain: Information about Its Uses and Effect on Property Owners and Communities is Limited," GAO.gov. http://www.gao.gov/new.items/d0728.pdf. The report noted: "The matter of eminent domain remains largely at the level of state and local governments that, in turn, delegate this power to their agencies or designated authorities. Since multiple authorities have the power to take private property within the same jurisdiction without any centralized tracking of eminent domain use, data such as the purpose for which eminent domain is used or the number of times eminent domain is used in a given locality are not readily available."

in the past 65 years the Supreme Court has increasingly expanded the government's eminent domain powers through a series of holdings, culminating in *Kelo et al. v. City of New London et al (2006)*, discussed below, in which the Court ruled that eminent domain could be used for economic development purposes, even absent a finding of blight. *Kelo* sparked a marked increase in the use of eminent domain and prompted 43 states to pass laws attempting to limit its use. Even so, a 2010 UPI news story reported:

> Thousands of families continue to lose their homes every year, though most were lost to public works projects rather than economic development projects like the one in New London. ... (T)here are indications that as stimulus funds make their way to the state and local levels, more property than ever may be at risk.[759]

Similarly, a 2009 Georgia State University study found that, left unconstrained by state law, state and local governments use eminent domain powers to expand control over privately owned resources.

> The empirical results show that the breadth of eminent domain power affects the size of the public sector; states that explicitly empower their local governments to use eminent domain for private economic development have larger state and local public sectors than those that do not.[760]

During the American Revolution, the colonial government occasionally seized private property without compensating the landowner, in order to build roads or to assist the war effort.[761] Though neither the Bill of Rights nor the Constitution address eminent domain by name, the Fifth Amendment includes language intended to limit the government's power to take private property: "No person shall be ... deprived of life, liberty, or property without due process of law; nor shall private property be taken for public use, without just compensation."

The Takings Clause of the Fifth Amendment grants the federal government the right of eminent domain, but provides two specific limitations on its power. First, the federal government can only take

---

759 Cook, Steve. "Eminent Domain is Alive and Well," UPI.com. http://www.upi.com/Real-Estate/2010/01/21/Eminent-Domain-is-Alive-and-Well/5911264089147
760 "Do Broader Eminent Domain Powers Increase Government Size?" The Berkeley Electronic Electronic Press, Review of Law and Economics, Vol. 5 (2009).
761 Williams, Amanda. "Examining the Current Abuse of the Doctrine of Eminent Domain," Lethbridge Undergraduate Research Journal, 2009 Volume 3, Number 2.

private property for a "public use." Second, if the government appropriates property, it must pay the owner "just compensation," which courts have generally interpreted to mean fair market value. In the first years of the United States' existence, the Supreme Court highly esteemed property rights as unalienable, and thus narrowly interpreted the government's eminent domain powers.

> The right of acquiring and possessing property, and having it protected, is one of the natural, inherent, and unalienable rights of man. … No man would become a member of a community, in which he could not enjoy the fruits of his honest labour and industry. The preservation of property then is a primary object of the social compact, and, by the late Constitution of Pennsylvania, was made a fundamental law.[762]

In ruling for the private property owners and against the government, the Court declared:

> It is, however, difficult to form a case, in which the necessity of a state can be of such a nature, as to authorise or excuse the seizing of landed property belonging to one citizen, and giving it to another citizen. It is immaterial to the state, in which of its citizens the land is vested; but it is of primary importance, that, when vested, it should be secured, and the proprietor protected in the enjoyment of it.[763]

Until the early mid-twentieth century, eminent domain annexations, in keeping with the original intent of the Fifth Amendment, were limited to legitimate, widely-accepted public uses, such as constructing roads, bridges, schools, parks, and public facilities. Congress took the lead in expanding the use of eminent domain, and the Supreme Court afforded great deference to Congress's determinations. In 1945, Congress passed the District of Columbia Redevelopment Act (DCRA). Unlike railroad and utility takings, which afforded public use of the land taken, the DCRA specifically declared that land could be taken for redevelopment and subsequent sale or lease.[764]

In *Berman v. Parker*, (1954), the Supreme Court unanimously upheld the constitutionality of DCRA and the use of eminent domain for urban

---

762 Vanhorne's Lessee v. Dorrance, 2 U.S. 304 (1795) 2 U.S. 304 (Dall.)
763 Ibid.
764 Berman v. Parker, 348 U.S. 26 (1954).

revitalization, using terms like "public interest," "public need," "public welfare," "public ends," and "public purpose" to justify its decision. Its ruling redefined "public use" to mean "public purpose," thus profoundly expanding the reach of the state's power. The Court explicitly rejected the contention that the Fifth Amendment prohibits the taking of private property if such taking results in the transfer of ownership from one private property owner to another, noting:

> In the present case, the Congress and its authorized agencies have made determinations that take into account a wide variety of values. It is not for us to reappraise them. If those who govern the District of Columbia decide that the Nation's Capital should be beautiful as well as sanitary, there is nothing in the Fifth Amendment that stands in the way.
>
> Once the object is within the authority of Congress, the means by which it will be attained is also for Congress to determine. … We cannot say that public ownership is the sole method of promoting the public purposes of community redevelopment projects.[765]

The *Berman* decision opened the door for government and private developers to use eminent domain to circumvent the free market in the name of urban renewal.

In *Berman's* wake, governments began vastly expanding the definition of blight so they could condemn perfectly fine properties for private development under the pretense of urban renewal. In addition, many state supreme courts adopted the rationale of *Berman*, reading their public use clauses the same way. Continuing down this slippery slope, governments began to bypass the charade of declaring an area blighted and instead used eminent domain to take homes and businesses so that the land could be given to other private parties who the government believed would produce more tax revenue than the current owners.[766]

In 1984, the Court added redistribution of property to its growing list of justifications for eminent domain takings. In *Hawaii Housing Authority v. Midkiff* (1984), the Court upheld Hawaii's Land Reform Act of 1967, a law designed to break up perceived oligopolies.[767] The Land Reform

---

765 Ibid.
766 "History of Eminent Domain and its Abuse," Castle Coalition. http://www.castlecoalition. org/index.php?option=com_content&task=view&id=512.
767 Hawaii Housing Authority v. Midkiff 467 U.S. 229 (1984).

Act established a condemnation process to redistribute property from native Hawaiian property owners to the people who had been leasing land from the native Hawaiian property owners. The Act asserted that condemning the subject properties constituted a "public use and purpose." The Supreme Court unanimously ruled that state and federal legislative bodies could declare the redistribution of property as a constitutional "public purpose" to use eminent domain powers. The Court held that that the Fifth Amendment did not literally require that seized private property be put to public use, and thus "the mere fact that property taken outright by eminent domain is transferred in the first instance to private beneficiaries" did not the prevent the government from meeting the Fifth Amendment standard, so long as its exercise of eminent domain was "rationally related to a conceivable public purpose."[768]

Both the *Berman* and *Midkiff* opinions narrowed the thin ledge on which private land owners could stand in defense of their property. In order to prevail in an eminent domain claim, property owners had to prove that the sole purpose of the government's taking was to transfer property from one private owner to another; even if the transfer was the direct effect of such taking, the property owners would lose if there was a conceivable rationale for the government's stated public purpose.

In the most recent attack on property rights, *Kelo et al. v. City of New London et al.* (2005), the Court specifically embraced economic development, absent any allegation of blight, as a constitutionally valid public use under the Fifth Amendment: "Clearly, there is no basis for exempting economic development from our traditionally broad understanding of public purpose."[769]

The *Kelo* controversy surrounded a proposed Pfizer research facility in New London, Connecticut. As part of the city's economic rejuvenation plan, the New London Development Corporation (NLDC) offered Pfizer an incentive package to lure the company to build a $300 million research facility in the Fort Trumbull area of New London. In 2000, responding to Pfizer's requests for more attractive surroundings for the new research facility, the New London city council authorized the NLDC to acquire properties for commercial development adjacent to Pfizer's proposed site through eminent domain. Plaintiff Susette Kelo and eight other New London property owners sued to prevent the City of New London from taking their property for the project. The planned complex, which would

---

768 Ibid.
769 Kelo v. City of New London 545 U.S. 469 (2005).

border the Pfizer site, included a waterfront conference hotel, retail shops, a pedestrian walkway, approximately 80 new residences, a renovated marina, and a new U.S. Coast Guard Museum.

The Court ruled in favor of the city and refused to include even a basic requirement that a government must demonstrate a "reasonable certainty" that the alleged public benefits would accrue from the taking. Justice Sandra Day O'Connor, dissenting, concluded that the *Kelo* ruling rendered the Takings Clause meaningless. [770]

> If predicted (or even guaranteed) positive side-effects are enough to render transfer from one private party to another constitutional, then the words "for public use" do not realistically exclude *any* takings, and thus do not exert any constraint on the eminent domain power. ... Any property may now be taken for the benefit of another private party, but the fallout from this decision will not be random. The beneficiaries are likely to be those citizens with disproportionate influence and power in the political process, including large corporations and development firms. As for the victims, the government now has license to transfer property from those with fewer resources to those with more. The founders cannot have intended this perverse result.[771]

New London's taking of the plaintiffs' private property to sell to other private property owners cannot be rectified with the history of the Fifth Amendment or its clear requirement of a "public use." But a majority of the Court, continuing on the path laid out in *Berman* and *Hawaii Housing Authority*, upheld the taking.

Professor Jonathan Turley of the George Washington School of Law, after noting that over 90 percent of Americans opposed the decision, wryly commented, "You might debate what public use means, but it is clear what it doesn't mean. It does not mean private use."[772] On November 9, 2009, four years after the widely-excoriated *Kelo* decision, Pfizer announced it would close its $300 million global research and development headquarters in New London.[773]

---

770 Ibid.
771 Ibid.
772 Gross, Martin L. National Suicide: How Washington is Destroying the American Dream From A to Z. New York: Penguin Group (2009).
773 Gershon, Eric. "Pfizer Inc. Plans to Vacate its R & D Center in New London," Hartford Courant. http://www.courant.com/business/hc-pfizer1110.artnov10,0,5205001.story.

As O'Connor predicted, *Kelo* created an economic incentive for ambitious private developers and tax-hungry local governments, which could now partner with one another to acquire land through the economic development-based exercise of eminent domain. By carefully targeting private property, the commercial developer could collect a tidy profit while the local government gained a richer tax base. The only losers would be the landowners that would be forced to sell their property and find another place to live. In 2006, the Institute for Justice, a self-described libertarian public interest law firm, issued a report detailing the deluge of new assaults against the property rights following *Kelo*.[774]

In the year after the *Kelo* ruling, local governments threatened or condemned more than 5,783 properties for private projects, more than half the number of properties threatened or taken by eminent domain in the five years between 1998 and 2002. Cities have become more aggressive in threatening condemnation, armed with *Kelo's* expansive holding. They know that many homeowners will give in rather than attempt to overcome *Kelo's* nearly insurmountable burden.[775]

Among the more common purposes state and local authorities cited for exercising eminent domain, according to the 2006 GAO report, was infrastructure, such as road construction; elimination of blight; environmental remediation; and economic or community development.[776] Constitutional concerns identified by the GAO in its study of eminent domain cases included a lack of timely notification about public hearings and inadequate compensation as two concerns that needed addressing. It also noted that property rights advocates described other concerns, such as the high cost of challenging property valuations, the intangible impact on neighborhoods, and misinformation given by authorities concerning condemnation proceedings or appraisals.[777]

In light of the popular notion that liberals are the champions of the poor, it is ironic that the five most liberal Supreme Court justices made up the majority in *Kelo*. These are the justices who, like Obama, believe that property is not an inviolable personal right but a valuable government resource for building a better society. *Kelo* sets the constitutional bar exceedingly low

774 "History of Eminent Domain and its Abuse," Castle Coalition. http://www.castlecoalition. org/index.php?option=com_content&task=view&id=512.
775 "Opening the Floodgates: Eminent Domain Abuse in the Post-*Kelo* World," by Dana Berliner, Published by Institute for Justice, June 2006 http://www.castlecoalition.org/ pdf/publications/floodgates-report.pdf
776 "Eminent Domain: Information about Its Uses and Effect on Property Owners and Communities is Limited," GAO.gov. http://www.gao.gov/new.items/d0728.pdf
777 Ibid.

for local governments in eminent domain cases. The government will always be able to conjure up some vague public good, but if private property can be taken for most any use, including private use, the court has rendered the Constitution's "public use" requirement meaningless.

Redistributing Property

It is disheartening that the Court has been repeatedly hoodwinked by the public purpose assertions in eminent domain cases because government will always allege a legitimate public purpose, such as combatting "concentrated property ownership." The legal burden these decisions heap upon private property owners defending against a greedy government is practically insurmountable. Even more frightening is the Court's ever-expanding tolerance for takings that transfer property between private persons, particularly when coupled with Obama's blatant disregard for individual property rights.

Obama believes that private property, such as bank accounts and land, do not truly belong to people, but are subject to the state's redistributive powers. In a 2001 public radio interview, Obama, then a law professor, lamented that one of the "tragedies" of the court-centered Civil Rights Movement was that it failed to bring about "redistributive change."[1]

When Joe Wurzelbacher, a.k.a "Joe the Plumber," burst into national headlines in mid-October 2008, the public did not understand the implications of Obama's now famous comment, "I think when you spread the wealth around, it's good for everybody."[2] In the context of Obama's 2001 public radio interview endorsing redistributive change, his "spread the wealth" comment seems more like social dogma than a casual remark.

Redistributive change is predicated on a misguided, zero-sum-game view of economics.[3] In this view, the only way the Have-nots can prosper is to take from the Haves. Government redistributive policies provide an ostensible legal basis for

---

1 "You know, if you look at the victories and failures of the civil rights movement, and its litigation strategy in the court, I think where it succeeded was to vest formal rights in previously dispossessed peoples. So that I would now have the right to vote, I would now be able to sit at a lunch counter and order and as long as I could pay for it, I'd be okay, but the Supreme Court never entered into the issues of redistribution of wealth, and sort of more basic issues of political and economic justice in this society. One of the, I think, the tragedies of the civil rights movement was, because the civil rights movement became so court-focused, I think that there was a tendency to lose track of the political and community organizing, and activities on the ground, that are able to put together the actual coalitions of power through which you bring about redistributive change. And in some ways we still suffer from that." Source: http://beldar.blogs.com/beldarblog/2008/10/obamas-2001-app.html

2 "Joe the Plumber, a Transcript," October 19, 2008, http://www.tampabay.com/news/perspective/article858299.ece

3 Source: "Money, Greed, and God: Why Capitalism Is the Solution and Not the Problem," speech by author Jay W. Richards delivered May 6, 2009 http://www.heritage.org/press/events/ev050609a.cfm

the taking.[4] By this logic, justice is not achieved simply by treating every person the same under the law and guaranteeing equal opportunity under the law for all persons; instead, "redistributive justice" is required to level the playing field between the haves and have nots. Obama has openly championed a "spread the wealth" system of taxing the wealthy to fund tax breaks for the middle class. Considering the Supreme Court's prior endorsements of government-facilitated takings between private individuals for the purposes of economic development and social engineering, there is nothing to stop the government from exacting redistributive change through takings.

Redistribution is the unifying theme of Obama's ideology. Following the Alinsky method, Obama is using every policy decision, appointment, and opportunity to achieve this end. The tax code, the judicial system, health care legislation, education, stimulus bills, budget priorities, cap and trade, green jobs, financial regulatory reform, and government takeovers of the private sector are all tools for redistributive change, and Obama's personal interpretation of fairness is his level. His socialist vision is expanding the welfare state, exacerbating chords of divisiveness, sapping the country's wealth, undermining the great American work ethic, feeding an entitlement mentality, and threatening the nation's security.

4   It is not surprising that Obama subscribes to this philosophy. Saul Alinsky, the father of community organizing, explicitly articulated this view in his organizing handbook, Rules for Radicals. Michelle Obama also advocated this new philosophy of leadership during the 2008 presidential campaign:"The truth is… someone is going to have to give up a piece of their pie so that someone else can have more."

The legislative action limiting the use of eminent domain, taken by all but a few states since *Kelo*, shines a ray of light for fearful property owners, but more time is needed to judge the impact of such laws. Residents of states like New York, which has yet to pass a post-*Kelo* law limiting the government's exercise of its eminent domain powers, remain the most vulnerable. The Institute for Justice issued a report in October 2009 that labeled New York as one of the worst states with a record of abusing the power of eminent domain. An example of how the state stacks the deck against homeowners is its 30 day window for homeowners to file suit after the state announces its intention to possibly seize the property by eminent domain at some unspecified future date. If the property owners miss the window, they are left without recourse when the condemnation actually occurs years later.[778]

The legal burden these decisions heap upon private property owners defending against an overreaching government is huge. Even the threat of an eminent domain action exacts an emotional price on landowners, whose

778 Berliner, Dana. "Building Empires, Destroying Homes: Eminent Domain Abuse in New York," Institute for Justice. http://www.ij.org/index.php?option=com_content&task=view&id=3072&Itemid=165.

homes or business may be put under a cloud of uncertainty for years, even decades. Often, homeowners give in to government pressure and sell so that they can retrieve their lives from legal limbo.[779]

> Based on a review of news reports, The Institute for Justice estimated that between the years 1998-2009, 2,226 properties (homes, apartment complexes, businesses, etc.) in New York were condemned or threatened with condemnation for private development and 74 projects used eminent domain for private development. The group's analysis also revealed that in New York eminent domain for private use is disproportionately focused on the poor and on minorities.[780]

The Supreme Court's sanctioning of government takings that transfer property between private persons is unworthy of a free society and a shocking affront to the rights of citizens. When the government tramples upon private property rights, whether tangible or intangible, it displaces families, disrupts communities, destroys businesses, discriminates against some citizens in favor of others, and ultimately destabilizes the nation's social fabric. It diminishes trust in government and exacts a heavy emotional toil upon the public. More important than the private property the government is taking is the freedom it is usurping: the freedom of citizens to have control of their own lives, homes, and businesses; to enjoy the fruits of their labors; to be unburdened by excessive government intrusions; to abide by their consciences; and to live in a society that recognizes their God-given rights to life, liberty and property.

---

779 Ibid.
780 Cook, Steve. "Eminent Domain is Alive and Well," UPI.com. http://www.upi.com/Real-Estate/2010/01/21/Eminent-Domain-is-Alive-and-Well/5911264089147.

Epilogue

Few Americans are naïve enough to believe that corrupt politics and lying politicians are newcomers to Washington, D.C. *Of course* there have been disreputable, self-serving politicians holding office since the founding of the country. Sin didn't wash ashore in America during the most recent hurricane season, (curiously, despite global warming warnings of increased mega-storm activities, 2009 seemed essentially hurricane-free), but we can no longer afford an it's-always-been-that-way, head-in-the-sand avoidance of the lack of integrity in politics. Given the country's dangerous fiscal and moral morass, anyone who ignores overwhelming and incontrovertible evidence of the political establishment's ongoing breach of public trust is complicit by default.

The truth is arrogant, self-serving politicians once were the exception in Washington, D.C., not the rule. There *is* a difference between principled leadership and Machiavellian deception. There *is* a difference between facts and spin, between reality and fantasy, between patriotism and partisan pandering. The flood of money into and out of Washington has sickened the political culture. The centralization of federal power is a chain around the neck, worn every day by American citizens who once looked to Washington for little, but now are increasingly dependent on its handouts and subject to its intrusions.

It is human nature to defend persons in whom we have invested our trust and our vote, politicians with whom we identify by political party affiliation and/or ideological perspective – as well we should – *when those persons honor that trust* by serving in office with integrity, humility, and competency. We want to *believe;* as relational beings it's part of our human nature. But *change we can believe in* must be more than a campaign slogan. Actions must follow words. Promises must be kept. Reality must bear at least a passing resemblance to rhetoric. And the change delivered must be constitutional, legal, ethical, and sensible.

These are basic standards for evaluating any candidate for office. Disreputable candidates count on a disengaged or easily deceived populace. If the bulk of a candidate's positions and promises conflict with his or her longstanding track record, there is no reasonable basis for trusting that candidate (short of dramatic evidence of a major turning point in the person's worldview). In that case, the relevant issue is no longer the candidate's *trustworthiness* but the voters' capacity for *self-deception*. Before we can hope to hold politicians accountable to the truth, we must stop lying to ourselves. Citizens have only themselves to blame if they trust persons who have amply demonstrated their lack of trustworthiness.

There is no lack of proposals for remedying the serious crises facing America. A modest start-list of promising possibilities might include cutting federal spending, simplifying the tax code, balancing the federal budget, enacting term limits, banning earmarks, prosecuting criminal activity by politicians and bureaucrats (what a novel idea!), requiring sunset provisions on all legislation; eliminating all corporate welfare, dissolving antiquated federal agencies; streamlining cabinet agencies, ending the practice of gerrymandering congressional districts to aid incumbents' reelection, and eliminating hundreds of wasteful/overlapping programs.

As the federal deficit and cumulative national debt explode further into the unsustainable range, politicians will routinely call for fiscal responsibility. Most such calls will be nothing more than empty rhetoric. Voters must learn which politicians have the intent, the will, and a proven track record of actually working for a return to sane financial policies.

Most, if not all, of the above proposals deserve enactment. However, they do not ultimately hold the power to cure what ails America. At most, they will simply stabilize the patient. America will reclaim its greatness only when it restores the principles of limited government enshrined in the Constitution and when together its people recommit to our founding document's inspired vision of equal opportunity and unalienable rights for all.

The journey to a nation's wholeness is not fundamentally different than the journey to personal wholeness. My hope for this book is not that readers will agree with all the arguments made in it; that would be a manifestly unreasonable and unwise expectation. Undoubtedly, at some not too distant point in the future, *I* will not agree with every assertion made herein. When we grow, we change; our views must grow with us. An entrenched ideology closed to new ideas is the enemy of wholeness.

My hope is the same for the reader as it is for me: that we continually seek Truth and that we consistently live up to that which we know to be true. Critical thinking is a must; otherwise self-deception will bring recurring, painful detours and dead ends. Reason can be a powerful advocate in that search. The federal government's continued profligate spending is irrational because it is self-destructive and unsustainable. Consideration of a massive and expensive government health care entitlement, when Social Security, Medicare, Medicaid, and the federal prescription program are already bankrupting the country, is unreasonable.

Reason is a valuable asset, but it is a neutral player, as willing to be co-opted for evil purposes as for good. Reason, for example, cannot account for the unconditional love that grace offers, the redemption that forgiveness ushers in, or the joy that putting the needs of others first brings. Science, likewise, has much to offer, but falls woefully short whenever the question of how gives way to the question of why. Critical thinking demolishes indiscriminate good intentions, which feel warmly self-righteous at the time but invariably lead to painful, unintended consequences (a specialty of Congress for generations).

As we seek Truth, we must know that the pull of modern society is relentlessly deceptive. The tone of modern American politics tempts with invitations to indulge in class warfare, cynicism, uncritical thinking, self-serving votes, willful self-deception, quick-fixes, blame-games, partisan bickering, and perhaps worst of all, an ends-justifies-the-means mindset that ensures personal and institutional corruption.

The deficit of trust generally in society, and in politics in particular, complicates and impoverishes our lives at every level. Trust, the essential building block of any society, is built one person at a time, one day at a time, one principled decision at a time. Only trustworthy people foster healthy relationships, which build strong friendships, families, and communities. America's historically rugged individualism must be tempered by a call to live in community with one another, regardless of differences of race, religion, income or politics. America's political system will never be stronger than the character of its people and its local communities.

Parents, especially, face difficult decisions every day that are magnified by the societal decline in personal integrity. Sleepovers and group camping trips must be considered with an increased concern for our children's personal safety. Predators lurk outside schoolyards, on the Internet, in neighborhood parks, at shopping malls. Decisions regarding our child's education must be measured against legitimate concerns of political indoctrination.

The recent spate of automobile recalls by Toyota highlights how trust affects us in the everyday world. Is the family car safe to drive? Does one trust the assurances of an automobile maker that has long-enjoyed a sterling reputation, or the National Transportation Safety Board, which has the responsibility of helping ensure the traveling safety of the general public? How does one weigh the potential conflict-of-interest caused by the government's majority ownership in a major American automobile manufacturer?

Another example is the H1N1 (swine flu) scare. The federal government has a responsibility to help inform the public and to make needed vaccines available, but when strong-armed bureaucrats and hypocritical politicians undermine the government's credibility, the government's ability to adequately respond to public safety crises is jeopardized by the public's understandable lack of trust in the federal machinations.

Examples of the burden caused by the trust deficit are endless, and affect every issue, from gun laws and gun rights, to property rights, to health care, to web surfing, to business expansion. Will the government preserve the right of citizens to defend themselves and their families? Will the value of a land purchase be devastated by zoning changes, or EPA regulations, or eminent domain? Will private medical information given to a doctor be safe from government misappropriation? Are emails and the record of visited websites safe from government spying? Will a business's hiring of new workers prove too costly in light of pending tax increases or other government mandates, or will the government fulfill its obligation to provide a stable environment for the private sector? As the federal government flexes its muscle in regulating every facet of life, even freedoms Americans have long taken for granted are burdened by the dearth of trust. Will effective but out-of-favor political speech by a citizen be met with personal smears, an IRS audit, or even prosecution? Will participation in a tea party event risk being labeled as an extremist by elected officials?

America can no longer afford a citizenry that blindly votes according to party allegiance. The paradigm has changed, and extreme political elements have been mainstreamed into the body politic. Deeply embedded in both political parties is a philosophy that purposely runs roughshod over the Constitution in a continual push for more government power and control. Citizens must be willing to identify and let go of personal viewpoints that may have held merit in past time periods but no longer apply, while holding fast to nonnegotiable principles of integrity.

Citizens of every legitimate ideology - liberal, conservative or libertarian; Democrat, Republican or Independent - should unite to peacefully, but vocally, insist that politicians govern transparently, speak honestly, and respond to voters' concerns respectfully. Likewise, every citizen should reject every politician who sacrifices principle for party or personal gain. Those who fail to do so should be summarily voted out of office. When political leaders demonize those who stand in the way of their policy objectives, citizens should unite in condemning the demagoguery.

The road to redemption for America begins with each of us. Politics will not lead the way; it's a journey of the heart. The current political and financial instabilities portend more trouble; those who know who they are and what they believe will be better prepared for whatever lies ahead. Persons who place their trust in the superintending providence of a just and loving God will find Him to be trustworthy - an inexhaustible reservoir of strength and a sure guide through the difficult times ahead.

Someone once observed that in a constitutional republic the people ultimately get the government they deserve. The point is well-taken: a responsible, trustworthy government flows from a responsible, trustworthy electorate. Every personal act of sound character is a deposit in the trust bank. We build trust assets in any relationship one deposit at a time. Every act of deceit, every failure of responsibility, exacts a large withdrawal of trust assets. When we reward duplicity for partisan, personal, or philosophical reasons, we enlarge the nation's trust deficit. We build trust by *being trustworthy* and by *properly valuing trustworthiness*, in ourselves, in others, in government.

Jesus answered, "I am the way and the truth and the life. No one comes to the Father except through me."
John 14:6 (NIV)

He [the devil] was a murderer from the beginning, not holding to the truth, for there is no truth in him. When he lies, he speaks his native language, for he is a liar and the father of lies.
John 8:44b (NIV)

Index

A

Abortion xvii, 19, 33, 35, 36, 37, 38, 92, 93, 178, 184
Abuse of power 39, 193
Accountability
  Accountability in the financial system 49
  Accountability structures 95
  Attempt to evade 50
  Avoiding accountability 91
  Lack of accountability xii, 195
  (Promise of) higher standard of accountability 77
  (Promise of) new era of responsibility and accountability 74
  (Promise of) unprecedented accountability 51
  Public accountability 61, 92
  Recovery Accountability and Transparency Board 51
  U.S. Government Accountability Office 250
ACORN 19, 21, 54, 55, 56, 57, 58, 59, 60, 129
Ageism 185
AIG 12, 47, 48
Alinsky, Saul 3, 128, 150, 258
American Medical Association 188
Anarchy 101
APOLLO Group 129
Arizona law 242, 243
ARRA (American Recovery and Reinvestment Act) 51, 66, 72, 73, 143
Art 12, 21, 65, 129, 147, 150, 161, 162, 163, 164
Articles of Confederation 101, 120
Audacity of Hope 15, 27, 31, 32, 33, 37, 150, 196
Axelrod, David xvii, 126, 130
Ayers 40
Ayers, Bill 40, 108, 126, 127, 129, 152

B

Bailout 8, 12, 47, 49, 50, 62, 65, 78, 79, 121, 122, 123, 203
Baird, Brian 78
Balanced budget 88
Bankruptcy Clause (see also Bankruptcy law) 120
Barofsky, Neil 49, 50
Baucus, Max xv, 133, 134, 135, 147, 175, 188
Beck, Glenn 39, 70, 95, 100, 145, 170, 198, 199, 249
Bernanke, Ben 61, 78, 82

Militia Movement 133
Miranda 12
Mortgages 46, 48, 65
Moveon.org 20
Muslim 25, 26, 27, 41, 94, 160, 222, 237

T

LaVergne, TN USA
26 October 2010
202221LV00004B/1/P